THE SOURCES OF THE OLD TESTAMENT

THE SOURCES OF THE OLD TESTAMENT

A Guide to the Religious Thought of the Hebrew Bible

JAMES E. ATWELL

T & T CLARK INTERNATIONAL
A Continuum imprint
LONDON • NEW YORK

Copyright © 2004 T&T Clark International
A Continuum imprint

Published by T&T Clark International
The Tower Building, 11 York Road, London SE1 7NX
15 East 26th Street, Suite 1703, New York, NY 10010

www.tandtclark.com

British Library Cataloguing-in-Publication Data
A catalogue record for this book is available from the British Library

Typeset by BookEns Ltd, Royston, Heuts
Printed and Bound in Great Britain by The Cromwell Press Ltd, Trowbridge, Wiltshire

ISBN 0-567-08473-6 (hardback)
ISBN 0-567-08463-9 (paperback)

Contents

Preface

This script is written from the conviction that the Hebrew Scriptures are an Aladdin's cave of treasures with universal human significance which are all too often overlooked and unrecognized. Those who, by virtue of their religious or cultural inheritance, have access to the Hebrew Scriptures need nudging as to their importance. The Hebrew Scriptures unite us with humanity's 'primaeval youth'; they connect us with the initial flowerings of human civilization. For that very reason, from the crossroads of the ancient world, they pose the big questions. Those questions relate individuals to their cosmic environment and they probe the significance of life in the face of the universal certainty of death. They contemplate the balance and harmony of things, fairness and unfairness, beauty and ambiguity. All these questions are set in the context of weighing life's meaning and God's purpose. The Hebrew Scriptures are written from a perspective which is convinced of God's involvement in history and that he values the human story. Once some of these issues are comprehended, the Bible is a book it is impossible to put down.

My very grateful thanks are due to those who have encouraged me in this pilgrimage of understanding over several decades. The research work of this book is drawn from an Oxford B.D. thesis. Without the liberal support, understanding and encouragement of Professor Graham I. Davies of the Cambridge University Divinity Faculty, the thesis would never have emerged, nor would I have had the confidence to turn it into a book. Anything of worth in this study I owe to him and the fact that he uses his considerable scholarship always to encourage and gently probe, and never to intimidate. My grateful thanks are also due to Professor Carolyn Sharp of Yale Divinity School who very kindly undertook to read and comment on the initial draft of the text.

My own family have lived with this interest, for my wife Lorna throughout our entire married life and for our children, Luke, Elizabeth and Mary, for their whole existence. I am grateful for their tolerance in allowing me chunks of time, usually commandeered from holidays and days off, to pursue this interest. Of course, colleagues, parishioners, seminars and diocesan study groups have contributed to the process. A short residential stint of training for clergy from the Diocese of Europe held in Spain in 1997 was the occasion which enabled me to enunciate the three sources as Tent, Temple and Tutor; the positive feedback there made me feel the insight was worth pursuing.

The script for this book has been painstakingly typed up over various recensions by Mrs Tessa Rodgers, who is Dean's Secretary at St Edmundsbury Cathedral. I am grateful for the enthusiasm for the project and the gift of assembling academic material which she has brought to the endeavour. The map of the Ancient Near East I gratefully acknowledge as the work of Robert Sunderland. The other illustrations have been painstakingly and generously undertaken by Leonard Goff; my considerable thanks are due to him. Quotations from untranslated German material have been rendered into English by Lucy Parkes. Biblical quotations are normally from the N.R.S.V.

Like the world which is presented by the Hebrew Scriptures, so this work has many connections and interactions by which it has been fed: for all of them I am truly grateful. Not least, I suspect, are inspirations from my formative years when my parents brought me up on a farm in the West Country and taught me of that wholesome but complex relationship which human beings have with God's good order.

James Atwell

St Edmundsbury Cathedral
Michaelmas 2003

PART I

The Generous Provider

Those who have visited the Holy Land may have penetrated the Golan Heights. From there it is possible to look across to the great Hermon range in the distance. The snow-capped peaks of that towering landscape hold the secret of the River Jordan. But it is quite possible to visit the River Jordan and know nothing of the massive landscape that is its generous provider. In this the River Jordan offers us a parable. It is possible to read the Bible and be totally unaware of the towering theological landscape from which it has emerged. The equivalent of the Hermon range for the Hebrew Scriptures is the theological and cultural context of the Ancient Near East.

CHAPTER 1

Surveying the Scene

A. The Broad Horizon

The significance of the religion and culture of the Ancient Near East for biblical faith can hardly be overestimated, yet it is often unappreciated. At the two poles of the region were Mesopotamia where, at Sumer (modern Iraq), in the final quarter of the fourth millennium, civilization began, and ancient Egypt, which was but moments behind in developing her own unique and unsurpassed culture. These first and timeless flowerings of human civilization feed the biblical traditions. Those who study the Scriptures are directly in touch with the initial combustion of civilization, which is humanity's common heritage and the universal creator's gift. Here are the first charted reflections on human destiny. We are consequently alerted to the profound significance of knowing about the cradle of biblical thought. The witness to a common human journey and the universalism of creation theology is at the very source of biblical theology.

At the crossroads of the Ancient Near East was the land of Canaan. When the Hebrews settled there they encountered the local Canaanite culture. Its religious practice is, of course, popularly associated particularly with the god Ba'al. Our knowledge of Ba'al has been at secondhand through the Hebrew Scriptures where the bad press he receives is not entirely without bias. Now the discovery of primary religious texts allows us direct encounter with that religious source. The Ugaritic Texts[1] have introduced us to a religious tradition that, at heart, is a conflict between Ba'al, the divine champion of order, and Yam (Sea), mythical representation of the lurking threat of disorder. The

3

triumph of Ba'al is the triumph of order and establishes the stability of the cosmos over the threat of chaotic forces.

The crossroads of the Ancient Near East was responsible for a particular signal of universalism. It was the western Semites who invented the alphabet in the seventeenth century BCE. The Ugaritic texts are evidence of the way the wedge-shaped cuneiform writing of ancient Mesopotamia had been developed into an alphabetical script. Ugarit still claims the earliest recovered list of letters that have been arranged in alphabetical order (called an abecedary). The invention of an alphabet meant that reading and writing were no longer simply the prerogative of a relatively few highly educated scribes, but, potentially, became universally available. It was an enormous human development.

It is of some significance that from the diversity of concepts in cultures as various as those of Egypt, Mesopotamia and Canaan there is yet a unifying vision. It was what we would call 'creation theology'. There was a single source for all theology and philosophy. It was based on the observation of and reflection upon the single great order of the natural world with its mysterious but precarious harmony. That common ground makes it possible to talk of a particular pattern about creation and world order throughout the entire region that was the cradle of the Hebrew Scriptures. In drawing attention to this broad consensus, inevitably justice is not done to minority voices and to complexities of detail. Nevertheless, the profile which emerges is remarkable for its clarity.

The miracle of creation for the peoples of the Ancient Near East was not that something should be created out of nothing.[2] That was not yet a significant theological idea. The miracle of creation was the marvellous order of the world. What they valued, marvelled at and reflected upon was the order, regularity and harmony of the universe. The opposite of creation was not nothing; the opposite of creation was a material world existing in raw potentiality without the familiar rhythm, order, form or even number. The pre-creation existence could only be described in negatives. The one event that mattered, the one truly new thing ever achieved, was in the moment at which this raw material was acted upon and in consequence a regulated, patterned and beautiful world had come into existence.

Creation in the Ancient Near East was about order and it was called forth from the pre-existent material that was the stuff of the pre-creation universe. The two poles of 'Before Order' and 'Order' are commonly referred to as a pair of opposites: Chaos and Order; however, the appropriateness of the use of the concept of Chaos has recently been challenged.[3] The retention of the concept of Chaos makes the point that although the 'Before Order' state represents 'potentiality in waiting', it can also represent threat. Inasmuch as the ordered world might be drawn back into its pre-creation formless state, that state represents a continuing threat of disorder. Viewed from the perspective of the ordered world the threat of a return to the pre-ordered state is a collapse of the familiar and the invasion of the topsy-turvy. In that sense the primordial world can represent the threat of chaos, and is often cloaked with that perception. It can take the guise not simply of the 'before creation' but also of the 'anti-creation'.

The picture from ancient Ugarit of the rolling breakers, seemingly resisting any control or restraint, is a powerful image of the threat to order. In ancient Egypt the annual flooding of the Nile obliterating familiar landmarks and contours carries the same significance. In the Osiris myth, which was a profoundly Egyptian myth about society and kingship, it was the sinister character Seth who similarly articulated the lurking threat of chaos. Ancient Mesopotamia, in the older traditions, emphasized the ordering of the world rather than the resistance of the materials.[4] However, the later military analogy required fierce subjugation before peace and harmony could be set forth.

With these qualifications in mind we may yet reach for a single parable that gathers the significance of the primal word. The analogy for creation in the Ancient Near East is close to the Speaker crying 'Order! Order!' to an unruly House of Commons. From the total absence of co-ordination – even at times Babel tongues and random confusion – there emerges a logic, a precedence, rules, regulations and a proper procedure. The spoken command 'Order!' creates not a series of interesting isolated fragments, but rather knits together a corporate, integrated whole. At best, the Speaker's word results in an end to confusion and the establishment of something whole and harmonious. Similarly, theological reflection within the environment from which the Hebrew Scriptures emerged is driven by its respect for, its fascination with, the priority it gave, to the miracle of order.

The mystery of the created order and of human existence that comes to us from the Ancient Near East is not the one that keeps many a contemporary youngster awake at night almost on the verge of panic: 'Why is there any existence at all?' The mystery they grappled with was: 'How come this harmony?' 'How come we are all fragments of a much greater whole?' They perceived an order to the heavens, to the seasons, to nature, to society which they just could not take for granted. The connectedness of everything was a truth they readily comprehended but could only wonder at. Any myth of creation had, therefore, to be able to explain who first proclaimed 'Order!'.

Ancient Egypt affords us the classic articulation of the nature of order. It was personified as a goddess whose emblem was a feather and whose name was Ma'at. Like righteousness and peace in the psalms, so Ma'at was never far from the side of the creator. She represented the precious order established by the creator at the beginning that ran through creation like a golden thread. Ma'at was the order of the harmonious universe, she was the delicate ecological equilibrium of nature, she was the stable reference point of society and the truth by which the judges regulated their courts. Ma'at signified one single principle of order which embraced all things. Just as the Pharaoh wore a double crown, and Egypt itself as upper and lower Egypt was appropriately symmetrical and balanced, so order was only static in so much as it too was delicately poised and undisturbed.

The tomb of Mereruka at Saqqara near Memphis is from the pyramid age. Its walls are beautifully illustrated with scenes of daily life. Typical of Egyptian detail, one representation of the Nile includes pictures of fish. The fish are not representative stereotyped pictograms, rather, each one is delicately drawn to represent a different species. It is a small indication of the way the variety and complexity of the natural order was observed, recorded, understood, respected and enjoyed. Somewhat later, from the New Kingdom, this same appreciation of the order of things is inscribed in a Hymn to Amun:

You are the sole one, who made all that is,
the solitary and only one who made what exists.
From whose eyes men came forth,
and from whose mouth the gods came into being.
Who creates the herbs that give life to the cattle,
and the fruit trees for mankind.
Who makes that on which the fishes in the river may live,
and the birds under the heaven.
Who gives air to what is in the egg
and nourishes the young of the serpent.
Who makes that on which gnats may live
and worms and flies likewise.
Who supplies the needs of the mice in their holes
and nourishes those things that fly, in every tree.
Hail, you who did all this,
solitary sole one, with many hands,
who spends the night wakeful, when all the world sleeps,
and seeks what is useful for his flock,
Amun, who endures in all things,
Atum and Harakhti,
praise is yours when they all say:
'Jubilation for you, because you weary yourself with us,
honour to you, because you created us!'
Hail to you, because of all cattle,
jubilation to you, because of all foreign lands,
to the height of the heaven and the width of the earth, and to the
depth of the sea![5]

The mention of 'All foreign lands' reminds us that creation
theology has no artificial boundaries. There was conceived to have
been a single act of ordering in the light of which all things are
relative. Everything was comprehended within that single great
order, and every constituent part had been allocated its task. The
corresponding concept in Mesopotamia was expressed as destiny
or fate. In contemporary vocabulary we would express a similar
understanding in terms of the given ecological niche. Every
fragment of creation in one way or another served the purpose
of the whole.

Egypt was typical of the Ancient Near East in making no
distinction between the physical order, the order of nature and
the human order. No differentiation was made between the
natural world and the achievements of human struggle that had

constructed canals, created cities, built temples or developed crafts and cultural skills. The correct social order and political order were conceived as a continuum with the order of nature which as a totality was invested with primal significance. The marvel of creation for the peoples of the Ancient Near East was the harmonious single order of the universe which embraced the physical order, the natural environment, and the social, political and cultural ordering of society.

In ancient Mesopotamia, successful handling of the processes of the universe required a degree of shrewdness, even cunning. Order was often conceived to be somewhat indifferent to human beings and therefore had to be played and carefully worked. For instance, if a bad fate had been decreed for an individual, but discovered in advance, a substitute might be slipped in and cosmic honour thereby satisfied. This shrewd anticipatory thinking is evident, in one particular way, that ancient Mesopotamia reconciled the human aspiration to succeed with the relentless mechanisms of cosmic order. The science of omen reading was as prolific as the Wisdom literature of ancient Egypt, made equal claim to be based on empirical observation, and was similarly categorized and ordered.

The Babylonian urge to understand and predict a regular universe, in which human beings might feel at home, has left a particular literary deposit. The Babylonians established and researched huge catalogues of what were claimed to be precedent on the meaning of particular omens. Such omens might involve the movement of the heavens, the path taken by flocks of birds, the occurrence of chance events on auspicious days or the shape of a sacrificial liver. Three hundred of the tablets recovered in the library of the Assyrian king Ashurbanipal were devoted to this science, only two hundred to epic literature. As it happens, our scientific world-view is compatible with the Egyptian attempt at categorizing nature, but is fairly bewildered at the Babylonians' lists and precedents. Yet the two endeavours have a basic similarity: the will to find order, pattern and meaning in a world which so often defies human logic. In their – to us – rather strange way, the scientists of ancient Babylon were struggling towards their own sense of unity, order and regularity in the universe. The universal respect for their astronomy is evidence of their ordered approach to the challenge of the universe. They believed that the cosmos was a fundamental unity with reliable repetitive processes such that the flight of a bird, the position of a planet, the shape of a sacrificial liver or the paths taken by a colony of ants might well carry a message that related to human destiny if precedent could be consulted and interpreted correctly.

Throughout the Ancient Near East it was taken for granted that order, even though established, remained vulnerable and had to be cherished if it were not to break up into disorder. The ordered world required to be sustained. The only way it could be effectively achieved was by lifelines and connections running back to the moment of creation itself. Any religion worth its salt had to have dependable ways of channelling power from the primaeval moment into the present lest the ordered cosmos should slip back into its pre-ordered state and consequently be overwhelmed by chaotic forces. The sort of anxieties that gave rise to the suspicion that the ordered world might be slipping back into its formless origin where everything was slack and unmanageable were wide in scope and included the languishing of nature in a drought, the neglect of justice, the invasion of an enemy and the failure of kingship.

The disintegration of the social fabric was a primary indicator of cosmic order breaking up; it was perceived as a threat to the very structure of being. Indeed, in ancient Egypt of the First Intermediate Period social collapse was grounds for throwing yourself to the crocodiles. Egypt in that period was going through one of its phases where social order was disintegrating; a sage named Ipuwer deliberately paints a picture of the disorder and confusion as resembling a return to the primaeval state. This concern can take on a humorous dimension from our perspective, but it was real enough. He cites the servant in place of the master, the rich in the place of the poor and the washerwoman refusing to carry her burden.[6] This vignette of disorder is understood as the anti-creation. As the obverse of order it witnesses to that single continuum which was conceived to embrace not only the physical and natural world, but also the political and social order. It illustrates the need for order to be guarded and nurtured.

From the opening of the second millennium onwards the vulnerability of the ordered world and the need for its sustaining received particular expression. The story of a flood, including a hero who builds an ark, became incorporated into a standard way that the creation and human beginnings were recounted in ancient Mesopotamia.[7] In this Genesis 1–11 has a greater context in ancient Babylon and Assyria. The story of an archetypal flood which threatens to overwhelm the ordered world is a sort of 'creation shadow' and expresses how precarious and delicate the order of the world truly is. The flood story powerfully expresses the fact that order cannot be taken for granted, but must be continually worked at and sustained.

At the source of the Hebrew Scriptures is the profound witness of the Ancient Near East to the significance of the creator's work of ordering. This is not simply because the Genesis 1–3 creation accounts come at the beginning of the Bible, but because the very soil in which the whole Hebrew Scriptures were nurtured, the very principles upon which they were founded, were of the stuff of order, harmony and regularity which were reckoned to be of cosmic significance. The biblical tradition was weaned within a wider culture for which the fundamental insight was of a single great order of creation. That primal order provided the standard against which all else was understood, compared and categorized. The maintenance or sustaining of that order was the goal of existence and the necessary prerequisite of creation's survival.

The once-accepted wisdom of the scholar G. von Rad that creation theology is secondary within the theological framework of the Hebrew Scriptures has had to be fundamentally revised. He maintained: 'The doctrine of redemption had first to be fully safeguarded, in order that the doctrine that nature, too, is a means of divine self-revelation might not encroach upon or disturb the doctrine of redemption, but rather broaden and enrich it.'[8] The opposite turns out to be the case. It is summarized in the subtitle of the perceptive essay by H. H. Schmid: '"Creation Theology" as the Broad Horizon of Biblical Theology.'[9]

B. Three Classic Pictures of Ordering

In this section there are identified three classic pictures of divine authority ordering the raw material of creation from the Ancient Near East. They come in the colour, the clothes, the cultural language of their age. In each the cry 'Order! Order!' is directed at the great primaeval ocean. Water proved to be a particularly powerful and appropriate metaphor for the pre-creation existence that could only be described in negatives.[10] It could enable primal existence to be pictured in a mode which was limp, slippery and unmanageable, yet full of potential. Here was an analogy for existence prior to any form, number, order or structure. In this, Genesis 1 is part of the received science of the Ancient Near East when it recounts that prior to order there was a dark, formless, watery waste waiting to be divided and organized. A watery description of the condition before creation is characteristic of many traditions throughout the Ancient Near East, including the three we must now consider.

There is, firstly, the Canaanite god Ba'al vanquishing Sea to which we have already referred. Secondly, there is the city-god of Babylon named Marduk vanquishing Tiāmat (also Sea). Thirdly, there is the Pharaoh presiding over his kingdom as the image of the sun-god who brought order at the first time when he rose from the primaeval ocean (Nun). These three enable us to encounter traditions from the three major areas of the Ancient Near East.

Firstly, let us consider the drama associated with the Canaanite god Ba'al. The texts from the ancient Canaanite city-state of Ugarit include a number of mythic cycles relating to the god Ba'al. The foremost is one which relates a struggle in which Ba'al and Yam (Sea) wrestle for kingship. In the city-states of ancient Canaan it was the king who was responsible for their corporate life in guaranteeing security, justice and good husbandry in agriculture: that is, for the totality of good order. In the mythic battle for divine kingship it is cosmic order that is at stake, and with it the steady procession of the seasons which deliver the autumn rains after the summer drought. Good kingship is code for 'order' within a complex integrated environment.

In this episode Ba'al is the vigorous storm-god, the warrior of the gods who themselves are all terrified by the challenge of Yam or Prince Sea. Ba'al is not the creator; in the Canaanite context that is the high god El. However, he stands close to that concept as the champion of order; he is the one responsible for the sustaining of the regularity of the earth's cycles. The conflict of divine order, vested in Ba'al, with the threat of chaos, personified as Yam, is of the soul of Canaanite religion. That conflict harnesses as its mythic setting the imagery of the naked power of the pealing thunder and flashing lightning unleashed every autumn over the rolling breakers of the Mediterranean Sea. Such imagery reverberates through the biblical psalms.[11] It captures the thrill of the moment when the summer drought gives way to the winter rains.

The drama of the battle as recounted in the Ugaritic texts is gripping. Ba'al's bravery and the pathos of the story is highlighted as he sinks under the throne of Yam. Colour and excitement are added by the special weapons manufactured for him by the craftsman of the gods. Inevitably, Ba'al finally succeeds in bringing down Yam and triumphs; the cry goes up:

> Yam is indeed dead! Ba'al shall be King!
> Ba'al has won the right to be King.[12]

Remember good kingship is code for 'order' within a complex integrated environment. But one thing remains; Ba'al's kingship is only recognized when he has a temple, that is a palace, from which to reign. Ba'al's victory is not secure until permission is won from the high god El for a temple to be built. It is with this 'planning permission' that the significance of Ba'al's victory becomes clear:

> Now at last Ba'al may appoint
> a time for his rain,
> a time for his barque to appear in the snow
> and for the sounding of his voice in the clouds
> for him to release lightnings on the earth.[13]

The temple is built, there is feasting, a victory march, and the cycle ends with Ba'al enthroned thundering through the window of the temple. The complex order of the world is secure and properly harmonious; the sustaining of its regular cycles is guaranteed.

The universal story of order is related to the immediate situation through the celebration of the local temple festival. As the people of Ugarit gathered in the temple every autumn to celebrate, with their earthly king, the enthronement of the divine King, they felt that they themselves directly participated in and benefited from Ba'al's victory. If Ba'al's kingship was secure and his rule over an ordered universe was guaranteed, then the local would benefit from the universal. The very existence of the temple locked the particular and the immediate into cosmic myth.

Secondly, we must consider the epic battle undertaken according to Mesopotamian tradition by Marduk. The pre-eminence of Babylon, and therefore of Marduk the city-god of Babylon, dates back to the eighteenth century BCE and the rule of the famous monarch Hammurabi. He was responsible for turning the city-state of Babylon into an empire.[14] He then established a legal and administrative system with a single language for the whole of Sumer and Akkad based on Babylon. Consequent upon his imperial power he brought a unity to his territories which guaranteed a system for taking grievances to be properly heard so that justice might be obtained. Although it is not possible to date the famous creation epic known as *Enūma Elish*[15] with Marduk as its hero, back to his time, there is no doubt that Hammurabi established the momentum which made it possible to achieve the transfer, by analogy, from Babylon as seat of civil order to Marduk as champion of cosmic order. Good kingship is again the access point for contemplating cosmic order as civil order writ large. The body politic is a vivid analogy for a true universe – a single complex order presided over and held as a unity by the creator.

The *Enūma Elish* creation epic recounts the battle between Marduk as warrior-god and the provoked primordial goddess Tiāmat, bent on annihilating the younger gods. Tiāmat represents water in its manifestation as the briny ocean.[16] Initially, at the challenge of Tiāmat the other gods are fearful, which serves to highlight Marduk's unique courage. Then, like a typical storm-god, he rides off in his chariot to do battle. He takes with him 'an armour of terror' for his cloak and the four winds for weapons, as well as lightning, bow and net. On meeting Tiāmat he challenges her to single combat, and they join battle. According to the account Marduk uses the wind to distend Tiămat's belly, and then drives an arrow down her open throat into her heart. The despatch of Tiămat completed, her consort and accomplice Kingu is bound. Next, Marduk splits the watery carcass of Tiămat; with the two parts of her severed body he establishes the heavenly firmament and the earth. He then goes on to arrange the rest of cosmic order, including the heavenly bodies. His final act is to create human beings, using the blood of the executed god Kingu; they are condemned to toil in order that the gods may go free. Human destiny is to release the gods from their labours and to bear the burden of creation. Their place is 'below stairs'. Marduk's victory is marked by the building of his temple Esangila at Babylon. His kingship, too, is made manifest by the building of a palace.

Despite the strangeness with which this creation epic confronts the contemporary reader, perhaps raising unexpected and darker issues of male violence against the female body, it carried a vision of some daring in its context. It articulated a proper universe, a single great cosmic order. It presented it in the context of responsible monarchy.

Perhaps the most universally appreciated feature of the Babylonian and Assyrian civilization is its respect for law. The oldest written laws yet recovered are those of Ur-Nammu, first king of the third dynasty of Ur (the last flowering of Sumerian civilization that brought the third millennium to a close). He claims to have established justice in order to protect the orphan and the widow against the rich and powerful. The most famous Akkadian law code is probably that associated with the name of Hammurabi.[17] The laws are inscribed on a stele dedicated to the sun-god Shamash, who was responsible for justice. Reference is made to the two senior gods Anu and Enlil. In the prologue it is claimed that:

> Anun (Anu) and Illil (Enlil) for the prosperity of the people called me by name Hammurabi, the reverent God-fearing prince, to make justice appear in the land, to destroy the evil and the wicked that the strong might not oppress the weak, to rise indeed like Shamash over the dark-haired folk to give light to the land.[18]

The theological implications of the Babylonian concern for justice enabled the transference of the regulation of the state to the order of the cosmos. There was a new analogy for understanding the significance of the universal order established at the moment of creation. If redress can be obtained in a human court there must be a writ which is cosmic. If responsible kingship is viable on earth then it must be effective from heaven also.

The temple festival at Esangila again enabled the universal to lock into the particular. The re-enactment of Marduk's victory and the reciting of the Epic became part of the ceremonies of the Babylonian New Year festival.[19] The king was crucial here to the associated observances. A procession occurred in which the king 'took the hand' of Marduk's statue and set out from the Temple to a ceremonial building known as the Akitu House. There, Marduk's victory over Tiāmat was acknowledged and symbolically re-enacted.[20] A triumphal return to the temple enabled the 'proclamation of destinies' and secured for contemporary king and people all the benefits of order including political security and agricultural fertility. Time was suppressed; the original act by which Marduk was conceived to have ordered the universe touched and refreshed the present. The contemporary threat of disorder was overcome; creation was sustained.

Thirdly, we must visit ancient Egypt. Throughout the dynasties of Egypt the ordering of the primordial material is, by contrast, rather gentler. The representation of potentiality, the primaeval ocean, was known as the Nun. From it had emerged the first land, the primaeval hill. The Nun was not a threat to be vanquished; by analogy with the Nile in flood, its watery formlessness contained life-giving potential. At the 'First Time' the sun-god Re' had majestically risen from the Nun over an ordered world and every morning the rejuvenated sun emerged from the Nun following its nightly bath in its fertile waters. The Egyptians never ceased to rejoice in the divine order called into being by the rising sun. From the time of the temple murals of the Old Kingdom dedicated to the sun-god they celebrated the variety of life – agricultural, animal, human – that the sun drew from the Nile valley. Akhenaten's 'Hymn to Aten' from the New Kingdom, which has strong affinities with the biblical Psalm 104, takes up the same theme. Here, characteristic of Akhenaten's brief religious experiment, the sun-god is called Aten:

The earth becomes bright: you have arisen on the horizon. As Aten you shine by day and have driven away the darkness. You shed your rays, and the two lands are in festive mood. The men of the sun are awakened and stand upon their feet; you have raised them up. They wash their bodies and take their clothing, their arms are bent in worship, because you appear. The whole land goes to work. All beasts are satisfied with their pasture, the trees and plants become green. The birds flutter in their nests, raising their wings in worship before your spirit. All the lambs skip around, the birds and everything that flutters live because you have risen for them. The ships sail upstream and down, every way is open because you appear. The fish in the river dart before your face, for your rays penetrate into the depths of the sea.[21]

In ancient Egypt the very presence of the god-king on the throne was reckoned to guarantee for the contemporary world an intimacy with the First Time. According to the theology native to the ancient city of Heliopolis (On), the sun-god Re' was the divine prototype of the Pharaoh. From the fifth dynasty onwards 'son of Re'' is a regular royal designation. Re' was even claimed as the first King of Egypt. The king therefore shared in the authority of the creator. He was able to exercise his rule and establish order only inasmuch as he participated in Re''s original act of creating and ordering. He was the channel which enabled the original act of ordering to be effective in the present.

Three concepts whose primary association is with the First Time and which are the prerogative of Re' were also attributed regularly to the reigning Pharaoh. One was Ma'at, which we have already encountered as order, and which embraced in a single whole the natural order, nature, justice and harmonious society. Judges were priests of Ma'at. The other two were Sia⸮ (perception) and Ḥu (authoritative utterance). These latter two are concepts which enabled Heliopolitan theologians to articulate creation by the word as involving the double process of thought and speech. All three concepts transfer imperceptibly from the sun-god who creates order to the Pharaoh who refreshes it. Significantly, a single verb is used to denote either sunrise or the appearance of the king on his throne; it makes the same easy transference. The king as Son of Re' was a powerful and effective sign of universal order. The Pharaoh's kingdom was not simply analogous to cosmic order; it was part of and identical with cosmic order. The creator's task and the Pharaoh's task were seamless.

The temples of ancient Egypt were the palaces and courts of the gods. The regular ceremonial offering of Ma'at (order) in the temple was as important as proper respect for order in the practicalities of daily life. Symbol and incantation had a valid and effective part to play in managing cosmic stability. Theoretically, all offering was made by the Pharaoh, for whom the priests deputized. The validity of temple sites, without any sense of illogicality, was maintained by insisting that they were built on the site of the primaeval hill; sometimes the waters of the receding Nun were pictured on the external walls. Except at festivals, when the statue of the deity might make a public progress, probably by river, the affairs of the temple were private. Its visible presence proclaimed the partnership of the divine and the human in the service of cosmic stability.

It is clear from the three examples that have been considered that order and good kingship were concepts closely connected in the Ancient Near East. The way the king was charged with responsibility for holding together the complex elements of the daily life of a state in an organic whole was a microcosm of the way the universe was deemed to operate as a single great system under divine royal control.

It is also evident that cosmic order once established could not be taken for granted. The entropy of creation, what might be described as the gravitational pull of the original formless condition, was always a real threat. As well as a sort of impersonal universal friction working to wind things down, chaotic forces of destabilization also lurked in human and spirit form. For order to be maintained there needed to be channels from the original act of creation that would flow into, reinvigorate and refresh the present. All three examples evidence particular ways in which the present could come into direct relationship with the primal moment and so be brought back into order; the world was sustained in every original detail.

The three case-studies have underscored the two cardinal principles previously identified: 'Any myth of creation had to be able to explain who first called "Order!".' 'Any religion worth its salt had to have dependable ways of channelling power from the primaeval moment into the present lest the ordered cosmos should slip back into its pre-ordered state and consequently be overwhelmed by disorder.' The temple was the place that, by its very existence, proclaimed divine kingship and – by the regular round of worship and service of the deity carried out within it – contributed to the maintenance of good order throughout the cosmos.

The classic pictures of ordering taken from ancient Mesopotamia and ancient Egypt make it clear that the deity responsible for order had a status and a significance that were unique and exalted. The council of the gods tended towards functionaries within a given system for which the creator-god bore ultimate responsibility. The concept of earthly kingship and sovereign of empire transferred to the heavenly provided a model of executive authority. The situation in Canaan was more complex in that El was the creator and presided over the council of the gods, but Ba'al was the sustainer. However, creator and sustainer are very close concepts in the Ancient Near East, and that is confirmed, as we shall discuss later, by the fact that at Jerusalem the Canaanite deity El Elyon (God Most High) combined features of El as creator and Ba'al as combat-deity. Clearly in that situation, as for Mesopotamia and Egypt, the god who called 'Order' and presided over the council of the gods potentially truly was God.

C. The Significance of the Status Quo

The fact that kingship provided not simply a metaphor for cosmic order, but operated as a seamless part of that order, had far reaching consequences. The accidents of history that created the governing class and put in place arbitrary social structures were elevated to cosmic significance. A snapshot of the present was given the dignity of primal order and therefore installed beyond all contradiction. In other words, the religion of the Ancient Near East was committed to the status quo. It could be well summed up in a now rarely-sung verse from Mrs Alexander's hymn 'All things Bright and Beautiful':

The rich man in his castle,
The poor man at his gate,
He made them high and lowly,
and ordered their estate.

According to the main traditions of the Ancient Near East the world had been organized in a particular way because that was how God intended it to be and to remain. There could be no theological challenge to this 'establishment' way of thinking because the divine was itself conceived to be within and not outside the emergent universe. Divinity was the servant of stability from within, not a radical challenge from without. Some further theological delving is necessary to understand the full significance of this perspective.

The given science of the Ancient Near East maintained that there was a pre-existing raw material from which the ordered world was wrought. It takes a leap of understanding for the contemporary mind to grasp that this primaeval existence was deemed to contain the origin of the gods as well as the origin of the natural world. The idea that the gods developed from within the raw material of creation, indeed were identical with it, is standard in the Ancient Near East. The continuum between the divine and the natural order is therefore an original feature of the religion of the Ancient Near East; its pantheistic roots permanently marked its boundaries. Radical transcendence is theoretically excluded; the divine was not conceived to be outside, but within the creative process. The Primaeval Ocean precedes all else in the standard theology of ancient Egypt, and from it the sun-god Re' is born. According to the *Enūma Elish* all things began within the mingling sweet and marine water of the primordial divine pair called Apsû (male) and Tiāmat (female). It is from within them the ancient gods first emerge from whom Marduk is descended, and it is from Tiāmat's recycled body that the ordered world is fabricated. Ba'al is the sustainer as the storm god in the Ugaritic texts. He guarantees the return of seasonal order. The analogy for the sustainer is with the mechanic rather than the inventor.

There are a number of gods in the Ancient Near East whose inability to be proactive resembles the New Testament picture of 'Lazarus bound', waiting after his resurrection for others to

release him from his grave clothes. They, too, are as if bound in
grave clothes and unable to take any initiative. The mummified
Osiris of Egypt is a literal example of this. Dumuzi or Tammuz
of Mesopotamia is similarly unable to help himself. They are often
called 'intransitive' deities as they do not seek to control or
influence beyond the phenomenon they represent. They are
gods who are identified with the mysterious latent power within
nature to overcome death. They are captured seemingly without
resistance by death, yet the good offices of the living enable them
to resurrect in the cycle of nature they inhabit. T. Jacobsen has
suggested Dumuzi is a survival into the historic period of an
earlier concept of divinity.[22] The same may reasonably be
surmised of similar deities. In that case the concept of sustaining,
of coaxing renewal, of maintenance is clearly identified as an
older one than creative ordering in the Ancient Near East. For
as long as it remained fundamental and seminal to theological
reflection it bound religion to the status quo. It required of
religion, in the words of the biblical Book of Ecclesiastes:

> What has been is what will be,
> and what has been done is what will be done;
> there is nothing new under the sun. (Ecclesiastes 1:9)

Alongside Dumuzi and Osiris we may place Ba'al in another aspect
of his character which emerges in the Ugaritic text. This time
Ba'al's enemy is Mot or Death. In this other cycle Ba'al does not
resist. He is swallowed by Death with the effect that there is
infertility and drought. His cause is taken up by other gods,
primarily his sister Anat, which leads to his resurrection with the
apparent consequence that:

> The heavens rained oil,
> the ravines ran with honey.[23]

It seems that the combat between Ba'al and Death is about
divinity within not outside the rhythm of the seasons with their
annual cycle of life and death. According to this way of thinking
there is straightforwardly a continuum of the divine with the
created order.

The intransitive god was identified with the phenomenon he
or she represented and was not conceived as acting or willing
beyond it. In the practice of planting the beds of Osiris in the

Egyptian New Kingdom tombs, nature is presented as the body of the god.[24] Such a deity is wounded when the corn is cut or the grape is trampled. There need to be ceremonies to give permission for such activities to be undertaken without sinister consequence. Here we encounter the source of the development of the religion of the Ancient Near East; it is clearly evident in that aspect of Ba'al's character which relates to the cycle involving the conflict with Death.

It is not easy to reconcile Ba'al's battle with Death (Mot) where he is intransitive and passive, accepting of his fate, with the archetypal battle with chaos (Yam) when he is vigorous and proactive. Probably represented in these two aspects of Ba'al's character are theological developments over a millennium and more. The experience of the vigorous, proactive, assertive monarch in the historical period provided a new analogy for divinity. The warrior and organizer acted upon the object he wished to influence. Involved in this developing theological reflection is a sort of 'centrifuge' separating out the divine from the natural order and the consequent emergence of the potential for transcendence. It has as its consequence the de-mystification or de-sacralization of nature.[25] This process involves growing pains evident amongst the issues that fuelled the conflict of the prophets of Ba'al with the prophets of Yahweh. Like all growing up it involves both gain and loss. The gain is the freedom to view nature dispassionately and scientifically, freed from taboo. The natural world is no longer encountered as personal but as 'a thing'. The loss is the temptation to abuse nature, and to think of humanity as observers of and not partners with the natural order.

The wineskins had to burst for true transcendence to emerge in the Ancient Near East – and they do so finally within the Hebrew Scriptures. Nonetheless, we do see the Ancient Near East pushing them near the limits. In particular, this is true in the Egypt of the New Kingdom. The potential for radical transcendence is assembled but never triggered. The theologians of Memphis claim for Ptah creation by his word, seemingly pushing his utterance back into the space normally accorded to the primaeval ocean, Nun.[26] Amun, as primaeval deity identified with Nun but also conceived of as wind or breath of all existence, became in the New Kingdom period combined with the sun-god Re' who was responsible for universal order. As Amun-Re', the high god of the New Kingdom, expressed theologically the creator as the absolute origin and principle of being.[27]

But the skins were never quite exploded. Divinity never became a challenge to the status quo. The Ancient Near East did not dream of the transformation of the order of creation. It did not cry out for redemption. There were literary protests at creation's frustrations and the impenetrable mystery of death. There is a remarkable Mesopotamian work known as the *The Epic of Gilgamesh*. The hero Gilgamesh is driven by grief at the loss of his companion Enkidu to travel to the very boundaries of creation. Although he penetrates to the garden of paradise he is frustrated in his quest for eternal life. The story ends with him older and wiser accepting humanity's lot. There was also the response of cynicism to the insistence that this world would touch perfection if it were not for mischievous, mainly human, disturbances of its processes. Within the biblical tradition it is evident in Ecclesiastes; in ancient Mesopotamia it is foreshadowed by a work known as *A Pessimistic Dialogue between Master and Servant*.[28] But those voices could not shake the colossus of creation theology which was firmly installed in both the mind-set and the soul of the Ancient Near East. When the world was ordered, a definitive standard had been established for all time. That standard had to be universally recognized and upheld without hesitation or deviation.

The fact that the present arbitrary arrangement of things was accorded a primal status that it did not deserve had shortcomings. Social order was frozen; the status quo was sanctified. The future, officially at least, could hold no break with tradition, no adventure, nothing new. The poor were not to be raised up. The governing classes were confirmed in office. The social hierarchy could not be challenged. Order, a snapshot of the present, was arbitrary in the social conventions to which it accorded primal authority. Justice was administered within the given context of order. There could be no protest about the position into which one was born. The world as it manifests itself, and as it always had been since the day order was called, was to be accepted and not challenged. Leaven, salt and yeast were not welcome ingredients in an ordered society where disturbance represented the dark forces of anti-creation and disorder, which were heavy with the terrifying threat of the invasion again of primordial chaos.

However, there was considerable consequence to be drawn from the high status accorded to the present. Because of the intimate relationship the present was conceived to have with the moment when the order of creation was divinely established, there was immediate access to a sense of the unity, coherence and wholeness of the cosmos. It is, in particular, that vision which the Ancient Near East brings to the Hebrew Scriptures. The theology of the Ancient Near East never broke the world into isolated fragments. It was conceived of as a body; it was an organism. Everything was understood to be interrelated and interdependent: all things find their place in the whole.

The creation was not, therefore, simply a remote event of the distant past; it explained the present. It provided a map, an orientation, a key to the way things are arranged. That arrangement was not just concerned with the natural order, but also with the political, social and moral order. Properly discerned, they were all part of the single order of creation. To breach any one of them was to go against a divine ordinance, and thus rupture the cosmic harmony God intended, yielding dire consequences. The human community operated within the greater context of universal order. In ancient Mesopotamia human destiny was to serve the gods and that is how they related to the scheme of things. In ancient Egypt human beings were servants of cosmic order, and in one of her traditions, even 'images of God'.[29] Humans, in the estimation of the Ancient Near East, were never actors walking across a stage-set which served only as a disposable context in which they had no particular investment.

There was not one tiny aspect of human life that was not connected into the single great construction of world order. Precisely because universal order was an organic whole, if its right functioning were disturbed in one aspect it would have immediate repercussions throughout. There was thought to be a linkage between a human act and its consequence which might be far-reaching. Moral rectitude was based on the principle that it was not possible to live in an ordered world in a disorderly fashion without triggering a recoil. The harmony of the world had a

providential consequence. It was not that God or the gods had
to act; it was simply that to work against the grain of the universe
was, inevitably, to work in opposition to life and health. That was
the lot of the foolish person which issued in calamity and
disintegration. The psalmist speaks for the whole of the Ancient
Near East:

> See how they conceive evil,
> and are pregnant with mischief,
> and bring forth lies.
> They make a pit, digging it out,
> and fall into the hole that they have made.
> Their mischief returns upon their own heads,
> and on their own heads their violence descends. (Psalm 7:14–16)

To live a righteous life, that is, a life of frictionless integration
with established order – however at a particular moment that
might have been understood and conceived – was to embrace
peace and prosperity:

> My child, do not forget my teaching,
> but let your heart keep my commandments;
> for length of days and years of life
> and abundant welfare they will give you. (Proverbs 3:1-2)

When things are right there exists a sort of equilibrium, even a
communion, through which all things hold together. This has
been vividly and perceptively described as a cosmic Covenant.[30]
It receives tangible illustration when in ancient Mesopotamia a
ruler setting out to build a temple orders a time of absolute peace
and harmony. The mother must not scold the child, the mistress
must not strike her slave, the child must not answer back its
parent.[31] Illustrative of the same point was the importance within
the Babylonian legal tradition that after a dispute has come to
court and been decided, the antagonism should be ended and
harmony restored. Conversely, for as long as order is ruptured,
cosmic equilibrium is disturbed and communion is broken. When
Cain murders Abel, not only is their own relationship involved
but the very communion with the earth is broken:

> And now you are cursed from the ground,
> which has opened its mouth to receive your
> brother's blood from your hand. (Genesis 4:11)

Such is the unity of the cosmos that human justice and the integrity of creation cannot be differentiated.

There is a well-known representation from the *Book of the Dead* in ancient Egypt of the human soul being weighed in a balance against the feather of Ma'at (order) here representing truth. If the human life has been righteous the soul will not tip the balance. That equilibrium, which is just and just balanced at the fulcrum and related to human moral integrity, scaled up, provides us with a very effective image of cosmic order in the Ancient Near East. The cosmos is created by God as a single whole in relationship, in harmony and in balance. If it is to remain poised at the fulcrum human justice must play a significant part in the great scheme of things. Honouring God involves understanding, respecting and living with the truth of the complex order of creation and its need for responsible maintenance. That is the foundation upon which biblical theology is constructed. It is a truth much neglected, but in the process of being rediscovered by our own generation.

Points for Discussion

1. 'The spoken command "Order!" creates not a series of fragments, but rather knits together a corporate integrated whole.' Do you think of human beings as primarily part of creation or separate from creation? To what extent have we re-learnt the connection between human actions and the integrity of creation?

2. What analogies are there between the concept of the Ancient Near East that the created order needed sustaining and protecting, and our contemporary attitudes to the environment?

3. The earliest ideas of the divine in the Ancient Near East thought of it as the latent power for renewal within nature. What were the losses when the developing idea of transcendence brought a break between God and the natural world? Do you have any sympathy for 'New Age' religion seeking to reunite human beings with the natural rhythms and divinity in nature?

4. Where are questions continuing to be asked about the 'miracle of the universe' in our contemporary world? Should there be common ground here for questions of science and matters of faith?
5. How far do we continue to make ethical and moral judgements based on creation and 'natural law'; for instance, about marriage, human sexuality and the Aids epidemic? Do such judgements need to be tempered by a challenge to creation's order as necessarily sacrosanct?

Key Bible Passages

Psalm 104 (the miracle of order); Genesis 4:1–16 (justice and the integrity of creation); Psalm 37 cf. Psalm 112 (providential order); Ecclesiastes 1 (the eternal return).

Further Reading

H. H. Schmid, 'Creation, Righteousness and Salvation: "Creation Theology" as the Broad Horizon of Biblical Theology', in ed. B. W. Anderson, *Creation in the Old Testament*, London (1984), pp. 102–117.
Walter Brueggemann, 'The Loss and Recovery of Creation in Old Testament Theology', *Theology Today*, 53 no. 2 (July 1996), pp. 177–190.
R. Murray, *The Cosmic Covenant*, London (1992).

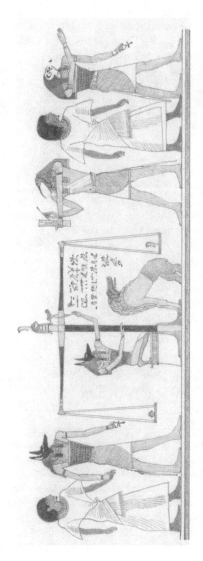

Figure 1. The weighing of the soul against the feather of justice (Ma'at) from the Egyptian *Book of the Dead*. Taken from the funerary papyrus of Hunefer c. 1310 BCE. (©British Museum).

Endnotes

[1] The ancient city-state of Ugarit was discovered by excavations at the modern Ras Shamra, a headland on the Mediterranean coast of northern Syria. The work was begun in 1929. Enormous quantities of clay tablets have since been uncovered from the region of the library attached to Ba'al's temple and also from the royal palace. They are inscribed for the most part with alphabetic cuneiform, and are to be dated to the mid-fourteenth century BCE. They are the deposit of a thriving city-state, whose prosperity was based on trade, of the Late Bronze Age. The city was destroyed by the coming of the 'Sea Peoples' in about 1190 BCE.

[2] The theological development that God creates from nothing is incontrovertibly asserted in 2 Maccabees 7:28. It is argued by M. Weinfeld ('God the Creator in Genesis 1 and in the Prophecy of Second Isaiah', *Tarbiz* 37 (1967/8), pp. 105–132) that Isaiah 45:7 which maintains that God creates the darkness as well as the light is actually in contradiction with Genesis 1:2–3 where the primordial material is the start of the creator's activity. In other words the Priestly creation account is still early on in a process of theological debate and development which eventually crystallizes into the distinctive notion of *creatio ex nihilo*.

[3] The use of the concept of Chaos in the context of ancient Mesopotamian myth has been questioned in particular by W. G. Lambert. With reference to the famous *Enūma Elish* creation epic he maintains:

> At first the so-called 'chaotic' powers are entirely orderly and peaceful, namely Tiāmat and Apsû. They exist in harmony and mix their waters together thus creating generations of gods. The trouble begins when these gods so begotten begin to romp around and so deprive their two ancestors of peace: this is the first chaos! Marduk too adds to the chaos by making a 'wave' (1 line 107) in Tiāmat. Meanwhile Apsû has been killed because he was planning to kill the younger gods to restore peace. Here is no opposition of order and chaos, but a mix-up for which the younger gods were largely to blame. Tiāmat at that point was persuaded to take action to kill off the younger gods lest she too suffer annihilation. Again, no simple conflict of order and chaos, but both sides simply trying to save themselves from the result of previous events. So my opinion has not changed: the evidence from Mesopotamia has no place for chaos as a cosmic principle. (W. G. Lambert in private correspondence with the author, June 1999).

Lambert makes the point that 'chaos' is not here strictly primordial but is something that develops. However, under provocation the primaeval waters in the form of Tiãmat do become a threat.

The understanding of what is involved in creative ordering in ancient Mesopotamia develops from the Sumerian deities of the third millennium to the Babylonian and Assyrian context of the second and first millennia. The work of the Sumerian creating deities is portrayed with fairly gentle analogies taken from biology and pottery, as well as the spoken word. Subsequently, the military metaphor predominates; a ferocious battle and subjugation precede the establishment of law and order. The common factor remains that order, however established, requires regular maintenance. The continuing threat of disorder, whether or not dignified with the title Chaos, is therefore a significant element of the Mesopotamian cosmology.

[4] In Sumerian tradition of the third millennium BCE, four primary deities were involved in creative ordering (An, Enlil, Enki and Ninhursag). Although they can occasionally behave mischievously towards one another, they create co-operatively – rather like competent technicians – without encountering resistance or real difficulty other than the occasional compromised experimentation. However, the battle between Marduk and Tiãmat of the later Mesopotamian epic is foreshadowed in a Sumerian tradition of a battle between Enki and the primaeval sweet waters Apsû. That creation could carry a 'dark' or violent aspect is further reflected in the fact that the Sumerian expression U-ri-a ('on that day') which is used in a technical way about the events of the beginning, also becomes associated with times of catastrophe in Sumerian history.

[5] *Hymn to Amun* from 18th dynasty (1365 BCE). Translation from ed. W. Beyerlin, *Near Eastern Texts Relating to the Old Testament*, London (1978), pp. 14–15. Amun is here identified with Atum and Harakhti (aspects of the sun-god in the course of the day).

[6] *The Admonitions of Ipuwer*, First Intermediate Period (c. 2160–2040 BCE).

[7] The earliest witness to the Flood narrative is known as the *Sumerian Flood Narrative*, but literary indications are that the tradition originates from the early post-Sumerian period, that is, during the first century of the second millennium. The name of the hero is Ziusudra. The subsequent *Epic of Atrahasis* includes the account of the Flood with Atrahasis as the hero. It probably dates from the classical period of Babylonian literature – the early centuries of the second millennium. Chapter XI of the *Epic of Gilgamesh* also recounts the story of the Flood; here the hero is called Utnapishtim. This was the text that George Smith of the British Museum knew when he gave his famous lecture before Prime Minister W. E. Gladstone in December 1872. It is the latest of the

three pre-biblical witnesses. George Smith was able to draw attention to the episode of the sending out of the dove, the swallow and the raven in the ancient text:

> When the seventh day arrived,
> I sent forth and set free a dove.
> The dove went forth, but came back,
> Since no resting-place for it was visible, she turned round.
> Then I sent forth and set free a swallow.
>
> ..   ..
>
> Then I sent forth and set free a raven.
>
> ..   ..
>
> (Gilgamesh XI:146ff; translation A.N.E.T., pp. 94ff.)

[8] G. von Rad, *The Problem of the Hexateuch and other Essays*, Edinburgh & London (1966), p. 143; first published Munich (1958).

[9] 'Creation, Righteousness and Salvation: "Creation Theology" as the Broad Horizon of Biblical Theology' in ed. B. W. Anderson, *Creation in the Old Testament*, London (1984), pp. 102–17. It is the first chapter (abridged) of *Altorientalische Welt in der Alttestamentlichen Theologie*, Zurich (1974).

[10] Water was not the only metaphor taken up for the pre-creation condition. Its total opposite, the dry, arid desert, could also provide an effective analogy as it does in Genesis 2:5. In ancient Sumer, for instance, there seem to have been at least two major traditions about creation. One from the south (Eridu) envisages a watery origin for all things from the seminal waters of the Apsû, and one from the north, more dry and dusty, tells of the original division of heaven and earth, and human beings sprouting from the soil broken up by Enlil's pickaxe.

[11] Cf. Ps. 93:3–4.

[12] CTA 2, iv:32 (J. C. L. Gibson, *Canaanite Myths & Legends*, Edinburgh (1978), p. 45).

[13] CTA 4, v:68–71 (*Canaanite Myths & Legends*, pp. 60–1).

[14] Hammurabi defeated the Mari kingdom to the north and that of Larsa to the south.

[15] 'Enūma Elish' are the first words of the epic which translate as 'When on high'. The opening lines illustrate typical negative descriptions of the pre-creation condition: 'When on high the heaven had not been named, Firm ground below had not been called by name'. See *ANET* pp. 60ff.

[16] Whereas in the Ba'al conflict no distinction is made in Yam between salt and sweet water, in the Marduk conflict Tiāmat is sea as distinct from sweet waters (known as 'Apsû').

[17] The laws relate to slavery, adoption, marriage and land as well as containing a criminal code.

[18] G. R. Driver & J. C. Miles, *The Babylonian Laws*, Oxford (1952) vol. 2, p. 7.

[19] The textual evidence for the reciting is from the Seleucid period (that is, the third century BCE.). Evidence for a parallel ceremony at Ashur in Assyria involving the king in a dramatic episode at the 'Akitu House' comes from the time of Sennacherib and therefore dates back to the seventh century BCE.

[20] W. G. Lambert, *The Great Battle of the Mesopotamian Religious Year*, Iraq 25 (1963), pp. 189 ff.

[21] *Near Eastern Religious Texts Relating to the Old Testament*, p. 18.

[22] T. Jacobsen, *Treasures of Darkness*, New Haven (1976). He suggests that the specific cult of Dumuzi well documented from the third millennium identifies the general characteristics of divinity and religious concerns of the previous millennium.

[23] CTA 6: iii: 12–13 (J. Gibson, *op.cit.*, p. 77).

[24] 'Gardens of Osiris' from the Middle Kingdom and 'Beds of Osiris' from the New Kingdom are well known. In both practices seeds had been placed in the tomb and watered so as to germinate, in the second case in a shape that resembles the deceased Osiris on his bier.

[25] A process M. Weber has associated with the phrase the 'disenchantment of the world'. See H. H. Gerth and C. Wright Mills, *From Max Weber, Essays in Sociology*, London (1948), pp. 51 ff. The theological disputes of the Ancient Near East have a strangely contemporary ring. Many of the issues raised about nature and divinity are re-visited in the 'New Age' debate. See, for instance, D. Reeves, *Making Sense of Religion*, London (1989).

[26] Our knowledge of the Memphite tradition we owe to the Pharaoh Shabaka (716–701 BCE). During his reign an ancient text was discovered in a worm-eaten state which, out of veneration for the teaching of the ancestors, he had copied on a black basalt stone which is now in the British Museum.

[27] 'Alone of all the Egyptian gods, Amun's true nature is not comprehended in the phenomenon of existence.' J. P. Allen, *Genesis in Egypt*, p. 61.

[28] We may compare also from ancient Egypt a similar work known as 'A Dialogue of a Man with his Soul'.

[29] *The Teaching of Merikare* (First Intermediate Period); see *Near Eastern Texts Relating to the Old Testament*, pp. 45–6.

[30] R. Murray, *The Cosmic Covenant*, London (1992).

[31] Gudea, ruler of Lagash in Mesopotamia c. 2000 BCE.

PART II

The Three Sources

The nearby mountainous landscape feeds the Jordan, but not in one single act of benevolence. The River Jordan has its origin in three major springs fed from the Hermon range. The springs rise in three separate locations with their mysterious gift of life. Like the River Jordan, the Hebrew Scriptures have three great sources. We may call them Tent, Temple and Tutor. By Tent is understood the nomadic source of Israel's faith. By Temple, the implications of the construction that Solomon built as a wonder of its time – a wonder that related not to desert culture but to Canaanite religion. Finally, there is Tutor or Teacher, to remind us that Wisdom was a permanent feature of Israel's religious life. God speaks in the Hebrew Scriptures through the tensions, patterns and even contradictions of a multiple witness.

CHAPTER 2

Tent

A. The Patriarchs

There is, in Deuteronomy 26:5, an ancient credo in which Israel acknowledges her identity: 'A wandering Aramaean was my ancestor; he went down into Egypt, and lived there as an alien. . . .'[1] Israel's story begins on the edge of the desert. Wandering semi-nomadic Amorite tribal groups with tents and flocks are surviving on the border between desert and fertile pasture by seasonal movement. They most probably penetrated the settled land after harvest, and moved back into the steppe when the rainy season increased the area capable of sustaining flocks and herds. They wanted nothing so much as the guarantee of heir and offspring, and dreamt of places of permanence in a land of milk and honey. The time is the opening of the second quarter of the second millennium BCE. The native language is probably Aramaic.

What can be known of those early nomadic roots through the opaque glass of history? Surprisingly, it is possible to piece together some helpful clues which introduce us to the essentials of patriarchal 'Tent religion'. It was Albrecht Alt[2] who identified the significant characteristic of patriarchal nomadic religion as the Hebrew Scriptures present it to us. He spotted the significance of 'the God of the Father'. He recognized that Genesis has preserved the authentic tradition that the nomadic deities were identified by the name of the patriarch to whom they were reckoned to have revealed themselves. Presumably, these were originally distinct deities but of a particular religious type. We meet, for instance, the 'Fear of Isaac' (Genesis 31:42) and the

'Mighty One of Jacob' (Genesis 49:24). These, which have been called 'frozen archaisms',[3] seem to witness to genuinely ancient tradition. In Genesis 31:44ff. the making of a treaty is recorded between Jacob and Laban; it contains authentic early material. A careful reading soon perceives that it betrays the primitive days when each group had its own 'God of the Father' before the traditions were reworked:

> The God of Abraham and the God of Nahor . . .
> judge between us. (Genesis 31:53)

It seems that the God of the Father revealed himself to the leader of a clan and henceforth entered into a special bond of relationship with that group to whom he gave his protection, guaranteed issue and provided the assurance of eventual settlement. It is a religion of revelation, of divine self-disclosure and adoption whereby the initiative is with the deity who makes himself known. There are certain basic characteristics of nomadic religion as we encounter it at the dawn of biblical religion that we can deduce from Alt's insight.

Firstly, the God of the Father is a pilgrim God tied to people rather than to place. He is not to be sought at a sanctuary, but rather accompanies his people in their journeying. That presence emphasizes the vertical axis for patriarchal religion – the relationship between God and people. Austere desert religion had no developed mythology. This is in stark contrast to the major religious traditions of the settled land within the Ancient Near East. For them it was more usual for colourful myths of temple building and cosmic battles to highlight relationships between the gods and marginalize people. The God of the Father had no such playmates in heaven. His preoccupation is with the Father and the associated clan. His presence with his people offers immediate protection and guidance and, in the longer term, guarantee of offspring and a future. The primary focus is on the divine care for the adopted community.

Secondly, patriarchal religion is a kinship religion. This fleshes out the bond between the pilgrim god and his people. The god was conceived of as bound to the group as a relative. The name Ab-ram means: 'The (Divine) Father is Exalted'. At the very beginnings of biblical religion we meet the significance of the term 'Father' for expressing the human relationship with God. Other Amorite names expand the analogies of relationship to include brother, uncle, kinsman, relative by marriage.[4] There is an intimate and mutual relationship between the god and the clan expressed in terms of the nomadic community's greatest responsibility – to their kith and kin.

The fact that the bond between the clan and the deity is expressed in kinship terms reflects the significance of the social and personal bonds that unite a familial group. We might expect, therefore, within nomadic communities a particular consciousness of mutual responsibility, trust and a strict code of community behaviour. Responsibility for and towards other people who share a clan identity is paramount for survival. Abraham's reputed words to Lot in Genesis 13:8 are certainly realistic: 'Let there be no strife between you and me, and between your herders and my herders: for we are kindred'. Abraham's responsibility for Lot even after they have separated involves the risk of planning a raid and taking strategic action to intervene on his behalf.[5] There could be no shirking such a basic responsibility. A nomad knew that he was his brother's keeper.

No doubt a mixture of ethical responsibility and passionate vengeance for perceived wrongs inflicted operated between different clans. Either way, an honour and a morality was recognized. Some words credited to a nomadic woman speaking in praise of her husband some two millennia later than Abraham bear calling to mind: 'His swords are straight and long, ready for attack or defence. The pile of ashes speaks of his hospitality. At his dwelling are consultations held.'[6]

Even today in the Sinai desert it is commonplace to see bags containing personal belongings hanging on acacia trees. They are the possessions of a Bedouin community which will be reclaimed when they return in that direction. They can be left in safety; other groups who pass that way will respect the ownership of the property such is the strict code that operates between and within Bedouin communities.[7]

Thirdly, the fact that each clan had only one God of the Father was of considerable significance. Only one divine 'next of kin' was responsible for the welfare of, and intimately bonded with the fortunes of, the travelling community. There was effectively

only one god that mattered and to whom each group was linked
as if to a relative. This is not yet technical 'monotheism' but it
is what is known as 'monolatry'. The god had chosen his people,
and once the relationship had been entered into there was
established a reciprocal responsibility of the clan towards the deity
who became their divine kinsman. There was understood to be
an exclusive, we might say monogamous bond between the god
and the clan. The nature of this relationship is at least compatible
with the later concept of covenant so characteristic of Israelite
religion.

There is a fourth significance we must consider. Morris Seale
in his book *The Desert Bible, Nomadic Tribal Culture and the Old
Testament*, looks to the evidence of nomads immediately prior to
the arrival of the Islamic faith for an understanding of ancient
Bedouin culture which he insists had changed little since the days
of Abraham. It is an interesting exercise, but any deductions need
to be handled with great care. One of the points he makes is that
poets are highly regarded in nomadic society. He draws particular
attention to an Arabian poet 'Urwa ibn al-Ward in the following
way:

> As a poet 'Urwa made his name by singing the exploits of his tribe,
> the 'Abs, in their forty year war with the Dhubyan, a rival tribe, at
> the close of the 6th century AD.[8]

In identifying the importance of the recounting of the human
story for the nomad, Seale certainly makes a valid point.

For the patriarchal clans we noted that there were no colourful
divine myths of the exploits of the gods to recount around the
campfire, but there was a rich human story to tell. What
characterizes much of Canaanite and Ancient Near Eastern
culture are vivid tales of jealousies, intrigues and exploits of the
gods. These were recounted both at religious ceremonies and
for popular entertainment. How Ba'al's palace came to be built
never ceased to fascinate and excite the agricultural communities
centred on the city-states of Canaan. Myths are the great cultural
and literary legacy of the people of Ugarit. But for ancient Israel
it is the epic tradition of her adventures and encounters in
history which she remembered, cast in poetry and handed on.
In this she is true to her identity and her roots. The tales of the

campfire for the nomad were about jealousy, intrigues and exploits, no doubt; but they were related to human figures. They were about people who led clans, planned marriages, protected their kith and kin from ambush or attack and planned strategies of migration to cope with famine or pressure of numbers. God is bound into, and his will made known through the unique events of history and the human heroes those events call forth.

A sense of history is peculiarly compatible with patriarchal tent culture. Whereas for a settled agricultural religion both the tasks of life and the festivals that celebrate them are cyclic, seasonal and repetitive, this is not so obvious in the case of the nomad. Each day is different and brings unique encounters. It emphasizes the significance of people, of decisions and of relationships. There is a sense of pilgrimage, that is, travelling to a destiny. The God of the Father promises protection through unique events, guarantees offspring and eventually holds out the hope of settlement and land; there was an immediate goal and a distant one. Life was working to an end, in the sense of a purpose. There was a human story to be told.

It has been possible to piece together, if tentatively, something of the nature of patriarchal religion; we must also note the moment at which it is introduced to us in Genesis. We first encounter the Hebrews at a boundary. The tent is being exchanged for the house: tent pegs for beams: goatskins for stones. The association of patriarchal names with particular fixed local sanctuaries witnesses to hopes fulfilled and a change of life-style in the process of happening. We can identify Abraham with Hebron, Isaac with Beersheba, Jacob with Penuel. Incidentally, these separate locations suggest similar but not related groups undergoing the process of settlement. Only later were they assembled into a family tree. Certainly at the sanctuaries, and perhaps in some cases earlier, the patriarchal deities became identified with the single high god El who was the creator and father of the Canaanite pantheon. The exclusive claim of the God of the Father on his people made the identification with the high god the most natural transfer. It was mediated through the El-divinities of the local sanctuaries, such as El-bethel 'God of Bethel' (Genesis 35:7). In this identification of the God of the Father with the creator-god El, two profoundly different ways of reflecting on the divine were brought together. A tension is set up which was to permanently become part of Israel's story.

Normally, as the wandering clans became sedentary, that is, changed their way of life to a settled agricultural existence, so their religion inevitably changed. Agricultural religion was related to place; its concept of the world was cyclic, based on the procession of the seasons. There were many gods – of thunder and storm, of grain, of the vine, of fertility and so on. Not only were you allowed, but you were expected to worship several gods. It was assumed that the successful sustaining of the vibrance of nature and the security of the city-state depended upon it. Nomadic communities were continually faced with this transition and no doubt went through a difficult *rite de passage* in which they adopted the new way of life as farmers and let go the nomadic past, including their religion. The uncomfortable transition was quickly forgotten and the stability of a new status quo embraced.

Against this background, Hebrew religion was virtually unique in holding on to this moment of transition. The Hebrews never abandoned their identity as 'wandering Aramaeans' throughout their long history. They remained with that uncomfortable boundary experience and therefore never threw off the claims of the faith of the desert. It made for tension; they could never be quite at home in their new life so long as they carried the baggage of the steppe. There would always be dilemmas, confused loyalties, inner controversies, the sense of impermanence as the divine Father called from the wilderness.

Clearly the essentials of Tent religion offered a critique of the established Canaanite religious conventions relating to settled agriculture and state security. The loyalty to the God of the Father challenged the perceived unfaithfulness of relationships with many gods. Conventions such as cultic prostitution that were practised in the name of religion conflicted with the strict morality of the clan. The embryonic sense of history was quite alien to the world of timeless myth, which seemed to suggest the gods were more absorbed with their own schemes and little to be wearied by the fortunes of the human community. The presence of the Hebrews within Canaanite culture put a little grit into the system.

The Hebrews were able to be a leavening agent within their cultural context because they retained the sense of transition. They never forgot that their identity was bound up with being wandering Aramaeans as much as farmers in the land of Canaan. Why, as was the case with every other nomadic group, was this particular example of austere and simple desert religion not simply swallowed up and absorbed into complex Canaanite religion tailor-made for the farmer? Why did the enzymes of Canaanite religion not succeed in breaking down this manifestation of desert religion? The answer seems to be: because of the unique experience of the Exodus under Moses. It was Moses who introduced God as 'Jehovah', or, as the name is now more correctly written, 'Yahweh' to the Hebrews.

B. The Mosaic Era

One section of what was to become the tribes of Israel and eventually the Hebrew nation had a truly foundational experience of deliverance at the Red Sea (Sea of Reeds).[9] It impressed itself as a moment of divine revelation and awesome rescue. These Hebrews, probably attracted to Egypt at a time of famine as the Bible suggests, had eventually been forced to sell themselves and their families for food in order to survive. They were no doubt one of many groups of foreign extraction that became trapped in Egypt and subject to the forced levy by which Rameses II 'the Great' and his immediate successors built the 'store cities' Pithom and Raamses in the thirteenth century BCE.

The pill of servitude became too bitter to take. This particular group had the opportunity to escape their serfdom, seized it and fled into the wilderness (Exodus 14:5a). They were pursued by their Egyptian hosts bent on making them an object lesson for others who contemplated a similar manoeuvre. At the moment when it looked as if the runaway slaves were about to be helpless victims of ruthless Egyptian vengeance they were saved against all the odds. A sudden change in the forces of nature protected the fugitives from annihilation by engulfing their pursuers in the sea.

It may be that the oldest witness to this event is contained in some early poetry from the Book of Exodus often called 'The

Song of the Sea'. The initial verses of the poem are here quoted
from the translation by F. M. Cross who sees in them a storm at
sea which throws the Egyptians from their boats.[10] Perhaps the
Egyptians were taking a short cut across the water to catch up
with the Hebrews who had travelled a longer route by land when
the events unfolded:

> Sing to Yahweh,
> For he is highly exalted
> Horse and chariotry
> He cast into the Sea.
> This is my God whom I exalt,
> The god of my father whom I admire.
> Yahweh is a warrior
> Yahweh is his name.
> Pharaoh and his army
> He hurled into the sea.
> His elite troops
> Drowned in the Reed Sea.
> The deeps covered them;
> They sank in the depths like a stone. (Exodus 15:1b–5)

Such was the searing effect of this event that not only was it
remembered by the descendants of those who had experienced
it, but was strong enough to bond that group with others of a
similar itinerant stock who had remained in Canaan and had not
shared the same experience. They, too, would have been
worshippers of the 'God of the Father', in the settled land
identified with the high god El. They now knew their god as
Yahweh. From the Exodus onwards Yahweh was the definitive
name for the God of Israel; he had a special relationship with
the Hebrews which E. W. Nicholson has expressed this way:

> Yahweh was acknowledged to be the God who alone stood at the
> foundation and beginning of Israel.[11]

The consequence of the Exodus experience of deliverance was
to reinforce the essentials of Tent religion. According to a passage
that has been traditionally identified as coming from one of the
early epic strands within the narrative contained from Genesis
to Numbers (known as the Elohist) the call of Moses at the
burning bush is firmly connected with patriarchal religion: 'I am
the God of your father, the God of Abraham, the God of Isaac,

and the God of Jacob' (Exodus 3:6). The parallel epic tradition
of the Yahwist similarly records the divine order to Moses to go
to the elders of Israel and say: 'The Lord, the God of your
ancestors, the God of Abraham, of Isaac, and of Jacob, has
appeared to me' (Exodus 3:16). The significance of the rescue
at the sea in theological terms was that the pilgrim god had saved
his people with his protection and guidance. He had revealed
himself as saviour. They owed their very existence to this single
act of divine election and compassion. The bond of familial
relationship demanded that loyalty, affection and commitment
be given to Yahweh in return. This bond of relationship became
the unassailable basis of Israel's religion. It assured continuing
protection in the precarious business of journeying in the
wilderness, it gave reason to hope for the renewal of the
generations and the eventual goal of land and settlement.

It is the company of the Exodus escapees gathered at Mount
Sinai that gives expression to the warmth of relationship and the
thankfulness of response in the face of divine initiative. The story
of the rescue from Egypt and the account of the events at Sinai,
despite their evidence of independent development,[12] are
securely bonded by two significant features. These are the human
name Moses and the divine name Yahweh. The close association
of Moses with Midian, the tribal inhabitants of the Sinai area, is
noted in the Bible. The father-in-law of Moses is a Midianite
priest.[13] Hobab, who acts as guide to Moses in the wilderness, is
identified as a Midianite and a kinsman of Moses.[14] The tenacity
of these traditions, in the light of the bitter hostility between Israel
and Midian which later prevailed,[15] seems to witness to a truth
which could not be conveniently forgotten or suppressed. But
Moses is an Egyptian name.[16] It has been expressed this way:

> And it is a fact of some significance in human history that the founder
> of the Yahweh religion had an Egyptian name.[17]

It places Moses firmly and indisputably within the Egyptian setting
of the Exodus. Correspondingly, Yahweh is the divine name that
the earliest traditions associate with the Exodus rescue as was
noted with the Song of the Sea (Exodus 15). He is also in the
very earliest traditions connected with Sinai (Judges 5:4; Deut.
33:2). He is clearly integral to both cycles.

It seems a reasonable supposition that the name and character of Yahweh is mediated by the tribal traditions of Midian and Sinai. In that case Yahweh is certainly identified correctly by the ministers of the King of Aram in 1 Kings 20:23 when they complain of the Hebrews:

> Their gods are gods of the hills,
> and so they were stronger than we;
> but let us fight against them in the plain,
> and surely we shall be stronger than they.

If the worship of Yahweh originated with nomadic tribes inhabiting the mountainous region of Sinai[18] then that worship was not at home with the settled agricultural existence distinctive of the plain. There is a recognition of the distinction between tribal and agricultural religion.

There is one major difference between nomadic religion as we have previously identified it and the association of Yahweh with Mount Sinai. At Sinai we find a connection with place which was not true originally of the 'God of the Father': This is perhaps a feature distinctive of Midianite religion, for Sinai identifies place in the context of the religion of nomadic tribes. Yahweh's association with Sinai and with the numinous natural phenomenon of a mountain, whether storm or volcanic activity, does not prevent him coming to the Hebrews as a pilgrim god and travelling with them in their escape. However, there is no doubt that the association of Yahweh with Mount Sinai is very ancient. It was for worshippers of Yahweh regarded as the Mountain of God. It was the place to seek out for communion with God, as Elijah was reported to have done in the days of Ahab.[19] The presence of the Hebrews on Mount Sinai is in origin probably not to receive the law but to establish their relationship with the God who had rescued them from Egypt. It was above all a place of communion, where their adoption by Yahweh could be properly acknowledged and the assent of their loyalty formally given. If Sinai sealed the adoption by, and the kinship of, Yahweh with his people, then inevitably the responsibilities were mutual. Yahweh had taken the Exodus community as his own, but that bond of relationship immediately involved the recognition of reciprocal obligations on the part of the people.

In acknowledging Yahweh, God of Sinai, as the God of the Exodus rescue, the seal was set on Israel's spiritual life at the boundary. She was to carry with her into the settled land an identity that ultimately could not be shaken or exchanged. Her identity as a tent people was now fixed once and for all in her consciousness.

We have come a long way from the statement of a distinguished scholar with reference to the one context he reckoned the Mosaic tradition to be originally at home in, namely the 'guidance into the arable land':

> Moses entered into this narrative because his grave site lay on the path of the Israelites who were occupying the land.[20]

The human name of Moses and the divine name of Yahweh, the God whom Moses introduced to Israel, bridge the two traditions of Exodus and Sinai. Here we encounter a real and foundational experience of rescue which became the basis of a profound sense of adoption by God and gratitude to God. That adoption and gratitude is focused in the journey to, and the communion at, the Mountain of God. The tradition of Moses' death in Transjordan,[21] before the Exodus community enter the promised land, further links the traditions of Exodus and Sinai with the settlement, the open future, and the expectation that the faithfulness of the pilgrim community to Yahweh would be rewarded in offspring and land. The nomad's dream found fulfilment.

It is perhaps enough that Moses led the Hebrews out of Egypt to Sinai, that he was founder of Israel's Yahwistic faith, that he presided over the establishment of a bond between the people and God, and that he inspired the hope for an open future that the divine adoption guaranteed. History cannot claim for him that he was the lawgiver in the way that tradition came to affirm him. The episode of Sinai has attracted an enormous collection of law that enabled Israel to offer her daily life to God once she had settled in the promised land. It is in that offering of her life to God that we may still claim the link with what Moses did and was.

In that weight of legislative material that is so characteristic of the Pentateuch, the most prized and well known is the

Decalogue or Ten Commandments.[22] If these were not chiselled in stone by, or for, Moses where do they come from? All we can say is that evidence of the stream of tradition with which they are to be associated certainly emerges with the prophet Hosea in the eighth century. That may be a clue as to their age. Hosea proclaims:

> Swearing, lying, and murder, and stealing, and adultery break out; bloodshed follows bloodshed. (Hosea 4:2)

Did Hosea already know of the Ten Commandments, or is he in the heat of the ferment which was to produce them? The jury is still out.

The question remains as to why the proclamation of law should have become in the tradition so intimately associated with Sinai, that the weight of it now overwhelms the narrative context. Perhaps it was because the law presented the mechanism whereby Israel's life was offered to God. It may be that the account of Moses' father-in-law advising Moses how to delegate the burden of judgement (Exodus 18:13–27) provided the initial occasion for the wholesale legal adoption of the Sinai episode by Israel's lawmakers. But it is also true that already the germ of the first two commandments are contained in the Sinai story.

The first two of the Ten Commandments, which insist on the worship of Yahweh alone and forbid images, have a tradition history separate from the community regulations of the following eight commandments. Now, on the one hand it can be argued that these commandments would not be relevant until the Hebrews entered the land of Canaan and encountered a plethora of gods and goddesses. On the other hand, the two initial commandments would have had much relevance to a people coming out of Egypt where both gods and images were numerous (Joshua 24:14). It has been argued above that for 'the God of the Father' there was already an exclusive bond once the clan had been adopted by the deity, as Yahweh had adopted the Exodus community. There was surely, therefore, an awareness that the relationship entered into on Mount Sinai was an exclusive, monogamous as it were, commitment to Yahweh. It is tempting also wonder whether the geographical link between Yahweh and Sinai may have rendered any other representations of Yahweh superfluous to the point where convention had abandoned them. Human beings need tangible ways of focusing their religious devotion; perhaps Yahweh of Sinai needed neither ark nor statue because he had a sacred mountain which could localize his numinous presence.[23] In that case it is possible, and we can say no more, that communion with Yahweh from the beginning of Israel's faith involved, if not yet a demand, certainly the assumption of total loyalty and the recognition that images were superfluous.

In new circumstances, away from the nomadic way of life, these quite natural customs and conventions became a peculiar badge of identity. Their maintenance may at that stage have become a matter of regulation and prescription. The living community of faith, true to its nomadic roots, further extended these 'commandments' to make clear that loyalty towards God, of necessity, involves responsibility towards one's neighbour. If this further development is taking place at the time of Hosea in the eighth century then it is interesting to note that precisely then the Hebrew religious tradition reasserts its tent roots and challenges conventional religion. With the eighth century prophets, in particular, the grit is evident in the system.[24] It is at this time, indeed in the ministry of the prophet Hosea, that the relationship between the Hebrews and Yahweh first becomes dignified with the technical term 'covenant'.[25] The concept of an unconditional relationship involved in election between God and his people is shaken in favour of a conditional bond with obligations on both sides if the 'vow and covenant' is to remain valid.

The notion of covenant reflects a developing sense of the transcendence of God, and with it the heightened awareness of God as judge as well as sustainer. It involves a recognition of the uncomfortable, challenging identity of Israel's boundary faith. The divine is threat as well as comfort. The eighth century prophets were crucial catalysts in this process. They interpreted the changing and menacing political circumstances, which lead firstly to the demise of the northern Kingdom and eventually to the exile of Judah, as evidence of God's judgement and the consequences of his holiness. In the changed theological perspective we see Hebrew faith flex its muscles and break the mould of the Ancient Near Eastern perspective based on an unassailable natural bond between God and his people. It is a development which enabled the survival of Yahwistic faith through the soul-searching and questioning of the Exile. It is an issue to which we shall return in due course in discussing the significance of the prophetic ministry for Israel's developing faith. The uncomfortable, boundary nature of Israel's faith was never without its witnesses.

C. Living at the Boundary as Evidenced by the Yahwist's Primaeval History

A *rite de passage* is devised in order to help an individual or a community through a significant period of transition. That transition may involve heightened joy or grief or even a mixture of both. It is also a moment of vulnerability, of often painful exposure and anxiety. It is not a comfortable experience although it may be a very rich and productive one. It is a necessary phase, but not normally a place to remain.

Something analogous to this must have been the experience undergone by countless nomadic groups who made the transition from the life of Bedouin to the life of peasant farmers. As they crossed the boundary from the semi-fertile steppe to the fertile land, so they crossed a major cultural bridge. They had to let go of the lifestyle, the customs and the religion of their old life in order to embrace the potential rewards of a settled agricultural existence. In the context of the biblical traditions it has been referred to as 'that other Exodus'.[26]

For the Hebrews it was different. They were destined to remain spiritually poised at the point of transition. Mosaic religion decisively located them in an uncomfortable place; to some extent they were permanently exposed and vulnerable. Against all the odds they did not simply enter the promised land and cast off their former identity. Despite the Davidic monarchy clothing them in the mindset and the conventions of Canaanite culture and the abundant archaeological evidence of religious syncretism, an integrity was sustained. The ability of Yahwistic faith to reassert its identity decreed that they were to struggle with tensions of belonging and not belonging, of hearing a call from somewhere else, of not being able to throw off the moment of transition. They were not to be totally at peace with themselves, but to struggle with their identity, with their vocation and with the turmoil of inner controversy. Yet the experience of being permanently on a boundary and at the margin was potentially rich and fruitful in its consequences. It was the ingredient that made Israel distinct, and in the end enabled her to find a unique vocation. There was always a minority, often an irritating minority, that carried the memory of Hebrew identity.

The telling of the human story remained throughout Israel's history one of the hallmarks by which it can be verified that she remained true to her unique religious identity. Not only was she conscious of but also cognizant of the confession: 'A wandering Aramaean was my father'. F. M. Cross in entitling his book *Canaanite Myth and Hebrew Epic* drew attention to one of the distinguishing features of Israel against her context. Whereas a characteristic of Canaanite culture was its rich mythology and the complex tales of the drama of the gods, the identity of Israel is bound up with her ability to tell the human story in the context of her relationship with Yahweh and to carry her own colourful history in epic tradition.

The identity and the escapades of many of Israel's judges, kings and prophets are recorded with a vividness that is often arresting. It is of some significance that it is possible to make a strong case for two early epic sources (J and E) commencing in Genesis, one with the creation and the other with the call of Abraham, which are traceable at least to the Mosaic era. The continuing interest in the epic tradition is taken up with great fervour in the period of the Exile when the priestly school was occupied editing a history of God's covenants from the creation through the Patriarch Abraham to the time of Moses. That is contained in the bulk of what we know as Genesis to Numbers. Concurrently, the Deuteronomistic historians were editing a history of the Hebrews from the wilderness wanderings to the Exile and drawing lessons from history and recounting God's dealings with his people as they interpreted them. That record is contained in books beginning with Deuteronomy and continuing through to 2 Kings.

The preoccupation with telling the human story, the consciousness of history and the sense of God accompanying his people in their changing fortunes is both characteristically Israelite and peculiarly compatible with her origins in tent culture. That this specific identity could remain with her through her long history witnesses to the power of the Exodus experience to freeze in her memory a moment of transition and, in a very remarkable way, sustain her in that uncomfortable but creative pose. There must have been particular vehicles of memory and there must have been specific circles who transmitted an uncompromising Yahwistic faith.

The tradition of telling the human story and God's intimate involvement with it was directly related to the uncompromising demand of Mosaic religion that Yahweh alone demanded Israel's total loyalty. It was an uncomfortable legacy of the Tent tradition that Israel found herself in the settled land where the support system of religion that had evolved to meet the specific needs of an agricultural community not only allowed but required polytheistic worship. Yet the demands of her religious identity ran counter to that culture. In so far as she honoured that loyalty then not only was Yahweh alone the God of Israel, but the consequence was that the human story, and especially the story of Israel, took on a particular significance. As C. Westermann has expressed it:

> Where God is unique, (and all that is not God is but humanity and the world), where there is no place for excitement and drama in the realm of the divine such as love and conflict, birth and death, rise and fall, then this unique being which is not God, namely the individual and his history in the world, becomes of great importance.[27]

The verdict of history is that until the ministry of the eighth-century prophets the significance of Yahweh-only for Hebrew religion was neither recognized nor observed in popular practice. Yet the deposit of Israel's epic literature witnesses to a tryst honoured, whatever the evidence from the sources of the burden and heat of the day borne by the few rather than the many.

The earliest epic strand is that of the Yahwist. It has been identified by G. von Rad as a product of the Solomonic enlightenment,[28] and by J. Wellhausen as early in the eighth century.[29] Those two scholars provide the boundaries as regards its dating.[30] It is a remarkable 'first', in a vibrant way gathering Israel's history into a single whole and for the first time relating it to the great traditions of creation and the origins of civilization encountered in the settled land. Whether it ended with the death of Moses or in the settlement remains an open question. It is early in the process of Israel's reflection on her identity, and yet the synthesis is evident between the Yahweh-only demand of the Tent inheritance and the claims of divinity as creator-sustainer in the settled land. It witnesses to the rich and fruitful consequences of Israel's unique identity living at a boundary. It is also evidence of the fact that the success of monarchy, not simply the leanness of exile, was able to stimulate quality theological reflection. On the evidence of the Yahwist the ministry of the eighth-century prophets intensified and brought to a crescendo a spirit and an identity already, at least in certain circles, integral to Israel's developing faith.

Including a Primaeval History, very much a fruit of encounter with the religious perspective of the settled land, and in such a way as not simply to preface but to transform Israel's history and give it a whole new purpose, is certainly due to the Yahwist's originality. He portrays the call of Abraham as the divine response to the instability and dilemmas of Primaeval History. In so doing he turns religious convention upside down, for which creation and Primaeval History stabilized the present. We may therefore use the Yahwist's Primaeval History within Genesis 1–11 as a valid sample.[31] Through it, using a compact text, we may gauge the Yahwist's purpose and illustrate something of the potentially distinctive quality of Israel's Tent-faith, the hallmark of which was the telling of the human story, as it encounters the rich culture and customs of the settled land.

Four features stand out as particularly significant in the way the Yahwist presents Primaeval History. The first, crucially, relates to its developed quality of story-telling and 'joined up' thinking. The Yahwist presents an epic history of the Hebrew people, which is leavened by acquaintance with the significance of God as creator. He presents his narrative in such a way that his respect for tradition enables him to take the individual pearls and string them so that a connecting thread brings goal, purpose and unity to a mass of received pieces, to shrewd human observation and to perceived divine purpose. If we take seriously von Rad's identification of a 'credo' in Deut. 26:5 ff., then tradition gave the Yahwist a basis upon which to work. Bringing together that tradition and presenting it in the context of a Primaeval History was the Yahwist's own particular genius.

Despite being, as far as we know, a first attempt at connecting Israel's history and sense of vocation to the great received tradition of creation and the origins of civilization, the Yahwist achieves remarkable seamlessness. As we noted, the Primaeval History is far from being a disconnected preface to the unfolding history that begins with the call of Abraham. The Primaeval History is bonded into the total work so that it transforms the whole. God's call of a people is set in the context of his creation of the nations, and therefore his purpose for the world. Of this initiative of the Yahwist in prefixing the Primaeval History to Israel's epic traditions it has been said that he:

> Thereby simultaneously invested his work with that theological breadth and depth that make it one of the most important components of the transmitted Pentateuch.[32]

The Yahwist's connecting link is achieved by the verses in Genesis 12:1–3, which recount the call and blessing of Abraham.

> Now the Lord said to Abram, 'Go from your country and your kindred and your father's house to the land that I will show you. I will make of you a great nation, and I will bless you, and make your name great, so that you will be a blessing. I will bless those who bless you, and the one who curses you I will curse; and in you all the families of the earth shall be blessed.

These are familiar words of blessing normally reserved for a king. They find a close parallel from that context in Psalm 72 v. 17. The form is very similar; the king's blessedness will overflow upon his people and bring universal blessing. That blessing transferred to Abraham at once looks forward to the blessing that Israel will bestow by her presence throughout her history, but also carries the resonance of the global nature of the primaeval traditions. The fact that the blessing is uttered upon Abraham, of course, makes it effective for the whole story he initiates. However a blessing in the ancient world always follows the naming of the creator. When Melchizedek blesses Abraham in Genesis 14:18–20 it is in the name of 'God Most High, creator of heaven and earth'.[33] The very nature of a blessing binds it to the primaeval creation traditions.

By anchoring a blessing upon Abraham at the very foundation of sacred history the Yahwist has been able to introduce the primaeval traditions in a way that makes them an integral part of a single narrative. The Tent tradition, which stimulated the telling of the human story, has interacted with the creation traditions, reaching a new level of skill and attained a classic form in this author. He is helped by the influence of the Wisdom tradition, which, for instance, in the narrative of Joseph in Egypt, had developed the ability to recount a complex, connected story in a way that is full of emotion, irony and unexpected developments. The story of the Hebrews begins, from now on, with the story of human origins and the creation of the world. The Yahwist's work certainly deserves the title 'epic history'.

The second feature is of enormous significance. In the Yahwist's Primaeval History the 'monolatry' of the Tent tradition is worked out in a vibrant and evident monotheism which is a further remarkable achievement. The potential of the Tent tradition is again translated into actuality. It is achieved by the association of monolatry with the creator. Any reference to plurality in heaven is now something of an archaism. The only place where the tradition of the council of gods familiar to the Yahwist from his environment enters the narrative untamed in the whole of the Primaeval History is the episode of the sons of God and the daughters of humankind (often called the Angel Marriages) in Genesis 6:1–4. The place where the transformation from polytheism to monotheism can most obviously be exposed is in the way the Yahwist treats the flood narrative.

The sole effective presence of Yahweh in heaven has radically changed the divine context of the drama of the flood. In the Yahwist's account the 'dissension between the gods becomes the dissension within God'.[34] What in Mesopotamia is a conflict within the heavenly council between those gods intent on destroying human beings and those scheming to preserve them, in the hands of the Yahwist has to be reconciled in the emotions of a single divine personality who is both creator-sustainer and judge. The decision to bring about a flood has taken on a moral dimension so that it has become not a response to the commotion of human beings whose proliferation provides a threat to the gods, but rather a verdict on the wickedness of the human race. Incomprehensibly, Yahweh God who made the human creatures also brings about their destruction. The Yahwist has to bring to birth a new theology which is subsequently and much later articulated from the exile by Deutero-Isaiah when he proclaims:

> I form light, and create darkness,
> I make weal and create woe;
> I the Lord do all these things. (Isaiah 45:7)

The Yahwist's conclusion is that God cannot judge his own creatures without pain. A similar pain of Yahweh in judging his own people is at least implicit in the subsequent prophetic message, for instance in the prophet Hosea (see Hosea 11:8–9). It is the pain of God which is the most original contribution of the Yahwist in his own prologue to the traditional flood story in Genesis 6:5–8. If God has brought about such a terrible judgement it can only be at enormous cost to himself. We are aware of the searing effect of such a dreadful decision in the Mesopotamian epics. It is opposed by the god Enki (the advocate of human preservation) and the mother goddess weeps. In the Atrahasis Epic, Atrahasis (the hero of the story who prefigures Noah) cannot eat as he contemplates the event and 'vomits gall'. All that tension and pain is taken up by the Yahwist into God:

> And the Lord was sorry that he had made humankind on the earth, and it grieved him to his heart. (Genesis 6:6)

The emotions expressed in this verse are strong.[35] Even from the Yahwist, who has accustomed us to expect descriptions of God which have a childlike simplicity and boldness, there is a vividness to his portrayal of the feelings of the Almighty which borders on the shocking. The strong emotions certainly link the regret and the grief of God directly to the terrible episode of the destruction of humankind.

It is the text of Deutero-Isaiah that presents us with a theology of the suffering servant, but it is the Yahwist who dares to perceive suffering in the heart of the Master and thereby acknowledges its potential role in the process of redemption. He has plumbed the depths and explored the consequences of the taking of the Tent tradition, with its insistence on Yahweh-only, into the settled land with its particular cultural, literary and creation traditions. He has dared in his testing of the boundaries of Yahwistic monotheism to interrogate the psychology of God.

Our third point is a development from the monotheism of the Yahwist's narrative. It has previously been noted that the consequence of the absence of any divine counterparts for absorbing the divine energy in heaven is the highlighting of the significance of the human story and God's emotional involvement with his human creatures. Throughout the Primaeval History we can detect a human-centredness.

Every conversation of Yahweh is with human beings, apart from one instance alone when he addresses the serpent (Genesis 3:14). Any occasional reference to the council of gods as we noted above has become redundant. For instance, in the Babel story when Yahweh reflects: 'Come, let us go down, and confuse their language' (Genesis 11:7) it is an indication of the pre-history of the text in a polytheistic environment and no longer relevant to the new context. It serves to remind us that in other contexts the primaeval story was told very much more as a conversation between the gods, and human affairs were relatively marginal.

Every emotion of Yahweh is generated by response to human deeds and actions. After the taking of the fruit in the garden the dialogue between Yahweh and first Eve and then Adam is full of drama and tension. A similar emotive and dramatic conversation is repeated as Yahweh interrogates Cain as his brother's blood cries out from the ground. In particular, Yahweh's strong emotions generated by human behaviour are expressed in the Yahwist's account of the flood narrative where, as we noted, regret and vexation are attributed to him (Genesis 6:6).

The way creation is presented by the Yahwist has a domestic and human-scale context. Human beings are created in a garden which represents a small and relatively secure world. When the creation of animals is recounted it is not, as in the Priestly creation account, for their own sake and as part of a greater order. They are created as a first attempt at bringing companionship to Adam (Genesis 2:18–20) which is subsequently found in Eve (vv.21–23).

There is, further, in the Primaeval History 'an enigmatic divine restraint'[36] which spares human beings the real consequences that their actions should bring upon them. There is a divine warmth towards human beings. A sort of irrational love of Yahweh for Solomon at his birth (2 Samuel 12:24) which is a feature of the 'Succession Narrative', is, in the Yahwist's Primaeval History, directed towards human beings as a whole. Adam and Eve are given coats of protection by God as they are driven from the garden, Cain is saved from the natural consequences of his murder by a mark of Yahweh's protection, the ark itself in the Yahwist's flood story is emphatically an ark of grace which assures humankind a future. The discord of Babel is followed by the blessing of Abraham.

Throughout the Primaeval History the arena of Yahweh's emotions and relationships is presented as directly concerned with human beings. The creation traditions are a feature of the high civilizations of the Ancient Near East in which the Canaanites participated. The human-centredness of the Yahwist's account is not. It relies for its inspiration on the Tent tradition for which the axis lies not between God and the gods, but between God and human beings.

We must turn to a fourth and final point. The Yahwist's articulation of monotheistic faith brought us to an encounter with God as judge in addition to God as creator and sustainer. It is of some significance that the Yahwist portrays Yahweh God as judge, as uncomfortable to live with and as in moral controversy with human beings.

The Primaeval History as the Yahwist has transmitted it to us has a conspicuous identity brought to it by the colourful primaeval stories. The Garden of Eden, the Cain and Abel narrative, the Flood, the scattering of the Nations (through the Genealogy of the Peoples and through the narrative of Babel) are representative of the way a developing and unfolding account is presented, connected by the thread of genealogy, through which the evolution of the natural order, the human environment and complex civilization, is presented. It is a hallmark of the Yahwist's narrative that the primaeval period develops through the hidden activity of divine providence rather than a series of divine interventions. However, the presence of Yahweh and his direct

personal encounter with his creatures is also a feature of
Primaeval History as nowhere else either in the Yahwist's own
epic or indeed in the biblical narrative. Characteristic of this
presence is the sense of a court in which Yahweh himself is both
counsel for the prosecution and judge. The direct dispensation
of justice is exactly as Job had prayed to experience it:

> O that I knew where I might find him,
> that I might come even to his dwelling!
> I would lay my case before him,
> and fill my mouth with arguments.
> I would learn what he would answer me,
> and understand what he would say to me. (Job 23:3–5)

Throughout the Primaeval History in a direct and immediate way
Yahweh does 'tear open the heavens and come down' (Isaiah
64:1). In these encounters there is always evidence of divine
mercy, yet they are in the nature of a dispute to be settled. The
presence of Yahweh is confrontational and challenges the moral
integrity of the human creature who is nevertheless able to hold
council with the creator.

The individual scenes of the primaeval narrative both present
the opportunities of the evolving complex patterns of human
society and culture within their environment, and also articulate
the shadow-side of progress. In particular, in the Yahwist's
assessment, the ability of human beings to pervert the good and
so distort and disfigure their environment is evident. Into that
world of distortion and disfigurement the presence of Yahweh
enters as conscience, judge and the one who challenges human
sin.

Yahweh confronts the human couple in the garden, he
challenges Cain for his brother's murder, he sees the wickedness
of human beings and makes the decision to wipe out the human
race with a flood, he scatters humanity from Babel. There is a
very close parallel with the ministry of the prophets. Yahweh's
challenging of Cain is reminiscent of both the prophet Nathan's
challenging of David for the state assassination of Uriah and of
Elijah's confrontation of Ahab for the murder of Naboth. The
finality of Yahweh's decision to bring about the flood has its echo
in the words of Amos: 'The end has come upon my people
Israel' (Amos 8:2b). The controversy of the prophets with the

people of God bears the stamp of similarity with God's dealing with fitful humanity in the Yahwist's Primaeval History.

It was the convention of classical prophetic confrontation, however hopeless the task, always to allow room for repentance and a change of heart. That this is not part of the dynamic of the Yahwist's Primaeval History is significant. It suggests that we are not dealing simply with another witness from the classic prophetic era, but rather with an earlier manifestation of the controversy of God before it had developed into the standard pattern: confrontation – room for repentance – judgement. The earlier parallels with Nathan and Elijah are significant here.

The fact that Yahweh is not portrayed simply as creator-sustainer, but also as judge and disturber of conscience has enormous implications. It represents a break with the traditional concept of deity in the Ancient Near East for which the divine was the servant of the stability of the natural order and the given social conventions. For the divine to challenge and upset the status quo means a break between the divine and the natural order, and a new emphasis on transcendence. The mould is being shattered, for which the maintenance of creation's equilibrium represents the limits of divinity.

The theological significance of a sea-change in the way divinity was perceived had enormous consequences. The world was no longer simply to be sustained in its present form and everything new shunned. The world might be transformed by confrontation with the divine. The presence of God was not simply to be understood as soothing and caressing, but also challenging and uncomfortable. God is not simply the servant of the status quo, but the Master of a potentially new order. The future need not necessarily be bound by the past. The possibility of redemption is articulated.

The potential to recognize God as transcendent and to articulate a break between the divine and the created order, creator and creature, was open to the whole Ancient Near East. It was the Hebrews who painfully and faithfully discovered it and proclaimed it. How did that come about? It was the strangeness of the Tent tradition carried into the settled land which acted as a disturber of the status quo, source of controversy and divine irritant. In so doing it triggered a potential assembled in the

Ancient Near East but never otherwise released. The call from
the desert sounded in the settled land as the voice of a stranger.
It came as a voice that unsettled and disturbed, and in so doing
revealed the presence of God as mysterious, 'other', holy and
transcendent.

The Yahwist's Primaeval History has enabled us to take a
sample from an early venture to write an epic history of the
Hebrew people. The very epic nature of the Yahwist's work is
evidence of its faithfulness to the Tent tradition, yet it would have
been impossible without the sophistication of Canaanite culture
and its creation theology. A vibrant monotheism has adapted and
transformed the polytheistic primaeval tales. The human-
centredness of the way in which the primaeval traditions are
presented represents a re-working of the given theological
perspective of the Ancient Near East. God is presented as judge
as well as sustainer. All these features witness to the fact that there
were those who were faithful to living at a point of transition,
and were willing to hold on to an uncomfortable boundary
experience. The consequences were rich and fruitful. The sample
explored has revealed to us evidence from the quarry-face of what
it meant faithfully to carry the Tent tradition deep into the
settled land. It later fell to the classical prophets to recall Israel
to that boundary place.

Points for Discussion

1. Of the four features of patriarchal Tent religion, which
   do you think was the most significant for Israel's future
   faith?
2. Can you think of ways, from your own experience, in
   which a moment of transition has been both challenging
   and enriching? In what sense is it true to talk of the change
   of lifestyle for the Hebrews from the steppe to the settled
   land as 'that other Exodus'?
3. The experience of the Exodus rescue was a truly
   foundational experience of deliverance for the Hebrews.
   What feelings are uppermost in the 'Song of the Sea'
   (Exodus 15:1–18)? How might the Egyptians have

understood God's involvement? Are you aware either for communities or individuals (yourself included) of any similar intense 'religious experience'?

4. What were the major contradictions between the perspective of Tent religion and the settled land?

5. How would you write your own recent story and express God's presence in it?

Key Bible Passages

Deuteronomy 26:1–11 (the context of Israel's 'credo'); Genesis 32:22–32 (Jacob associated with the sanctuary at Penuel); Exodus 15:1–18 (*The Song of the Sea*: an ancient poetic record of the Exodus-conquest); Genesis 6:5–8 (the Yahwist's own preface to the traditional Flood Narrative).

Further Reading

A. Alt, *The God of the Father, Essays in Old Testament History and Religion*, Oxford (1966), pp. 3–77.

F. M. Cross, *Canaanite Myth and Hebrew Epic*, Cambridge, Mass. (1973), ch. 6, 'The Song of the Sea and Canaanite Myth', pp. 112–44.

Morris S. Seale, *The Desert Bible, Nomadic Tribal Culture and Old Testament Interpretation*, London (1974).

Figure 2.   Rameses II (1304–1237 BCE), probably the Pharaoh of Israel's bondage, makes an offering: from his funerary temple at Abydos. Beside are his royal cartouches.

Endnotes

[1] 'Deut XXVI.5ff is a creed with all the characteristics and attributes of a creed, and is probably the earliest recognisable example.' G. von Rad, *The Problem of the Hexateuch and Other Essays*, Edinburgh and London (1966), p. 5 (German edition 1958).

[2] A. Alt, *Der Gott der Väter*, Stuttgart (1929). English translation: *The God of the Father, Essays in Old Testament History and Religion*, Oxford (1966), pp. 3–77.

[3] F. M. Cross, *Canaanite Myth and Hebrew Epic*, Cambridge, Mass. (1973), p. 5.

[4] F. M. Cross, ibid., p. 6, note 10.

[5] Genesis 14:13–16.

[6] Morris S. Seale, *The Desert Bible, Nomadic Tribal Culture and Old Testament Interpretation*, London (1974), p. 123.

[7] This story was told to a group on a diocesan training scheme at St Edmundsbury Cathedral. Later, a student told me that she had left her Bible, a notebook and her sandwiches hanging in a bag in the cloakroom. Afterwards she went to get her bag and found it had been gone through – the Bible and notebook remained but the sandwiches had gone! An illustration in reverse of the dimension of trust involved in leaving bags unattended.

[8] Morris S. Seale, *The Desert Bible*, p. 109.

[9] 'Certain indications suggest that the Exodus tradition was cultivated especially in the "house of Joseph" (cf. Josh. 17:17ff.; Judges 1:22,35), that is, in the later northern Kingdom . . . It is surely no accident that it is the Joseph narrative (Gen. 37–50) that unites the traditions of patriarchs and Exodus. In addition, the sons of Joseph, Ephraim and Manasseh (according to Gen. 41:50–2; 46: 20; 48:5ff.) had an Egyptian mother and were born in Egypt; while people living in the area of Ephraim have Egyptian names (Josh. 24:33; 1 Sam. 2:34).' W. H. Schmidt, *The Faith of the Old Testament*, p. 28ff.

[10] For the translation see F. M. Cross, *Canaanite Myth and Hebrew Epic*, p. 127 ff. Of this passage he says: 'In our view, the hymn is not merely one of the oldest compositions preserved by biblical sources. It is the primary source for the central event in Israel's history, the Exodus-conquest.' *Op. cit.*, p. 123.

[11] E. W. Nicholson, *God and His People*, Oxford (1986), p. 202.

[12] G. von Rad, *The Problem of the Hexateuch*, p. 19: 'We can say no more than this, that we have two traditions, one of which is incorporated into the other as a subordinate element.'

[13] Exodus 4:18–20; Exodus 18. 'Since Moses' father-in-law is also called a Kenite, it can be conjectured that the tribes of the Midianites and the Kenites stood in a relationship of kinship (cf. Enoch as a son or sub-group of Kain in Genesis 4:17 and of Midian in 25:4), that is, ultimately we have a single tradition. If, however, a distinction must be made between the two traditions, the connection with the Midianites must be regarded as the older. Israel's connections with them were, unlike those with the Kenites, tense at a later date.' W. H. Schmidt, *The Faith of the Old Testament*, p. 61.

[14] Numbers 10:29 cf. Judges 1:16, 4:11 where Hobab is identified as a Kenite.

[15] Judges 6ff.; Isaiah 9:3; 10:26; Hab. 3:7; Num. 25:6ff.; 31.

[16] 'The name Moses (Hebrew Mōše) is undoubtedly not of Hebrew but of Egyptian origin. Well-known personal names like Thutmoses or Rameses have the meaning "the god . . . is born, or has born (him)". Moses is an abbreviated form (attested also occasionally in Egyptian) of a type of name with the sense roughly of "son"; the theophorous element, that is, the divine name, has fallen out.' W. H. Schmidt, *The Faith of the Old Testament*, p. 67.

[17] J. Gwyn Griffiths, 'The Egyptian Derivation of the Name Moses', JNES XII (1953), p. 231.

[18] The Yahwistic tradition describes what could be a volcanic phenomenon (Exodus 19:18). That would locate Sinai in the nearest active mountain range in historical times which is on the far side of the gulf of Aqaba in north-western Arabia. The assumption would be that the Midianites had penetrated the area. The Elohistic tradition uses the physical circumstances akin to a thunderstorm to illustrate the local natural phenomenon of Sinai (Exodus 19:16,19). This would be compatible with the area of the traditional location of Sinai. 'The different names "Sinai" (J, P) and the (probably later) "mount of God" (E) and Horeb (D, and insertion into E) of themselves indicate something of the complicated course that the tradition later took.' W. H. Schmidt, *The Faith of the Old Testament*, p. 42.

[19] 1 Kings 19 cf. Exodus 3:1.

[20] Martin Noth, *A History of Pentateuchal Traditions*, Englewood Cliffs (1972), p. 173 (German edition 1948).

[21] 'In fact the tradition that Moses died outside the area settled by Israel and was buried at a place which was not precisely known by Israel (Deut. 34:5 ff.) must be historically reliable.' W. H. Schmidt, *The Faith of the Old Testament*, p. 67.

[22] Exodus 20; Deut. 5.

[23] If in origin images were redundant because of the numinous presence associated with Sinai, it is a little ironic to note that the prohibition of images would have tended, throughout the development of Israel's faith, to emphasize the transcendence of God and the distinction between creator and creation.

[24] In the eighth century the sense of judgement was increased by the menacing presence of Assyria on the world scene. The prophets who challenged Israel from within were Amos and Hosea in the north, and Isaiah and Micah in the south. See further, Chapter 6 below.

[25] E. W. Nicholson, *God and His People*, Oxford (1986) has thoroughly investigated the development of the concept of covenant and its significance within the life of Israel. He agrees with those scholars who see covenant as a relatively late concept, and identifies its first appearance

with the prophet Hosea. He returns us to older insights (p. 3ff):
'Wellhausen's reconstruction of the history of the Israelite religion led
him to the conclusion that the presentation of Israel's relation with
Yahweh in terms of covenant was a late development and came about
as a result of the preaching of the great prophets. In the period before
their time and beginning with Moses, the relationship between Yahweh
and Israel is best understood as a "natural bond", like that of a son to
his father.'

[26] Morris S. Seale, *The Desert Bible*, p. 23.

[27] C. Westermann, *Genesis*, p. 67 (translated from Biblischer
Kommentar, Neukirchen-Vluyn, 1/1).

[28] G. von Rad, *The Problem of the Hexateuch*, pp. 68–74. D. W. Jamieson-
Drake, *Scribes and Schools in Monarchic Judah*, Sheffield (1991) highlights
the reign of Hezekiah in the 8th century as potentially Israel's
enlightenment.

[29] J. Wellhausen, *Prolegomena to the History of Israel*, Edinburgh (1885),
pp. 7 ff. (German edition, Berlin 1883).

[30] This dating has been challenged. Three recent publications have
in common the fact that they pose fundamental questions to established
pentateuchal criticism since Wellhausen, and move the locus of historical
writing from the period of the monarchy towards the exilic period. These
are: J. Van Seters, *Abraham in History and Tradition*, New Haven and
London (1975); R. Rendtorff, *Das überlieferungsgeschichtliche Problem des
Pentateuch*, Berlin and New York (1977), and H. H. Schmid, *Der sogenannte
Jahwist*, Zurich (1976). In his assessment of the evidence, E. Nicholson
concludes: 'The recent attempts to date the origin of JE to the exilic
period are not persuasive, and the older view which dates it substantially
to the pre-exilic period remains much more plausible.' *The Pentateuch
in the Twentieth Century*, Oxford (1998), p. 239.

[31] According to the classic documentary hypothesis as expounded by
J. Wellhausen the Primaeval History contains a Priestly strand and a
Yahwistic strand. Both use the device of genealogy to give their accounts
a sense of evolution and development. The Priestly strand, with the seven
day account of creation, continues with the Flood Narrative presented
as a cosmic catastrophe and concludes with a tripartite genealogy of the
nations. The Yahwistic Narrative commences with the story of the Garden
of Eden, and continues to present developing complexity as both light
and shadow through a series of episodes. These include the story of Cain
and Abel, the Flood Narrative of forty days, the story of the Tower of
Babel and a preserved fragment of national genealogy. See Appendix
1 for a comparative chart of the two traditions within the Primaeval
History.

[32] M. Noth, *A History of Pentateuchal Traditions*, Englewood Cliffs (1972), p. 40.

[33] Compare also Ps. 115:15; 134:3.

[34] C. Westermann, *Genesis*, p. 408.

[35] 'The anthropopathy which attributes to Yahweh regret and vexation because he has created man is unusually strong. Although in the sense of a mere change of purpose, the former is often ascribed to God (Exodus 32:14; Jeremiah 18:7–8, 26:3 and 13; Joel 2:13; Jonah 3:10 etc), the cases are few where divine regret for accomplished action is expressed (1 Samuel 15:11).' J. Skinner, *Genesis*, ICC, Edinburgh (1930), p. 151.

[36] W. Zimmerli, *Old Testament Theology in Outline*, Edinburgh (1978), p. 172.

CHAPTER 3

Temple

A. Temple Liturgy

The Hebrew community penetrated deeply into the life, the culture and the religion of the settled land. The initiation was no charade; the evidence is at Jerusalem. It was at this city, which Deuteronomy was later to legislate as the single valid cult-centre for the worship of Yahweh, that Israel encountered the raw reality of Canaanite religion. It was a specific example of the very custom and practice which threatened to swallow up and digest, once and for all, the vestiges of nomadic religion.

Canaanite religion in its multiple manifestations was vigorous and evident throughout the settled land. However, once David had taken the Jebusite city of Jerusalem by stealth, made it his capital, spared its inhabitants and seemingly validated its religious traditions, then Canaanite religion had entered the fold.[1] It was now within Israel's core traditions. Potentially, Temple stood firmly alongside Tent. The mix could have extinguished the youthful identity of Mosaic Tent religion, already an alien in a strange environment. That it did not do so is witness not only to the resilience of Mosaic religion, but also to some unique features about the manifestation of Canaanite religion at Jerusalem. Is it possible that these features were recognized by David and that he adopted Jerusalem as his capital with more than astute awareness of its geographical and political advantages in mind?

Canaanite society was based upon a network of autonomous city-states. Each was under the authority of its own king. Responsible kingship was key for a healthy and secure community. Society was a more complex and sophisticated phenomenon than nomadic tribal units. It related to an agricultural way of life which depended upon the regularity of the seasons, the fertility of crops and the careful conservation and handling of water. It was maintained by laws relating to property, to boundaries and to inheritance. There were political and social structures that made possible commerce, trading and crafts, and that afforded protection to citizens, land and property from external threats.

It was the critical importance of these necessary structures and the crucial responsibility of reliable kingship if they were to be held together and maintained in good order which clothed religious identity. Divine authority was understood in terms of the exercise of responsible kingship on the cosmic level; the temple was adjacent to the royal palace. Indeed, the temple was conceived of as the palace of the divine king. Its very presence was tangible evidence of living in a complex ordered world under reliable divine control.

The religious preoccupation was with order. The maintenance of order including the regularity of the seasons could not be taken for granted; it required proper religious observation led by the king. The upholding of the political order of the city state, internally dispensing justice and good government, and externally guaranteeing firm military order against all threats to state security, was equally part of cosmic stability. These different spheres of order were conceived as one comprehensive unity such that the welfare of each part affected the whole. That single complex status quo was reckoned to be managed safely, provided the god of order reigned. The maintenance of stability and continuity, not guidance through the changing scenes of life, was required of religious observance in the settled land.

The nail-biting drama of the Canaanite story related not so much to human beings, who were considered somewhat peripheral to real issues, but to the world of the gods. It was the wrestling for kingship in the divine world upon which depended the outcome of order in the human world. The temple, a heavenly palace built to recognize the triumph of responsible kingship in the divine world, was part of the story of the gods and not part of the history of the human beings who had built it. Indeed, history was an alien concept in a world whose milestones were the revolving cycle of the seasons and recurring harvest festivals.

This was emphasized by the fact that the seasonal religious festivals, which took place at fixed sanctuaries to which the people travelled, were the vehicles of religious encounter. These were the occasions that were cloaked with significance. The daily round and common task were not, officially at least, dignified with the companionship of deity.

The opera of the gods necessitated a considerable cast; Canaanite religion was unashamedly polytheistic. The divine kingship related to the loyalty that the ruling deity might claim from the council of the gods rather than from human beings. Any personal relationship that might be established by the deity with human beings was secondary, and probably channelled through the earthly king as the viceroy or son of the divine king.

As *Father* was the key theological concept for nomadic religion, so *King* was the key concept for Canaanite religion. The move made by David from Hebron to Jerusalem was a move in the theological analogy from Father to King, and, symbolically, from Tent to Temple. When initially the adoption of kingship and then the building of a temple encounters prophetic resistance within Israel these are not momentary criticisms but fundamental concerns. These two institutions were the pillars of Canaanite society and related to the adoption of a new political, social and religious order. The soul of the new nation was at stake. The consequences of such a move needed careful weighing.

The first step to kingship was forced upon Israel by the need to meet the Philistine threat in an organized way; the prophet Samuel grudgingly acquiesces against his better judgement.[2] Its consolidation and the inevitable consequence of establishing a temple adjacent to the royal palace was deliberately promoted by David when he did not simply move his capital from Hebron to Jerusalem, but accepted and embraced the myths and traditions relating to kingship which were cherished there. Even so, he was restrained by the prophet Nathan from fulfilling his ambition to build a temple:

> Go and tell my servant David:
> Thus says the Lord: Are you the one to build
> me a house to live in?
> I have not lived in a
> house since the day I brought

up the people of Israel from Egypt
to this day, but I have been moving about
in a tent and a tabernacle. (2 Samuel 7:5–6)

The monumental acknowledgement of the full implications of
the new order that Israel had embraced in its kingship was
subsequently achieved by David's son and heir Solomon. He
built a temple for Yahweh on the Canaanite model with
Phoenician craftsmen.[3] The continuity with the old ways received
gentle reference; the ark – symbol of the wilderness period –
which David had brought up to Jerusalem[4] was placed in the
Temple as a symbol of Yahweh's presence.[5]

The term Canaanite is a word for a coherent culture rather
than a single people. It is a description that extends across
ancient Syria – Palestine, a wide geographic area of considerable
ethnic diversity. There must have been a substantial variety of
local customs between north and south, and between
communities along the Mediterranean coast and those of the
interior heartlands. Yet the evidence of a single culture which
can be identified as Canaanite throughout the area is convincing.
The correspondence between the vocabulary of the Hebrew
Scriptures and the texts discovered at Ugarit far away on the
Mediterranean coast of northern Syria is evidence of this. It has
been expressed by W. H. Schmidt:

> the verbal agreements of Old Testament and Ugaritic texts are so
> extensive that this position can only be explained by the assumption
> that the religious literature of Ugarit is entirely typical of Canaanite
> religion.[6]

We noted in an earlier context that for the whole of the Ancient
Near East there was a single great conviction that the miracle of
the universe was world order. The stability of that order could
not be taken for granted. It had to be upheld and its equilibrium
maintained. The preoccupation of religious activity was with this
process of sustaining, which could only be effective by virtue of
its closeness to the archetypal act of cosmic ordering. The religion
of Canaan represented a particular manifestation of the
articulation of world order and a distinctive set of religious
answers to the need for that order to be sustained. A notable
feature was a distinction drawn between the high god El who was

honoured as creator, and the younger god Ba'al, who was more relevant to the needs and concerns of those dependent upon an agricultural existence, as 'rider on the clouds', champion of order and sustainer. Ba'al is the classic example of a storm-god.

Throughout the whole area covered by Canaanite civilization there seems to have been a regular religious celebration of the timeless victory of divine order over unruly chaos. The festival took place in the autumn as the summer drought, accompanied by the waning of nature, gave way to the reawakening winter rains heralded by the rumble of thunder and the flash of lightning. The conflict was conceived to rage against the background imagery of the rolling breakers of the Mediterranean Sea stirred by the autumn storms and was dressed in the language, symbolism and colour of kingship.

We are already familiar with the classic illustration of the cosmic battle from the texts discovered at the late Bronze Age city-state of Ugarit. Ba'al is the divine champion of order who takes on the threat of chaos in the form of Yam, the Sea. The contest is for kingship, and Ba'al's victory means he can be proclaimed king. The proper recognition of his kingly status requires the construction of a palace or temple for which permission has to be secured from the high god El. Once this is done, and the building constructed, following a processional excursion, Ba'al, enthroned in the temple, presides over the freshly established world order which is now safe and secure for another year.

The fact that the drama had been followed through living liturgy in the local temple firmly related the universal, with all of its benefits, to the particular. The involvement of the local ruler of the city-kingdom was essential, and emphasized the earthly king's rule as a simple reflection or delegation of the heavenly king's responsibility for an ordered world. There was a tendency, not surprisingly, for the great powers of Mesopotamia, and particularly Egypt, to accord divine status to the reigning monarch. In Canaan such language was probably hyperbole. Nevertheless, the king was of considerable significance and placed in a cosmic context. The qualities of the 'primal man' full of beauty and wisdom were therefore considered as an appropriate and literal description of the kingly status.

The religion of Jerusalem seems to have been a specific local manifestation of universal Canaanite religious practice. In particular it shared the common mythic pattern of conflict and triumph resulting in the enthronement of the deity known as El Elyon or God Most High over personified chaos in the form of monstrous sea. The evidence from the psalms is that in all likelihood this was taken over by the Hebrews from the Jebusites and became the norm of Temple religion throughout the period of the Judaean monarchy. Each autumn would have witnessed a New Year Festal Liturgy, and the earthly king would have had a pivotal role in it. It presented the human environment in a cosmic setting, and acknowledged a complex interrelated world whose ecologies could easily be disturbed and needed constant refreshment.

S. Mowinckel suggested that the full gamut of emotions from lamentation to rejoicing found expression at the Festival.[7] In that case it perhaps began in a mood of lament, sympathetic to the languishing of nature at the end of the season of drought and consequent infertility. It certainly included some symbolic presentation of, or allusion to, God taking on the forces of chaos symbolized by sea, and triumphing. This would have taken place at a traditional site away from the Temple. We may note the association of the battle drama with kingship and creation in this excerpt from Psalm 74:

> Yet God my King is from of old,
> working salvation in the earth.
> You divided the sea by your might;
> you broke the heads of the dragons in the waters.
> You crushed the heads of Leviathan,
> you gave him as food for the creatures of the wilderness.
> You cut openings for springs and torrents,
> you dried up ever-flowing streams.
> Yours is the day, yours also the night;
> you established the luminaries and the sun.
> You have fixed all the bounds of the earth;
> you made summer and winter. (Psalm 74vv. 12–17)

This focal phase was, in all likelihood, followed by a victory procession to the Temple in which the divine presence was symbolized by the Ark carried shoulder high along a processional way. Messengers probably went ahead proclaiming the victory, announcing comfort and good news, much as runners took the news of victory from a battlefield to the waiting people at home. The mood is expressed in a verse from one of the enthronement psalms:

> God has gone up with a shout,
> the Lord with the sound of a trumpet. (Psalm 47:5)

When the procession arrived at the Temple area it halted at the closed gates. Psalm 24 takes up the story; a psalm that begins by announcing Yahweh's work as creator (vv. 1–2). Entrance was demanded by the pilgrims:

> Lift up your heads, O gates!
> And be lifted up, O ancient doors!
> That the king of glory may come in. (v. 7)

The ritual question of the priests who keep the gate is put in return:

> Who is the king of glory? (v. 8a)

The pilgrims, only moments before witnesses of Yahweh's mythic triumph in the battle for kingship, reply:

> The Lord, strong and mighty,
> the Lord mighty in battle. (v. 8b)

The gates swing open, the Ark is born to its place of honour in the Temple and the representatives of the people throng behind. As the Ark is placed beneath the Cherub throne so Yahweh is enthroned; it is nothing less than a renewed coronation. The ram's horn is blown and the people proclaim that God is King. This is the other focal moment. Now the order of the world is secure, the clouds will drop fatness, the earth may bloom and the unruly are subordinated. In the words of another enthronement psalm:

> The Lord is king; let the peoples tremble!
> He sits enthroned upon the cherubim;
> let the earth quake. (Psalm 99 v. 1)

A further reflection is necessary on the significance of the Ark. There was certainly a consciousness in Temple worship of the background of the Ark prior to its being brought to the Temple where it symbolized Yahweh's presence. The evidence for that is from Psalm 132. The Ark carried with it a sense of history both in what it represented as a symbol of Tent religion, but also in its being more than a timeless piece of Temple furniture. There was a moment when it had arrived at the Temple, and that was inscribed in the corporate liturgical memory. Certainly subconsciously, and perhaps also in some conscious liturgical way, the presence of the Ark wove into the New Year Festival a witness to the world of Hebrew epic during a celebration of a foundation Canaanite myth.

The insight into Temple worship during the period of the Judaean kings and the recovery of the significance of the autumn New Year Festival is in particular due to the research of S. Mowinckel.[8] He identified a group of psalms which celebrate the Kingship of Yahweh.[9] By conceiving of them in their liturgical setting he was able, in the words of J. Day commenting on Psalm 47, to make the point that: 'The whole context seems to imply an action rather than an eternal state.'[10] The refrain which recurs in the enthronement psalms, namely '*Yahweh mālak*', Mowinckel argued should be translated not 'Yahweh is King' but 'Yahweh has become King'. Translated into liturgy is exactly the picture presented when Jehu is proclaimed King following Elisha's clandestine arrangement for him to be anointed:

> Then hurriedly they all took their cloaks and
> spread them for him on the bare steps;
> and they blew the trumpet, and
> proclaimed, 'Jehu is King'. (2 Kings 9:13)

Mowinckel, therefore, proposed an annual enthronement festival at the autumn Feast of Tabernacles on the model to which the Ugaritic texts witness for Canaanite civilization.

The cluster of themes associated with the Festival, broadly as Mowinckel proposed it, reappear in the proclamation of coming release from Exile in Isaiah 40–55, and seem to be the motivation for its message. The prophet is familiar with the archaic vocabulary related to the victory over Sea (Isaiah 51:9–11), he refers to the feet of the messengers (52:7a), he mentions a processional way (Isaiah 40:3b), and proclaims the enthronement of God (52:7b). The late evidence of Zechariah connects the annual festival of the Feast of Tabernacles with the kingship of Yahweh and the fertile rains.[11] The circumstantial evidence bears out Mowinckel's case.

How could the coronation of God happen afresh every year? How could God become King again? In the world of myth as the rains arrived and seemed to overwhelm the drought and death of summer, the Kingship of God was something new and exciting to celebrate. There was a sense of participating in the divine victory of order over chaos – it was not long ago; it was now. In other words, there is a timelessness about the liturgical celebration of the overwhelming of chaos within the religious observance of ancient Canaan including Jerusalem. This was precisely why the Temple could be a threat to the Tent. Whereas a pilgrim people took time, history and events seriously, a cyclic, agricultural religion expressed its cultic celebrations in a timeless now. The only really true story for Canaanite religion was the story of myth which explained and interpreted the present in single archetypes, not as unique moments. Here, if anywhere, we perceive foaming at the confluence of the biblical sources.

The liturgy and worship of the Jerusalem Temple meant that Israel now had a religious tradition that took account of the created order and human beings as part of it. The significance of God as creator was now part of her core traditions. She had plugged firmly into the great religious vision of the Ancient Near East for which creation theology was its beginning and end. The scales of justice were not simply a family matter, they related to the very balance of creation itself. Human beings were not simply travellers in a stage-set; they were intimately related to their environment, in relationship with the created order and delicately knitted into a whole web of relationships. The world was presented as cosmos, a universe, an integrated whole. Humans were part of something bigger than themselves which they did not control, but whose well-being they might influence. Tent religion needed the additional source, the articulation of the order of creation, the sheer scale and beauty of Temple religion:

O worship the Lord in the beauty of holiness:
tremble before him, all the earth. (Psalm 96:9, A.V. translation)

B. The Kingdom of God

I give you the end
of a golden string;
only wind it into a ball,
it will lead you in
at heaven's Gate
built in Jerusalem's wall.

[*William Blake*]

No other city has had quite the ability to inspire, to transform its stones into poetry, to mediate eternity in the way that has been true of Jerusalem. Its very dust has been sacred to pilgrims and its fascination endured across more than three millennia. Yet it has no obvious source of wealth, its original community clung precariously to a stony hill-side drawn not by its loftiness but simply by a modest spring of water. It has never been the seat of a world power. It has often been the victim of the power hungry; not least was this true of the Babylonian conquerors in 587 BCE and of Roman imperial brutality in AD 70. Yet, even today, the peace of Jerusalem is bound up not simply with the peace of the Middle East but with the peace of the world. Its gates still stream with pilgrims from the three great monotheistic faiths. The enigma that is Jerusalem remains: 'the name with its originally limited geographical reference eventually becoming the symbol for the universal Kingdom of God'.[12]

The New Year proclamation of the reign of God at Jerusalem has had unique and unexpected consequences. The order which it proclaimed has been responsible for awakening a hope for the dawning of the Kingdom of God across all boundaries of time and geography. Echoes of the cry 'Your God reigns' have brought inspiration, consolation, comfort and hope to a myriad of human conditions. The germ of an explanation takes us back to a powerful set of traditions established at Jebusite Jerusalem before it became the City of David.

Jerusalem had had a long history before the arrival of David on the very eve of the first millennium BCE. Virtually a thousand years previously the Egyptian Execration Texts witness to a city already established.[13] The earliest substantial archaeological evidence for 'dense occupation of the hill on which the City of

David stood is from the eighteenth century BCE.'[14] A section of the city wall and the lower courses of what was probably a tower related to the 'Fountain Gate' (Nehemiah 2:14–15) remain from this period. The gate and its tower were probably intact until Nebuchadnezzar destroyed the city in the sixth century BCE. It is tempting to speculate that the political momentum evidenced in the erecting of the tower and its gate may correspond with the time when the traditions relating to Melchizedek had their origins. This would tie in with the historical context which can link Melchizedek with the era of Abraham in the pericope Genesis 14:18–20. It brings a sense of perspective to our understanding of the enduring nature of the Zion traditions and their very ancient and sturdy roots. The later El Amarna letters of the fourteenth century BCE include correspondence from Abdi-Hepa, the Canaanite King of Jerusalem, to the Pharaoh. At that time an Egyptian garrison was stationed there. The Jebusite phase may perhaps be dated to the time following the defeat by Joshua (Joshua 10:1–27) of the alliance led by Adonizedek of Jerusalem in the twelfth century.[15] The name of the king, like that of Melchizedek before him, would certainly seem to link the associations of Ṣedeq, or 'righteousness' to Jerusalem significantly prior to its Jebusite phase. However, it was to the Jebusite city that David came.

Three deities have clear and long-established associations with Jerusalem and must have been mediated by the Jebusites to the Hebrews. The primary deity is El Elyon, translated as God Most High. He appears amongst the Abrahamic traditions in Genesis:

> And King Melchizedek of Salem brought out bread and wine; he was priest of God Most High. He blessed him and said, 'Blessed be Abram by God Most High, Maker of heaven and earth; and blessed be God Most High who has delivered your enemies into your hand!' (Genesis 14:18–20)

This ancient designation for the high god of Jerusalem as 'Most High' continues to have a place in the biblical psalms.[16] Viewed against the perspective of the Ugaritic texts, El Elyon seems to have both El features as 'maker of heaven and earth' and Ba'al features as the combat deity.[17] In other words the Jerusalem version of the battle with watery chaos is a true creation myth.

God Most High combines in himself the task of warrior god and creator.[18] In the psalms, which reflect the worshipping life of the Temple, the battle drama and the order of creation are simply mentioned side by side.[19] This reflects the archetypal mythical timelessness of cultic practice which is not at home with narrative or history. When the action is removed from the cult in the context of Wisdom literature, a clear consequential link is presented between the battle drama and the ordered world.[20] It is significant that El Elyon's features do not include that aspect of Ba'al's character that related to the battle with Mot (death) which involved the cycle of death and resurrection. That had already proved incompatible with the dignity of El Elyon in Jebusite Jerusalem and earlier. That fact must have contributed to the compatibility of Yahweh with El Elyon; after all, Yahweh had been identified with El from the patriarchal traditions. The identification with Yahweh may well have accentuated El Elyon's transcendence, but his disassociation from Ba'al's involvement with the cycles of nature already suggests a divinity who is 'high and lifted up' as he is later encountered by the prophet Isaiah in the Temple.[21] El Elyon must have been almost uniquely placed among the gods of Canaanite sanctuaries to be identified with Yahweh. Perhaps David had already decided so before he became king at Jerusalem.

The name of El Elyon's priest in Genesis 14 acquaints us with another deity who seems to be firmly associated with Jerusalem. The name Melchizedek translates as '(my) King is (the god) Ṣedeq'.[22] Another King of Jerusalem, already identified above from Joshua 10, has a name compounded with the same divine name. He is Adonizedek which translates as '(my) Lord is (the god) Ṣedeq'.[23] We may perhaps add to this list the name of Solomon's high priest who appears in David's entourage after he has become King in Jerusalem, namely Zadok the priest. The word Ṣedeq is usually translated as righteousness; its personification as a god still lingers in the psalm which promises 'righteousness will look down from heaven' (Ps 85:11b).

In the context of the Jerusalem traditions, ṣedeq should be understood as 'right order'. Only secondarily does conduct in keeping with right order become righteous conduct. Ṣedeq is the Canaanite equivalent of the Egyptian Ma'at, the goddess of order. Ma'at is the companion of the creator, the golden thread of order running through all things, the foundation of the Pharaoh's throne. So also Psalm 89 praises God in the words 'Righteousness and justice are the foundation of your throne' (v.14a). Ṣedeq is the foundation of the creator's throne, his companion in his work, and represents the single correct order established by the creator throughout the length and breadth of creation. It is a concept which articulates the perceived miracle of the Ancient Near East, the establishment of an ordered universe. It expresses a connected, corporate, integrated global whole which only functions properly and as originally established when it is rightly ordered in all of its individual component parts.

The significance of the concept of Ṣedeq has been carefully researched by H. H. Schmid. He identifies six areas where the concept has particular and specific application, namely in the realms of justice, wisdom, nature and fertility, war and victory, cult and sacrifice, and kingship. In the areas of justice and wisdom, for instance, individual derivatives from the root Ṣedeq may become technical terms; applied to nature it may be used as a term of classification; in the cult it may relate to respect for taboo and so on. Yet all these areas are held also in a single whole and affect each other: 'Again and again the cosmic, that is to say the outer reaches of the concept, extending so far as to include all these areas simultaneously.'[24]

The significance of the third deity for Jerusalem we may glean from the name of the city itself. That is Jeru-salem or 'foundation of (the god) Shalem'.[25] In it there is a claim to divine origin. The god Shalem appears in the Ugaritic texts as one of a pair – Shachar and Shalem, Dawn and Dusk, sons of El. The divine name Shalem seems to be reflected in the name of David's son Absalom, although he was born in Hebron and not Jerusalem, and perhaps also in Solomon. It is likely that it was the god Shalem who bequeathed the abiding association of peace (Shālôm) to Jerusalem. The personification of two deities still obtrudes into the text of Psalm 85 in the charming line:

'Righteousness and peace will kiss each other. (v.10b)

It is perhaps not too far-fetched to imagine that the significance of 'peace' has to do with dusk, that is with the completion of the day. The setting sun gathers in the wholeness of the day and draws heaven and earth together. The repose of nature, the return of human beings from their labour to their hearth, the hush of busyness, all seem to speak of a single, complete and harmonious universe at peace with itself and its maker. The concept is not unlike that of God's rest at the conclusion of the seven-day creation account. God, according to priestly tradition, was satisfied when he contemplated the completion of the totality of a living, functioning, whole, ordered universe. Somehow the totality or the completeness of a thing is seen most obviously in its end. This concept with its ancient Canaanite roots would predate the commencing of the Hebrew day with sundown.

Whatever its linguistic roots, Shālôm identifies itself as related to the concept of 'right order'. H. H. Schmid states that the root ṣedeq is not the only one that witnesses to the reality of a world order, and amongst other concepts he includes that of shālôm. He suggests that whereas ṣedeq refers to world order analytically from the point of view of what is right and correct and as it should be, shālôm refers to that order from the point of view of its totality.[26] In other words, it represents that harmony and integration of a healthy and whole world across all the six areas identified by Schmid in connection with 'right order'. When the world order – including nature, politics, society and religion – is functioning harmoniously then creation exhibits a sort of bloom, and peace is established. We must understand the jubilation of creation when God reigns as an expression of universal peace and harmony:

> Let the heavens be glad, and let the earth rejoice;
> let the sea roar, and all that fills it;
> Let the field exult, and everything in it!
> Then shall all the trees of the forest sing for joy. (Psalm 96:11–12)

It has been possible to identify a sort of trinity of deities at Jerusalem in pre-Davidic times. The picture at the annual enthronement festival is of El Elyon, God Most High, presiding over the newly refreshed world order accompanied by Ṣedeq (Right Order) and Shālôm (Peace). It may well be that, already towards the end of the Jebusite period, Ṣedeq and Shālôm had become simply aspects of El Elyon and his work. Certainly, after El Elyon was identified with Yahweh their individual personae would have faded away. Yet, if they were now no longer proper nouns, the qualities which they represented remained valid and vigorous as descriptions of the Kingdom over which El Elyon was enthroned. Throughout the biblical tradition, in particular in the psalms and the Isaianic corpus, where the Jerusalem theology has been influential, these two concepts of righteousness and peace constantly recur. Deutero-Isaiah proclaims:

> O that thou hadst hearkened to my commandments!
> Then had thy peace been as a river,
> and thy righteousness as the waves of the sea. (Isaiah 48:18b, A.V. translation)

The boundaries of the Kingdom of righteousness and peace over which El Elyon presided officially knew no limits. The traditions of Jerusalem were cosmic and universal. But, unlike the universalism of Wisdom, the universalism of Jerusalem did not articulate a neutral concept of world order which thought of all human beings as equally 'before Yahweh' (Genesis 10:9). Rather, world order radiated out from Jerusalem, because it was there that the Most High had chosen to dwell. The Temple was no pretence. A psalm makes it abundantly clear:

> There is a river whose streams make glad the city of God,
> the holy habitation of the Most High.
> God is in the midst of the city, it shall
> not be moved. (Psalm 46:4–5a)

Zion as the residence of the Most High has attracted to itself descriptions which can only carry mythological rather than geographical significance. The mention of the river 'whose streams make glad the city of God' hardly squares with the city that requires Hezekiah's tunnel to secure its water supply. It does make sense in the light of El's abode described in the Ugaritic texts as at the 'source of the two rivers'. Again, Psalm 48:2 rejoices in the loftiness of Zion although the neighbouring peak of the Mount of Olives is higher. This inconsistent claim for Zion is overcome by giving it a future (eschatological) reference in Micah and Isaiah.[27] The point is that the reference to the height of Zion is a theological description suitable to a mountain designated as the dwelling-place of God. It is in that same context that we must understand Psalm 48:2 where the identification of Mount Zion with Mount Zaphon is made; in Isaiah 14:13–14 Zaphon is the abode of El and in the Ugaritic texts has become the holy dwelling-place of Baʻal. It makes good sense of the psalmist's universal claim in the same verse that Mount Zion is 'the joy of all the earth'. Such traditions seem to lie behind the witness of Ezekiel when he talks of the inhabitants of Zion dwelling 'at the navel of the earth'.[28]

Psalm 46:5 already leads us a stage further towards a natural deduction from the assumption that Mount Zion is the dwelling-place of God: the inviolability and impregnability of the Holy City. Certain psalms[29] witness to the repulse of an assault of the nations and their kings within the very sight of the dwellers of Jerusalem. It is portrayed as a miraculous deliverance due to divine intervention. The primaeval battle resonates in the mention of the waters (Ps. 46:3). The roots of this myth of miraculous deliverance are doubtless to be found in Zion's Jebusite inheritance, and associated with Zion as the fortress of the Almighty himself.[30] The threat to cosmic order may be focused and localized in the threat of the nations in the assault on Zion. Conversely the repulse of the threat has universal consequences:

> Be still, and know that I am God!
> I am exalted among the nations,
> I am exalted in the earth. (Psalm 46:10)[31]

The tradition that Zion is the dwelling place of God, and therefore the navel of the universe, the place from which universal righteousness and peace radiate forth, helps us to understand the significance carried by its earthly king. To the king is devolved the protection of the very seat of divinity and the fulcrum of cosmic order. In this task he had powerful backing from the throne of the universe. At his coronation the king became the adopted son of the Most High. Consequently, the king is the champion of the kingdom; in his hands are the protection and maintenance of universal order. Any rebellion or disaffection does not simply threaten local instability, but provides a direct challenge to cosmic order. The king's enemies are therefore the enemies of God, they represent a conspiracy of the nations, and are put down by divine authority:

I tell of the decree of the Lord:
He said to me, 'You are my son;
today I have begotten you.
Ask of me, and I will make the
nations your heritage,
and the ends of the earth your possession.
You shall break them with a rod of iron,
and dash them in pieces like a potter's vessel. (Psalm 2:7–9)

The responsibilities of the earthly king as son and viceroy of the heavenly king give access to the way the analogy of kingdom brought a sense of complexity held and managed in unity to the understanding of cosmos. An ordered kingdom required that agriculture, law, worship and sacrifice, military activity all be handled in such a way that together they contributed to a single reliable and healthy environment. The world, too, was understood to be a single complex environment requiring care for every small detail if global equilibrium was to be maintained. The components could not simply be got right individually, but were conceived to be part of a single order such that distress in one area created dis-ease throughout the whole.

Responsible kingship was required of the monarch. Crucial to that responsibility was the concept of justice (mišpaṭ) which was the king's primary responsibility. Justice was closely related to the maintaining of universal right order. Order therefore had a moral element. Justice and righteousness are balancing equivalents in the first verse of Psalm 72:

Give the King your justice, O God.
And your righteousness to a King's son.

The king is to be the champion of justice so that the very mountains deliver peace and the hills right order (Psalm 72:3), he is to defend the case of the poor and deliver the needy (v.4), he is to secure abundance of grain in the countryside and under him city life is to flourish (v. 16), and he is to bring a blessing upon the nations (17b). His son after him will be the Prince of Peace and will establish the throne 'with justice and with righteousness' (Isaiah 9:6–7). Indeed, what peace might mean as it breaks through all creation cherished by royal justice, in language rich with mythological imagery, is delivered in an oracle contained in the Book of Isaiah:

Righteousness shall be the belt around his waist,
and faithfulness the belt around his loins.
The wolf shall live with the lamb,
the leopard shall lie down with the kid,
the calf and the lion and fatling together,
and a little child shall lead them.
The cow and the bear shall graze,
their young shall lie down together;
and the lion shall eat straw like the ox.
The nursing child shall play over the hole of the asp,
and the weaned child shall put its hand on the adder's den.
They will not hurt or destroy
on all my holy mountain,
for the earth shall be full of the knowledge of the Lord
as the waters cover the sea. (Isaiah 11:5–9)

Because they shared in the Canaanite analogy of world order as a Kingdom, the Jerusalem traditions were able to introduce into the Hebrew Scriptures issues that have re-emerged in the contemporary world under the label of 'justice and the integrity of creation'. World order is such a unity, and the individual parts bound so closely with the whole, that moral deeds in one sphere have totally unexpected mundane consequences in a quite different and remote other sphere. Problems have to be tackled from a global perspective. It is expressed by H. H. Schmid in this way:

> Only from this background is it possible to understand, for instance, why in the whole Ancient Near East, including Israel, an offense in the legal realm obviously has effects in the realm of nature (drought, famine) or in the political sphere (threat of the enemy). Law, nature, and politics are only aspects of one comprehensive order of creation.[32]

It is small wonder that Jerusalem had the power to stir the heart. The proclamation of the coronation of God and the order of his kingdom, championed by the justice of the anointed king, held out a vision which reached every corner of creation with an intensity which set the ideal as within the grasp of the present. Zion spoke powerfully in symbol and word, through Temple and King, of a realm where the cherishing of righteousness and peace ensured a whole, harmonious, integrated and beautiful universe.

C. The Temple Witness to the Creator

When David entered Jerusalem as its king he accepted not simply a throne, but also a destiny. The ancient Canaanite perspective on kingship fell to an Israelite monarch. The stability of the Davidic house itself received its guarantee and authentication by being taken into the established order of things. The creation theology of the Ancient Near East and its underwriting of the status quo manifested in the good order and harmony of the world included the Davidic house itself. A Hebrew king was now a priest for ever after the order of Melchizedek,[33] a Canaanite priest-king. It was a theological hedge which enabled the Judaean monarchy to survive for almost four and a half centuries, and subsequently to become the source of the messianic hope.

There were incongruities in this match, which was almost in the nature of an experiment when David tested Jerusalem as his capital. Although the identification between El Elyon and Yahweh may have been seamless as El and Yahweh were already identified in the God of the Fathers tradition, yet the proclamation 'Yahweh has become King', with all of its associations with authority over the council of gods and the high drama of myth, was quite alien. Further, the timeless myth of kingship and the historical reality of David's conquest of Jerusalem went a little uneasily together. The cycle of myth had been punctured by a moment of history. Psalm 89 is specific and historical in its appointment of David:

> I have found my servant David;
> with my holy oil I have anointed him; (v.20)

However, it is timeless in the way it incorporates the Davidic line into world order:

> I will establish his line for ever,
> and his throne as long as the heavens endure. (v.29)

Similar were the circumstances of Yahweh's arrival, consequent upon the arrival of David. The Ark was brought up to Jerusalem as the symbol of the presence of Yahweh by authority of David.[34] This arrival of Yahweh was somewhat in contradiction to the timeless presence of the Most High in the city of divine foundation. Yet the Ark's historic arrival embedded itself in liturgical memory.[35]

No doubt the success of the monarchy under David and Solomon, the evident divine blessing, confirmed the experiment. The enthronement of Yahweh in the Temple produced a dynamic theological combination. Through the Most High, Israel now had a sophisticated witness to God as creator within her own traditions. Conversely, the fact that it was Yahweh's presence on the Cherubim throne no doubt shaped the way the Jerusalem cult and its customs developed. Schmid notes that within Israel two of the six areas in which the Canaanites applied the concept of ṣedeq diminished noticeably, that is to say, the spheres of nature and fertility. He suggests this may be the effect of Israel's historical thinking on the subject of order.[36] We have noted, too, that the presence of Yahweh would have accentuated divine transcendence and tended to diminish the significance of the council of gods. However, the Temple itself continued to play host to all sorts of religious practice; the hospitality to foreign gods was part of the exercise of diplomatic relationships with foreign governments. The evidence is that, until the stirring of the eighth-century prophets there was no cry for reform which involved exclusive acknowledgement of Yahweh. The major reforms are associated with Hezekiah in the eighth century and Josiah in the seventh century.

The fact that Israel now had a source of its own which acknowledged God as creator is of the utmost significance. The move from Hebron to Jerusalem, of necessity, connected the Abrahamic-patriarchal traditions of Hebron with the royal creation traditions of Jerusalem. Indeed, the pericope of Genesis 14:18–20 has done just that in insisting that Abraham was blessed by Melchizedek, King of Salem. The move from the one capital to the other was, we have claimed, responsible for the confidence of the Yahwist, the earliest of Israel's epic writers whose connected narrative has come down to us, to break new ground and set a primaeval history at the head of Israel's epic history.

The point has already been made that the crucial verses that connect the Yahwist's primaeval history with the subsequent history of the Hebrews are Genesis 12:2–3. They do so with a blessing upon Abraham. The blessing identifies itself as none other than a royal blessing familiar from the Jerusalem Temple transferred to the Patriarch. In all likelihood it reveals the Yahwist's source for asserting the significance of God as creator; it is drawn from the worship at the Temple. If this is so, then the effect of the Jerusalem Temple traditions on the Yahwist has not been to diminish sacred history, but to provide it with a new context. In an incredibly daring way he insists that the call of Abraham and the subsequent history of the Hebrews is actually divine response to the instability of primaeval time and creation's dilemmas. The call of the people of God is set in a universal context. In some way the existence of the Hebrew community is related to the welfare of the world. It was a tall order, in fact an outrageous claim for an obscure people, but seminal for all subsequent theological reflection.

The primaeval history of the Yahwist seems to be just beyond the breakthrough from monolatry (exclusive commitment to a single God) to monotheism. The monotheism that it exhibits is youthful and vibrant. The Yahwist's reworking of ancient texts to introduce a single presence in heaven is immaculate. There is a causative thread throughout the primaeval history which relates developments in terms of human evolution not divine intervention.

Consciousness of the historical process does not, however, prevent the Yahwist claiming for Yahweh – in the context of his version of the Flood narrative – control over the sustaining of the cyclical processes:

> As long as the earth endures,
> Seedtime and harvest, cold and heat,
> Summer and winter, day and night, shall not cease. (Genesis 8:22)

An indication of the significance of the Temple in inspiring these ideas may, perhaps, be gleaned from the association of this announcement with the immediately preceding building of an altar and sacrifice (vv. 20–21).

In the Yahwist we are encountering the 'new theology'. There is reflected here the influence of temple theology after Yahweh has tamed the council of the gods, but reflecting the control of God Most High over the cyclic processes. The generosity of the Yahwist's theology could well reflect recent memory of the success of the great empires of David and Solomon. It is evidence of the creative penetration of Israel's Tent identity into the religious tradition of the settled land at Jerusalem.

In the biblical primaeval history there is a twin creation tradition to that of the Yahwist's drama of the Garden in Genesis 2:4b–3:24. The other tradition is in Genesis 1:1–2:4a; it recounts creation over a six-day period with a seventh day of divine rest and is part of what is known as the Priestly strand of the Pentateuch. Although the Priestly strand with its creation narrative did not attain its present shape until the Exile, it is likely that the creation traditions which are so characteristic of it were absorbed into Hebrew tradition through the international cultural contacts of the time of David and Solomon, probably from ancient Egypt. The relevance of the creation traditions for Priestly faith would certainly have been a result of the insistence in the Temple theology that Yahweh is the creator. This supposition is confirmed by the fact that the narrative of creation and rest over a period of seven days is in all likelihood influenced by analogy with the duration of the New Year Festival celebrated in the Jerusalem Temple.[37] It appears that the Temple's influence in the Priestly strand, too, has had the effect not of diminishing the significance of sacred history, but of enabling it to be set within the context of an account of the creation of cosmos.

A strong concept of the transcendence of God seems to have been a feature of the worship at the Jerusalem Temple during the period of the Judaean monarchy. It receives classic expression from the prophet Isaiah of Jerusalem. The passage that recounts his calling commences:

> In the year that King Uzziah died, I saw the
> Lord sitting on a throne, high and lofty;
> and the hem of his robe filled the temple. (Isaiah 6:1)

As has already been suggested, this was perhaps also, at least to some extent, a feature of the cult of El Elyon. Jerusalem may already have been an example of the Ancient Near East testing the boundaries set by its own religious traditions. The New Year Festival is associated with judgement.[38] Presumably, the judgement was on those who were caught on the 'wrong side' of right order in any of its six sub-classifications. With the arrival of Yahweh that aspect of El Elyon would have been intensified as would have been the moral element associated with justice. The fact that Yahweh could not be represented in an image, and therefore his presence was signified by the Ark, contributed to the sense of a deity separate from and other than the created order. It is worthy of note that the prophetic articulation of a radical break between Yahweh and the order of creation took place at Jerusalem in the proclamation of Isaiah corresponding to the wider proclamation of the eighth-century prophets generally working from more conventional Yahwistic traditions.

This transcendence had two important consequences. Firstly, we find that the Jerusalem traditions, in common with other Yahwistic traditions, can be turned against themselves. That is to say, the Canaanite apparatus for stabilizing the world ceases to be unconditional. In this, Israel presents something of a unique case within the Ancient Near East. In other nations, military defeat was normally interpreted either as neglect of the proper processes of maintaining the status quo or as failure on the part of the nation's gods, although temporary divine anger might be involved.[39] In Israel the prophets could interpret God's judgement on his people in a final and radical way. In the preaching of Amos and Hosea, Yahweh is judge of his people, and his righteousness can turn against them in a way that threatens their very existence. All institutions of state or religion are, in the end, provisional. Similarly, the 'perfection of beauty' at Zion can become a standard by which Israel is judged, not a security upon which she can count. It is a sign that the Temple was truly integrated into the Yahwistic realm. Thus Isaiah, as an eighth-century prophet, uses the Zion traditions to confront, not to reassure. In this case righteousness is linked with the key related Jerusalem concept 'justice':

> And I will make justice the line,
> and righteousness the plummet;
> hail will sweep away the refuge of lies,
> and waters will overwhelm the shelter. (Isaiah 28:17)

This is a matter to which we shall later return in discussing the ministry of the prophet Isaiah.[40]

Secondly, the differentiation of God from the created order enabled the breakthrough to what is known as eschatology. God need not simply uphold the status quo or return it to its pristine original condition, he can bring about something entirely new. The presence of the holy God had the potential not simply to refresh and renew creation, but to judge, transform and change it. For the prophets this took the form of an expected renewal of history. God would create a new covenant (Jeremiah 31:31), he would replace the heart of stone with a heart of flesh (Ezekiel 11:19). Eschatology within the Jerusalem traditions is the mirror image of creation. It expresses the concept of a fresh initiative of God in consummation corresponding to his initiative in creation. The Jerusalem Temple theology annually rearticulated the language of creation at the service of the sustaining of world order and its continuity. It was uniquely poised for a mutation. For this to happen the timelessness of cultic worship, for which there was only one archetype, which telescoped every annual festival into a single mythical event, had to be confronted by the Hebrew sense of history which could tell the story of creation as a completed event.[41] Only then would myth not reduce all reality to a function of a single concept. There could be a history in God's dealings with his creation also; he might do a new thing in recreating that which was not contained within, or even intimated by, his original act of creation. The boundaries of Ancient Near Eastern religious convention would be decisively breached.

True eschatology within the Jerusalem traditions becomes evident subsequent to Deutero-Isaiah (who stands tantalizingly on the brink) and the Exile, in the work of Trito-Isaiah (Isaiah 56–66).[42] The raw material of the Zion traditions is of course cosmic and universal. Consequently, when eschatology is expressed it significantly carries a hope of redemption for the whole of the created order:

> For as the new heavens and the new earth,
> which I will make, shall remain before me, says the Lord,
> so shall your descendants and your name remain. (Isaiah 66:22)

It is in the fact that the Zion traditions, with some intensity, set a vision of the ideal as within the grasp of the present that ultimately transformed its claim for today into a hope for tomorrow, based on God's reliability. When righteousness and peace failed to materialize in the present, when the promise of each new royal child fell short of expectations, there grew the hope for a new act of God in the Kingdom of God yet to be revealed, heralded by an Anointed One yet to come.

Points for Discussion

1. For the civilization of ancient Canaan, 'kingship' was the key word for understanding God and 'Temple' was the most powerful symbol. What were the significant insights they expressed? Do those insights connect with contemporary concerns?
2. Why do you think that Jerusalem has become such a potent symbol for the universal Kingdom of God?
3. What do we mean by righteousness and peace? How different from that were the concepts at Jerusalem during the period of the kings?
4. What do we mean by 'justice and the integrity of creation'? Can we use the Jerusalem traditions to help us think about the issues involved and relate them to God as creator?
5. 'Kingdom' and 'Temple' became classic concepts for biblical theology. How helpful are they now in our search for word and symbol to talk of God? What analogies and symbols could speak with a similar power today?
6. In what ways were liturgy and life bound together in ancient Israel? Do contemporary liturgies raise a tension for us between the reassurance of celebrating the annual cycles and the uncertainties of specific events brought into worship such as the events of 9/11?

Key Bible Passages

Genesis 14:18–20 (Melchizedek); 2 Samuel 5:1–11 (David king at Hebron and Jerusalem); 2 Samuel 7:1–17 (David may not build a temple); 1 Kings 5 and 6 (Solomon's temple building); Psalm 24 (a processional psalm); Psalm 72 (a royal psalm); Psalm

74:12–17 cf. Psalm 93 (God's conflict with the waters); Psalm 96 (enthronement psalm).

Further Reading

W. H. Schmidt, *The Faith of the Old Testament*, Oxford (1983), ch. 13 'Zion', pp. 207–20.

J. Day, *Psalms*, Old Testament Guides, Sheffield (1990).

J. Day, *God's Conflict with the Dragon and the Sea*, Cambridge (1985), ch. 1, pp. 1–61.

S. Mowinckel, *The Psalms in Israel's Worship*, Oxford (1962), especially ch. V, pp. 106–92.

Figure 3. A reconstruction of the 18th century BCE Fountain Gate to Jerusalem with the stones still in position identified. (Taken from the *Illustrated Atlas of Jerusalem*, ed. Dan Bahat, reconstruction L. Ritmeyer.)

Endnotes

[1] 2 Samuel 5:6–10 is a tantalizingly brief record of the capture of Jerusalem. W. H. Schmidt writes: 'How close the contact between the two groups in the population was can perhaps be illustrated by one detail: the priest Zadok, who appears suddenly in David's entourage, with no indication of his origin, supported Solomon in the struggle for succession and finally replaced Abiathar who was from the older Israelite priestly family (2 Sam. 8:17; 1 Kings 1:7 ff., 34;2: 26ff., 35), was perhaps already a priest (although probably not like Melchizedek actually the priest-king) in pre-Davidic Jerusalaem.' *The Faith of the Old Testament*, p. 209.

[2] 1 Samuel 8.

[3] 1 Kings 5.

[4] 2 Samuel 6; cf. Ps. 132.

[5] 1 Kings 8:1–11.

[6] W. H. Schmidt, *The Faith of the Old Testament*, p. 136.

[7] S. Mowinckel, *The Psalms in Israel's Worship*, p. 141.

[8] P. Volz, *Das Neujahrfest Jahwes*, Tübingen (1912) first proposed a New Year Festival for Israel by analogy with the Babylonian New Year Festival. However, it was S. Mowinckel who drew his conclusions independently from the biblical evidence. See S. Mowinckel, *The Psalms in Israel's Worship*, Oxford (1962), translated and revised from *Offersang og Sangoffer*, Oslo (1951).

[9] Psalms 47, 93, 96–99.

[10] J. Day, *Psalms*, Old Testament Guides, Sheffield (1990), p. 78.

[11] Zechariah 14:16–17.

[12] Norman Porteous, 'Jerusalem-Zion: The Growth of a Symbol', *Festschrift für Wilhelm Rudolph*, Tübingen (1961), p. 236.

[13] 'The Egyptian Execration Texts are the first documents to provide data on the geography of the land of Israel during the twentieth and nineteenth centuries BCE. These are texts written on clay vessels, or on clay figurines in the form of slaves with their hands bound. The names and rulers of the cities of the country were inscribed on them. Two groups of Execration Texts have been discovered: the earlier writings, dating to the twentieth century BCE, were written on clay bowls, and the later texts, from the nineteenth century BCE, were inscribed on figurines. In the early group mention is made of a number of cities and the names of a number of rulers of each city. In the later inscriptions the number of rulers is reduced to one or two. The Execration Texts refer to two cities in the mountain region of the land of Israel – Shechem (Nablus) and Jerusalem. Only Jerusalem is referred to in both groups of inscriptions, but both these cities had important status in the region . . .' Dan Bahat, *The Illustrated Atlas of Jerusalem*, New York (1990), p. 22.

[14] Dan Bahat, *The Illustrated Atlas of Jerusalem*, p. 20.

[15] 'The weak situation of the Canaanite city attracted new inhabitants – the Jebusites. Allusions to the origin of this people, who constituted a new factor in the country, and their link to the Hittites, can be found in various places in the Bible. For example, Ezekiel 16:3 'Thus saith the Lord God unto Jerusalem; Thy birth and thy nativity is of the land of Canaan; thy father was an Amorite, and thy mother an Hittite.' Dan Bahat, *The Illustrated Atlas of Jerusalem*, p. 23.

[16] Pss. 46:4; 47:2.

[17] It is disputed whether El Elyon is a hybrid of El and Ba'al, or an independent deity whose character always combined these features. J. Day, *God's Conflict with the Dragon and the Sea*, Cambridge (1985), p. 129, cites the witness of Philo of Byblos 'who refers to Elioun as father of Ouranos (Heaven) and Ge (Earth)'. His contention is that the Jerusalem traditions witness to the specific features of the cult of this god who already had what we identify as Ba'alistic features as part of his character. On the other hand it is difficult to escape the hovering presence of Ba'al in the psalms which praise the storm-god's achievements, whose spear is lightning (Ps. 18:14), whose voice is thunder which makes the cedars of Lebanon quake (Ps. 29: 4 and 5), and whose home is Mount Zaphon (Ps. 48:2).

[18] There are striking comparisons that can be made with Marduk of Babylon. However, Jacobsen suggests that the origin of the battle imagery may have been with Ba'al and the Mediterranean coast and moved eastwards (T. Jacobsen, 'The Battle between Marduk and Tiämat', *JAOS* 88 (1968), pp. 104–8).

[19] Pss. 74:12–17; 89:9–14.

[20] Ps. 104:5–9; Job 38:8–11; Prov. 8:29.

[21] Isaiah 6:1.

[22] W. H. Schmidt, *The Faith of the Old Testament*, p. 209.

[23] Ibid, p. 209.

[24] H. H. Schmid, *Gerechtigkeit als Weltordnung*, Tübingen (1968), p. 166.

[25] W. H. Schmidt, *The Faith of the Old Testament*, p. 209.

[26] H. H. Schmid, *Gerechtigkeit als Weltordnung*, p. 68.

[27] Micah 4:1; Isaiah 2:2.

[28] Ezekiel 38:12.

[29] In addition to Ps. 46, also Pss. 48 and 76.

[30] See further J. H. Hayes, 'The Tradition of Zion's Inviolability', *JBL* 82 (1963), pp. 419–26. W. H. Schmidt, *The Faith of the Old Testament*, p. 214 has suggested that we have here a genuine Israelite development of the Jebusite myth of Zion as the dwelling-place of God. As there are no known parallels to this myth in the Ancient Near East he has suggested

that it is perhaps peculiar to Israel. In that case it would be a genuine Israelite 'historicization' of the mythic creation battle drama.

[31] The Ark with its military connotations (1 Samuel 4), may have helped reinforce this sense of security. The ancient title 'Lord of Hosts' (perhaps associated with the Ark) appears in the complex associated ideas of Pss. 46:7,11 and 48:8.

[32] H. H. Schmid, 'Creation, Righteousness and Salvation: 'Creation Theology' as the Broad Horizon of Biblical Theology', in ed. B.W. Anderson, *Creation in the Old Testament*, London & Philadelphia (1984), p. 105 (article first published in German in ZTK 20 (1973), pp. 1–19).

[33] Ps. 110:4.

[34] 2 Samuel 6.

[35] Ps. 132.

[36] H. H. Schmid, *Gerechtigkeit als Weltordnung*, pp. 171–3.

[37] J. E. Atwell, 'An Egyptian Source for Genesis 1', *JTS*, NS, vol. 51, October 2000, pp. 441–77.

[38] For instance, Psalm 96:10 'He will judge the peoples with equity'. If distributing justice was the task of the earthly king, by so much the more was it characteristic of the heavenly king.

[39] The ninth-century inscription on the 'Moabite Stone' erected by King Mesha of Moab to commemorate his victories over Israel offers an interesting perspective on the relationship of a state deity with his people; the god's name is Chemosh. The scene is set for the reversal of fortunes: 'Omri, King of Israel, he oppressed Moab many days, for Chemosh was angry with his land.'

[40] See Chapter 6 below.

[41] The Wisdom tradition was an ally of the Yahwistic historical consciousness in insisting on creation as a completed event, cf. Job 38: 10–11.

[42] See further discussion in Chapter 7 below.

CHAPTER 4

Tutor-I

A. Identifying Wisdom and Wisdom's Transmission

Where is Wisdom to be found? In terms of an authoritative starting point within the biblical tradition we must direct our search to the three books of Proverbs, Job and Ecclesiastes. These books have a distinct identity within the Hebrew scriptures which clearly sets them apart and marks them out as different, even strangers, in their context. They all share an absence of what is normally identified as distinctive Israelite theology. The name for God is Yahweh, the familiar, if refined, creation traditions relating to the primaeval waters are apparent, yet there is no special revelation and there are no chosen people. We search in vain for mention of the patriarchs, of Moses and the Exodus, for an interest in Davidic kingship or pride in Jerusalem, the Temple and the priestly sacrificial institutions. Instead we encounter a way of doing theology which is the common possession of the Ancient Near East and based on the principles of creation theology.

The key concept is the God-given universal order. The material of these three biblical books seeks to articulate, to explore and even to question the accumulated experience of the tradition as it discerns the sensible, healthy, successful way for human beings to live within the given order of the world. Beyond that, in the light of common observation, and evidence assembled by the tradition, to probe the universal human questions of meaning and meaninglessness, life and death, good and evil. The questions are all those which know no artificial boundaries erected by state, religion or race. This is the Wisdom tradition. The biblical books of Proverbs, Job and Ecclesiastes must provide the 'gold standard' of Wisdom, and, in making a judgement about whether Wisdom or Wisdom-influence is to be found in other parts of the Hebrew scriptures, they must be the guide.

The fact that Wisdom is a particular example of the application of Ancient Near Eastern creation theology means that it is an enterprise Israel shared with the world around her. The biblical Wisdom writings therefore have a context within the international literature and traditions of the Ancient Near East. Not only do we look to the three biblical Wisdom books as arbiters within the biblical tradition, but we must also look to them for some sort of definition of what is meant by international Wisdom. No collective self-designation existed for these texts within the world of the Ancient Near East. In his book *Babylonians*, H. W. F. Saggs discusses Babylonian literature and states: 'One might also include as literature in the narrower sense Wisdom texts, that is, compositions in the category of the biblical books of Job and Ecclesiastes.'[1] Wisdom is a category invented by biblical scholars, but nonetheless a useful and essential one. The Wisdom books, so obvious in the Hebrew context, are in their Ancient Near Eastern context simply a particular way of expounding its creation-theology principles. The fact that they enabled an international theological dialogue does identify them as special, but it is significant, too, that there was no obvious international community amongst those who handled them. It does suggest that the international Wisdom tradition was less monolithic and more casual than has sometimes been recognized.

It is interesting to note in this context that there was a key word associated with Wisdom in ancient Israel, which was not true in the same way for Egypt and Mesopotamia. The distinctive Hebrew word for Wisdom was ḥokmā, and those who spoke or interpreted Wisdom were the wise, ḥakāmim. Over half of the occurrences of this vocabulary in the Hebrew scriptures occur within the three books of Proverbs, Job and Ecclesiastes.[2] The wise delivered counsel 'ēṣâ. They are to be distinguished from the scribes (sopherim) who must have been associated with Wisdom's transmission as 'the men of Hezekiah' referred to in Proverbs 25:1 would suggest.

The three biblical Wisdom books cover a considerable span

of time. If we allow that Proverbs collects some material from early in the monarchy, then between them these books cover a period from soon after the formation of the monarchy, through exile and return, down to Ecclesiastes in the late third century BCE. Throughout that seven hundred years of developing tradition, often at the centre of Israel's institutions, biblical Wisdom retained its identity and distinctiveness and continued to operate within clearly defined parameters and conventions. There was a robust tradition with accomplished practitioners. It was not until the Wisdom tradition reaches Ben Sira's Jerusalem[3] and again in the later Wisdom of Solomon[4] that it ceases to have an identity distinct from Israel's theological concern with revelation and election. It is only with Ben Sira that the covenant and sacred traditions of Yahwistic faith become part of the world of Wisdom, and that the two ways of doing theology are united when Torah (by now specifically interpreted as the Law of Moses) is identified with Wisdom.[5] It is interesting that at this point Wisdom ceases to retain its distance from the rough and tumble of bitter politics. For instance, Ben Sira identifies three nations with special loathing,[6] something previously quite alien to Wisdom's vision. The Wisdom of Solomon has a distinct consciousness of God's election of Israel:

> That God's grace and mercy are with his elect,
> And that he watches over his holy ones. (Wisdom 4:15b)

Again, this too has been quite alien to the earlier witness of the Wisdom tradition. Ben Sira and the Wisdom of Solomon serve to throw the enigma of the canonical Wisdom literature into relief.

The question arises as to the transmission of Wisdom texts within Israel, and indeed how that relates to their transmission and dissemination throughout the Ancient Near East. Who wrote them and how were they handed down?

In the great civilizations of Egypt and Mesopotamia there was both the necessity for and the wealth to provide a major state bureaucracy. Highly trained and educated scribes were necessary for state administration, international diplomacy, legal, literary and religious tasks. There was, therefore, a well educated and motivated scribal class to create and use the Wisdom literature.

Moreover, the highly complex nature of Akkadian cuneiform and Egyptian hieroglyphics required long perseverance and concentrated coaching if they were to be mastered. The up-and-coming generation had to be trained. Schools were essential. We already learn of the events of a day at school from the Sumerian period.[7] If the right attitude for life could be inculcated by copying improving texts at the same time as learning the skills of literacy then so much the better. The finds from Ebla in northern Syria dating from 2500 BCE, amongst a wealth of administrative texts, reveal educational material including bilingual vocabularies and word lists. Stories, hymns and proverbs also figure amongst the collection.[8]

'Tutor' or 'Teacher' captures the likely provenance of at least some of the Wisdom texts from the great centres of culture in the Ancient Near East. Associated particularly with the royal courts, evidenced by the collection assembled at Ashurbanipal's library complex, and sometimes with temples in ancient Mesopotamia, the learned trained generations of young men for service. In the context of education and training in practical scribal skills, the academic mentor eagerly inculcated standards, self-discipline and principles that would enable the young men to succeed as worthy and successful citizens and be a credit to their educational institutions.

The tutors worked with classical texts which often endured for enormously long periods of time and expressed the common values which were reckoned to undergird stable society. No doubt the tutor sometimes added his own gloss. Presumably, the standards and principles commended were afforded limited debate, and occasionally, particularly in times of social upheaval and consequent demoralization, there might be radical questioning. Perhaps the brighter graduates, when fate seemed to have been less than evenhanded to their promising career, diverted their scribal skills to take solace in committing their emotions to the written text and occasionally something of real quality was produced.

To what extent can this model simply be transferred to Israel? The straightforward answer is that we cannot be certain. It has been expressed this way:

Besides this inability to discern absolute dates and functions of the literature, it is impossible to write a history of the institutions or persons responsible for compiling and transmitting the literature. Their origins are obscure, as is the overall development of the tradition.[9]

At one point the matter seemed settled. Von Rad established the consensus of a 'Solomonic enlightenment'. The court of Solomon, modelled on the scribal bureaucracy of ancient Egypt,[10] was conceived to be a source of new learning and, under the influence of Egyptian Wisdom, inspired the Joseph Narrative,[11] the Succession Narrative[12] and the Yahwist's Primaeval History.[13] It was even argued that the designation of Solomon's cabinet ministers was based upon Egyptian prototypes.[14] Israel participated, according to this view, in the very structures through which international Wisdom flourished.

There has been something of a reaction to this view. A modification of it is the simple relocation of Israel's 'enlightenment' to the reign of Hezekiah in the eighth century.[15] The potential for Wisdom's transmission to be associated with scribal training at the royal court remains. R. B. Y. Scott describes as 'late and largely imaginary' the claims for Solomon's great wisdom in 1 Kings 4:29–34. However, he does maintain that:

> Since no tendentious purpose can be suspected in the mentioning of the otherwise unknown 'men of Hezekiah', this is first-rate evidence that an organized literary Wisdom movement existed at Hezekiah's court and under his patronage.[16]

Scott suggests that 'the wise' as a class or profession emerge at this time,[17] and he notes Isaiah's oracles directed at the wise precisely at this period.[18] Certainly their existence as a definable group at court would allow a quite natural interpretation of Jeremiah 18:18 as making reference to three distinct classes of professional:

> for instruction shall not perish from the priest,
> nor counsel from the wise,
> nor the word from the prophet.

The implications for the scaling down of Solomon's court would be that he operated on an enhanced Canaanite model.[19] Already David had inherited, and no doubt developed, some sort of modest bureaucracy on the Canaanite model. One capable of engaging in correspondence with the Pharaoh in the Amarna period.[20] Further, there had been an Egyptian garrison stationed at Jerusalem at the time. It is a reminder of Egyptian influence, military and cultural, on Palestine during the New Kingdom period. Egyptian cultural contacts were not new. The fact that Solomon married Pharaoh's daughter suggests that those direct contacts remained vibrant. We must be aware, too, that Solomon's court was capable of making the complex arrangements for building and financing the Temple, as well as fortifying and equipping chariot cities (Hazor, Megiddo and Gezer) and undertaking engineering for complex water cisterns.

The Canaanite court reminds us that there would have been cultural exchange more locally. Edom and the 'people of the East', the setting for the Book of Job, were famous for their Wisdom. The well-known Wisdom of Ahikar, set in the Assyrian court, has sayings that probably originated in Syria and indicate Wisdom activity there. We know that Solomon had much to do with King Hiram of Tyre for his Temple building; trade rarely takes place in isolation from cultural exchange.

A reminder of the significance of the local also highlights the likelihood that 'clan wisdom' persisted in the corporate memory and that Israel would have had its own indigenous source of proverbial material.[21] This would highlight the family, and not just the sophisticated élite at court, in the origin of proverbs and embryonic collections of them. It is a reminder, too, of the significance of oral as well as literary tradition, and the cross-connections that can occur in popular tradition, for instance, with legal, ethical and liturgical material. It clearly does not, on its own, account for the highly sophisticated and developed international literary tradition of Wisdom.

A radical challenge to any enlightenment consensus, be it the reign of Solomon or Hezekiah, or any analogy for Israel of an educational context for Wisdom's transmission comparable with Mesopotamia and Egypt, has come from those who point out that the first actual evidence for a school in Israel comes from Ben Sira in the second century BCE.[22] All arguments for the existence of schools are therefore inferential. It is argued that there may well be no collective educational process for Wisdom to be associated with, whether at court or elsewhere. It is pointed out that the Hebrew language was written as a consonantal alphabet and so is immeasurably easier to grasp than cuneiform or hieroglyphs; it could be taught at home. The modest court scribal activities associated with a city-state could be accounted for by a hereditary profession with the father training the son. Further, it is maintained that a court scribal school is hardly appropriate to the material contained in the Book of Proverbs. The few references to the king can be explained by other circumstances.[23] It is summed up by Stuart Weeks:

> Were it reasonably clear that schools actually existed, then we might at least entertain the possibility that Wisdom literature was used in them, or even composed for use in them. However there is neither any strong evidence for schools nor any convincing reason to suppose that they would have existed. Our ignorance of educational methods in Israel remains profound, and claims for the use of Wisdom literature in schools are entirely speculative.[24]

It has been argued by R. N. Whybray[25] that Wisdom is simply an 'intellectual tradition' associated with no institution or collective undertaking. Wisdom existed, according to this conception, for the private edification and pleasure of a small literate class. This is seemingly confirmed by the logic of S. Weeks. However, Whybray's conclusion does contradict the urgent nature of the Wisdom material. It is difficult to resist the connection between a book as didactic as Proverbs, clearly not designed to stay on the shelf, and some interactive environment between teacher and pupil. Indeed, Proverbs seems to disclose just such a setting:

> I did not listen to the voice of my teachers
> or incline my ear to my instructors. (Proverbs 5:13)

It seems that the Tutor-teacher may be a valid inference for Israel after all; an analogy, if not identity, with practices in Mesopotamia and Egypt is valid. Further, Wisdom's home at the centre of power and close to state institutions is difficult to dismiss. John Day emphasizes the importance of connections between Israel and more local Wisdom as found in the nations around her. In accumulating the names of the local heroes of Wisdom he sums up:

Job, Daniel and Ahikar were all members of the ruling class, and Solomon, of course, was a king. The extent to which Wisdom should be seen as a product of the court and ruling class in Israel is currently disputed, but there is little doubt that this was one of the contexts in which it was cultivated.[26]

B. The Books of Proverbs, Job and Ecclesiastes

It is now time to review the books themselves, and the starting point must be the Book of Proverbs. Proverbs is full of practical advice. It sets out guidance for handling life successfully. Its focus is limited to human behaviour. When it makes reference to natural wisdom it is to draw analogies between the natural world and human behaviour from which a lesson can be learned. Its advice is given in two distinct forms, these are 'proverbs' and 'instructions'.[27]

The proverbial saying is virtually a universal human phenomenon, and is cast in the form of general observation. It is a particular feature of Mesopotamian Wisdom where it was popular:

> Fruit in the spring
> – fruit of mourning.
> A canal in the direction of the wind
> brings water in abundance.[28]

As we encounter these sentence proverbs in the biblical Book of Proverbs they seem to have no particular logic of arrangement, except perhaps for the occasional catchword. However, the individual fragments have been gathered so as to create a total landscape of integrated advice for the prudent person. They participate in a sort of 'Wisdom standard' of wise behaviour that is recognizable across the Ancient Near East, but which was adapted to local circumstances and conventions.

The typical Hebrew proverb (māšāl) is a straightforward sentence in two halves constructed with a parallelism similar to the psalms. Sometimes the second half contains a maxim which mirrors the first:

> Listen to your father who begot you,
> and do not despise your mother when she is old. (Proverbs 23:22)

Sometimes the second half contrasts with the first:

> A false balance is an abomination to the Lord,
> but an accurate weight is his delight. (Proverbs 11:1)

Sometimes a proverb can be constructed with 'counterpoise' so that a tension is set up in each half as well as between them.[29] The elegant poetic quality of the individual sentences reminds us that we are dealing with a sophisticated literary tradition far removed from the origins of the proverbial form in popular Wisdom. Although it is a general feature of Wisdom that it contrasts the wise and the foolish, the vigour with which that is done in Hebrew Wisdom literature and the presentation of the 'two ways' may be a case of Hebrew parallelism generating a specific theological perspective. In particular, Proverbs often speaks of the foolish as 'wicked' (rešā'îm).[30] In the opening section Lady Wisdom[31] and Dame Folly[32] personify the choice of life and death presented by the tradition:

> Those who keep the commandment will live;
> those who are heedless of their ways will die. (Proverbs 19:16)

The proverbial form is characteristic of both of the 'Solomonic' collections to be found in Proverbs 10:1–22:16 and Proverbs 25–29. The former is often reckoned to contain the oldest gathered material of the Book of Proverbs.[33] The latter collection has an interesting superscription: 'These are the proverbs of Solomon that the officials of King Hezekiah of Judah copied.' It is one of the crucial pieces of evidence for associating the court of Hezekiah with patronage of the Wisdom movement.

According to the first Solomonic collection, the good life has to do with hard work and industry, honesty and straight-forwardness, and no deceit on the weights. It is people who honour their parents, are humble, reserved in speech and even tempered, and err on the side of generosity and magnanimity, who are wise. Such people discipline their children (even grandchildren receive a mention), care for their animals, till their fields and are kind to the poor. They take counsel before making a decision and are not susceptible to bribes; they

respect justice and are loyal, their grey hairs honour them and
they are a blessing to their community. Good sense is preferred
to beauty in a woman; she is one who 'builds her house'. The
commendable wife is, in a patriarchal society, a credit to her
husband.

By contrast, the fool is lazy and devious; he is not to be trusted
with the scales. He is arrogant, hasty in speech and contentious.
He is cruel and mean, takes offence at rebuke and oppresses the
poor: one given to drink and brawling. His company is best
avoided. The contentious and fretful wife is warned against. The
'loose woman' also receives a mention but is not a preoccupation
of this section.

Clearly, it is practical management of daily living which
preoccupies this proverbial Wisdom. There is an almost prophetic
edge to the verse:

> To do righteousness and justice
> is more acceptable to the Lord than sacrifice. (Proverbs 21:3)

The instruction form is more discursive than its proverbial
companion. It is specifically addressed from father to son; cast
in the imperative mood, it gives its advice in the form of orders.
Often the reason for the advice is explained following its
annunciation:

> My child, if your heart is wise,
> my heart too will be glad.
> My soul will rejoice
> when your lips speak what is right.
> Do not let your heart envy sinners,
> but always continue in the fear of the Lord.
> Surely there is a future
> and your hope will not be cut off. (Proverbs 23:15–18)

The instruction form is well known from ancient Egypt where it
seems to be indigenous. There, it is particularly cast as advice by
the king or a high official to his son and heir. It may have had
its origin in tomb inscriptions. In the Book of Proverbs the
instruction genre appears in two major sections. It is present in
the initial section of Proverbs 1–9 and also again in the section
between the two Solomonic collections in Proverbs 22:17 – 24:22.
Let us consider the latter first.

Following the publication of the Egyptian New Kingdom work, *The Instruction of Amenemope,* it was recognized to have more than a passing similarity with Proverbs, and in particular with Proverbs 22:17 – 23:11.[34] It became evident that not only can the form of the instruction be associated with Proverbs, but a specific Egyptian work is linked to it. This highlights the international nature of the Wisdom tradition and the exchange of ideas it enabled throughout the Ancient Near East. It also shows how easily Proverbs connects with a work that is based on an awareness of Ma'at and the Egyptian sense of the order of the world as it relates to human conduct.

After his introduction Amenemope begins with an enunciation of the two ways:

> It is useful to put it (what is heard) in your heart,
> but woe to the one who neglects it. (3:11 and 12)[35]

The contents of the Instruction has a high moral tone; Amenemope is himself a civil servant, a tax official. The wretched are not to be robbed (cf. Proverbs 22:22), it is not right to take advantage of the weak or elderly, to infringe the boundary of widows' property nor tamper with any boundary markers (cf. Proverbs 22:28 and 23:10). The hot-headed man should be avoided (cf. Proverbs 22:24) and silence cultivated; it is always best to sleep on a response. Do not set your heart on riches (cf. Proverbs 23:4). Do not covet. Do not bear false witness. Do not speak first in the presence of a great man or eat bread before a noble (cf. Proverbs 23:1–3). The proverbial form also occurs several times in Amenemope:

> Better a bushel if God give it to you,
> than five thousand with injustice. (8:19 and 20)

The work even has a saying which, in the Hebrew context would sound suspiciously like Yahwistic Wisdom, but is part of the theology of the Instruction:

> One thing are the words which man says,
> and another thing is what God does. (19:16 and 17)

It concludes with a note that an experienced scribe will be found worthy to be a courtier (cf. Proverbs 22:29). There are coincidentally thirty chapters of Amenemope (cf. Proverbs 22:20).

Another Egyptian work, which most probably had an influence on Amenemope, is *The Instruction of Ani*. As we move to consider Proverbs 1–9, which forms a preface to the Book of Proverbs and clearly reflects the instruction genre, a quote from Ani is in order:

> Be on your guard against a woman from abroad,
> whom no one knows in her city.
> Do not gaze at her when she goes past,
> and do not know her carnally.
> She is a deep water, the extent of which no one knows.
> A woman whose husband is far away, says daily to you:
> 'I am polished (= pretty)!', when she has no witnesses.
> She waits and sets her trap. A great crime – and death,
> when it is known.[36]

The 'woman whose husband is far away' obtains a particular notoriety in Proverbs. Not only is she the one to be avoided by the young man for whom she spells death (Proverbs 7:6–23), but she attains to the anti-type of Lady Wisdom herself (Proverbs 9:14–18). Lady Wisdom preaches and exhorts from the city gate (Proverbs 8:3) and the acropolis of the town (Proverbs 9:3) that, whoever will, may attend her banquet of life. This personification of Wisdom pleading life is developed even further when Wisdom becomes the first-born of creation, the one present when the world was ordered (Proverbs 8:22–31). The preface in Proverbs 1–9 would seem to be, in terms of composition, the final and most theologically developed section of the whole book. It is well on the way to the theological developments of Ecclesiasticus and the Wisdom of Solomon. What it does is remind the reader that for all of its seemingly mundane advice for Monday morning, Wisdom in Proverbs is actually about a cosmic thread and respect for a divinely sanctioned order. Given the closeness of Egyptian thinking to this cosmic awareness, Kayatz[37] is probably correct to see the Egyptian goddess of order, Ma'at, behind Lady Wisdom. It was Ma'at who, as daughter of Re' delighted in the order of creation. Her representation holding the ankh, sign of life, could well be behind Proverbs 3:16:

> Long life in her right hand;
> in her left hand are riches and honour.

Of course, if Ma'at is the germ of the personification of Lady Wisdom, as we meet her in Proverbs she is very much the product of indigenous Hebrew theological reflection and development.

Before concluding this review of Proverbs, it may be noted that recent scholarship has argued for the influence of Wisdom outside what would be considered the normal boundaries of its activities.[38] Prophecy and Law have both been candidates for this agency. The ministry of Lady Wisdom preaching in the market place and at the city gate seems closer to what one might conceive as a prophetic ministry than the traditional concept of the wise man in his scriptorium. We have already noted the bite of Proverbs in its prophetic challenge:

> To do righteousness and justice
> is more acceptable to the Lord than sacrifice. (Proverbs 21:3)

The prophets and Wisdom share a very strong moral and ethical demand.

As regards law, there seems a valid comparison between the 'two ways' of Wisdom and the starkness of the choice it presents between life and death, and the exhortation of Moses in Deuteronomy:

> See, I have set before you today life and
> prosperity, death and adversity. (Deuteronomy 30:15)

Further, the world of the Instructions, with its imperative mood and absolute demands, does not seem a great distance from the world of the Ten Commandments. When we discussed the relationship between Proverbs 22:17 – 23:11 and the Instruction of Amenope we noted that there were thirty rather than ten instructions. Interestingly, they relate to honouring parents, not bearing false witness, not coveting and not committing adultery. There are connections to be uncovered and identified.

It does seem that the stream of Wisdom may have been more at home and more generally influential in Israel than once seemed possible. Far from being an alien force, it may have been seminal. If there was a class of the Wise, at least from the time of Hezekiah, it is likely that they were able to both practise the discipline of Wisdom and participate in Israel's national religious institutions. After all, a prophet could inhabit more than one form with integrity and respect the parameters of each one. Deutero-Isaiah uses the Oracle of Salvation and the Proclamation of Salvation, both adapted from Temple-worship, but also legal forms, Wisdom disputations, Hymns and so on. He can clearly handle this variety of forms using the rules and conventions by which they operate, even to the extent that sometimes, it can be argued, theological developments in one form do not transfer to another. There is no reason why the prophet should be unique in this ability to move across the boundaries of the way the theological enterprise was undertaken in Israel.

The Book of Job is set in the Land of Uz (Job 1:1), which is probably to be located in Edom. That very fact stresses the internationalism of the Wisdom movement:

> Since the Book of Job is widely agreed to date from c. 500–300 BCE, we thus seem to have here an Edomite as the hero of a Jewish Wisdom book at the very time when the Edomites were so hated by the Jews, apparently because of their connivance in the Babylonian destruction of Jerusalem in 586 BCE.[39]

In content, the Book of Job bears a striking affinity to a Sumerian work written some 1500 years earlier commonly, if anachronistically, referred to as *The Sumerian Job*.[40] Mesopotamia also provides another parallel, this time from Kassite times, in the work known as *I Will Praise the Lord of Wisdom*,[41] who in this case is the Babylonian deity Marduk. The theme throughout the Book of Job is one which knows no national restrictions; it is the question which undeserved human suffering puts to the goodness and justice of God. When God appears, the answer to which humanity is pointed is the mysterious universal order of creation.

Job questions Wisdom where it is most vulnerable. The principle of retribution has broken down. In an ordered universe why is God singling him out for seemingly unjust treatment? Job's 'comforters' give the traditional answers of Wisdom. The message of Eliphaz, Bildad and Zophar is one, and it is stated early by Eliphaz:

> Think now, who that was innocent ever perished?
> Or where were the upright cut off? (Job 4:7)

The only real development called forth by Job's continued protestations of righteousness is that none is upright before God:

> How then can a mortal be righteous before God?
> How can one born of a woman be pure? (Job 25:4)

This is a point that already seems to have won Job's assent.[42] Elihu, the youthful latecomer to the dialogue, in some ways anticipates the theophany and points to the loftiness of the creator, and the incongruity of human attempts to interrogate him.

How does the theophany answer Job's persistent challenge to the righteousness of God? It is not a direct answer. Rather, in chapters 38 and 39, in a way very reminiscent of the Egyptian Onomastica tradition, God recites his deeds in the ordering of creation which include the shutting up of the sea, the establishment of the treasuries of the snow and the hail, and also the creating of winds, lightning and rivers. He has created the constellations of the skies, he made the grass grow and he plants understanding in the minds of human beings. Chapters 40 and 41 set forth the might of God who can tame the wild beasts; at times it is difficult to tell whether these beasts are part of the natural world or the mythical monsters controlled at creation.

God's answer seems to deal with Job's questioning in two ways. Firstly, as we considered earlier, it is a return to first principles. Looked at across the complete spectrum it is a complex, orderly and beautiful world. Somehow Job's life must fit into that order; it is just that he cannot perceive how that can be. Order and justice are a continuum, and therefore the reassurance of order across the universe must also guarantee a justice operating for the individual at the 'local' level. Secondly, the scale of creation serves to undermine the partial human perspective, and remind Job of the profound mystery and unknowability of God. His ways are inscrutable; humanity cannot call God to task:

> Who is this that darkens counsel
> by words without knowledge?[43]

The answer apparently satisfies Job, he 'repents in dust and ashes' (Job 42:6). It is an outcome to be anticipated. Like Jacob wrestling with God, even if it cripples him, so Job will not let go. His very struggling is witness that he can accept no other answer than a mysterious confirmation of divine justice. But in the Book of Job we clearly perceive the vigorous questioning of a just and perfect order on the one hand, and the emergence of a theology of the unknowability and transcendence of God on the other.[44] Along with this latter goes its corollary, the wretchedness and creatureliness of human beings. In these intimations a tradition in part influenced by the optimism of the Egyptian vision of universal order has come close to confirming the assessment of ancient Mesopotamia as regards human destiny and dignity. It is 'the Preacher' (Qoheleth) of the Book of Ecclesiastes who turns this ultimate nightmare into poetry.

Qoheleth, writing in probably the late third century,[45] like certain sections of Proverbs, invokes the persona of Solomon thus claiming his instructions and sayings as within the great stream of Hebrew Wisdom. He leaves us in no doubt as to his universal concern. His work seeks to search out all that happens 'under the sun'[46] or, alternatively put:

> I applied my mind to seek and to search
> out by Wisdom all that is done under heaven; (Ecclesiastes 1:13)

His concerns are, through contemplating the order of the world, to reflect on meaning and meaninglessness, life and death, good and evil – issues of the human spirit which do not know boundaries of race or nation.

Here also, ancient Mesopotamia can provide us with a work that may be compared with that of Qoheleth. It is entitled *A Pessimistic Dialogue between Master and Servant*. One verse is sufficient to sample its evocative melancholy:

> Climb the mounds of ancient ruins and walk about:
> look at the skulls of late and early (men);
> who (among them) is an evil doer,
> who a public benefactor?[47]

Ancient Egypt, too, provides a parallel in *The Dialogue of a Man with his Soul*[48] in which a man tries to convince his soul that it is not worth remaining alive. The man's soul scorns the normal funeral procedure. Those entombed in pyramids are no different from 'the dead on the dyke' (i.e. the unburied). Qoheleth's was not a lone voice in his international setting.

Qoheleth no longer argues against the anxieties with which Job fought, but which he felt - in some innate way – could not be the final word. Qoheleth accepts that the principle of retribution has broken down:

> The same fate comes to all,
> to the righteous and the wicked,
> to the good and the evil,
> to the clean and the unclean,
> to those who sacrifice and those who do not sacrifice. (Ecclesiastes 9:2)

The way of Wisdom, as humans are able to perceive it, is no longer authoritative. At best it operates in a very pragmatic way that can, within limits, help one to bear the cruelties of life and its pleasures by accepting them as they come.[49] By living without too much excess one can minimize life's mishaps, so Qoheleth advises

> Do not be too righteous . . .
> Do not be too wicked . . . (Ecclesiastes 7:16 and 17)

There is still a dim hope that perhaps justice is simply slow when it looks absent,[50] or that humankind is being proved.[51] An explicit reference to the creation surfaces in the final chapter, albeit in rather a salutary context:

> Remember your Creator in the days of your youth. (Ecclesiastes 12:1)

But as far as Qoheleth is concerned the ways of God – which he does not doubt – are totally inscrutable and unknowable. It is because humankind cannot perceive the way God works that the wisdom of the wise has lost its unerring authority:

> Then I saw all the work of God,
> that no one can find out what is happening under the sun.
> However much they may toil in seeking, they will not find it out;
> even though those who are wise claim to know,
> they cannot find it out. (Ecclesiastes 8:17)

As we have already noted, the obverse of an emphasis on God's unknowability is human creatureliness. Here, too, Qoheleth's vision confirms the lowest moments of the Book of Job:

> Surely there is no one on earth so righteous
> as to do good without ever sinning.[52]

He would agree with Job's comforters in that. Altogether, Qoheleth has arrived at an assessment of life based upon God's unknowability and humankind's frailty, which represents the failure of Wisdom to live with its own vision of perfection:

> I saw all the deeds that are done under the sun;
> and see, all is vanity and a chasing after wind. (Ecclesiastes 1:14)

The books of Proverbs, Job and Ecclesiastes enable us to identify clearly the Wisdom tradition as part of Israel's theological enterprise. Wisdom provided within Israel's mainstream religious traditions a clear reflection on universal order. Proverbs is at the heart of orthodox reflection on order; Job, in the end, succumbs to the evidence of order's grand sweep throughout the universe; for Qoheleth, order has lost its glistening glory and has become tedious and capricious. Even with Qoheleth, however, reflection on order retains its scientific and detached methodology. The nature of Wisdom's integrity, its ability to retain a distinct identity in a pluralistic environment, meant that Hebrew religion was not without a witness to a common humanity and a common context with the rest of the Ancient Near East.

C. Order's Spokesman

If Order was the great marvel of creation for the Ancient Near East, then it was the Wisdom tradition which was the clearest spokesman for that insight. Wisdom most obviously and rigorously spelt out the significance of Order as the miracle of the universe. The Wisdom tradition was the intellectual companion of the Ancient Near East's single and most basic assumption about the nature of the universe. The divine voice that called the world to order imprinted upon it the principle of rationality so that it could operate as a breathtakingly beautiful and complex system of interrelated and harmonious parts. The biblical priestly creation account in Genesis 1 speaks about this with a single voice for the whole Wisdom movement: 'God saw everything that he had made, and indeed, it was very good' (Genesis 1:31a). A Wisdom-form adopted by the prophet Deutero-Isaiah of the Exile[53] enables us to touch and encounter the sheer thrill of this magisterial vision of the divine achievement albeit in interrogative form:

> Who has measured the waters in the hollow of his hand
> and marked off the heavens with a span,

enclosed the dust of the earth in a measure,
and weighed the mountains in scales
and the hills in a balance?
Who has directed the spirit of the Lord,
or as his counsellor has instructed him?
Whom did he consult for his enlightenment,
and who taught him the path of justice?
Who taught him knowledge,
and showed him the way of understanding? (Isaiah 40:12–14)

A rational, ordered universe could be counted on to be regular, repetitive and verifiable. There had to be a logic to its processes which could be anticipated, categorized, interpreted, even appropriately harnessed to human endeavour. In principle, all things could be understood provided the depth of insight was available. There was something approaching a scientific inevitability about the potential of the universe to yield to the right questions skilfully directed. There were no hidden tricks; it was not necessary to reach for interruptions or discontinuities to explain the proper processes. The consequence of this dependable and repetitive rationality of the universe was the recognition of the value of keen observation. It was possible to spot patterns and therefore predict future outcomes of similar situations. Inasmuch as Wisdom lived up to its own principles such deductions required a closeness to events and processes, accurate assessments and a continual willingness to revise provisional conclusions to take account of new evidence. At their truest, Wisdom principles required a continual willingness to learn from the school of experience and to be open to experiment and verification, as well as to look for unexpected and surprising connections and analogies.

Of course, only Wisdom was the companion of God in creation:

The Lord created me at the beginning of his work,
the first of his acts of long ago. (Prov. 8:22)

Only Wisdom, therefore, would be in a position to fathom totally the hidden depths of the profound rationality of the universe. It was beyond even the wisest counsellor to do more than probe the skirts of rationality. At different times of Wisdom's history optimism about this waxed and waned. The remarkable chapter

28 of Job likens the discovery of Wisdom to the mining of ore deep in the ground; if mining is difficult how much more dark and obscure are Wisdom's treasures:

> Miners put an end to darkness . . .
> They open shafts in a valley away
> from human habitation . . .
> That path no bird of prey knows,
> and the falcon's eye has not seen it.
> . .   . .
> But where shall wisdom be found?
> And where is the place of understanding?
> Mortals do not know the way to it,
> and it is not found in the land of the living.
> The deep says, 'It is not in me',
> and the sea says, 'It is not with me'. (Job 28:3a, 4a, 7, 12–14)

Nevertheless, the connection between the human intellect and the rational puzzle of the universe was recognized. What made human beings 'god-like' was the amazing, even unexpected, ability of the human mind to grapple with the logic of the universe. It was an ability whose ambiguity the sages were only too aware of, and which was often the subject of learned discussion. In the famous *The Epic of Gilgamesh* from ancient Babylon, the companion of Gilgamesh named Enkidu has to forego close companionship with the wild animals when he is introduced to civilization. His wild appearance is exchanged for wisdom and understanding. The cult prostitute, who is the agent of the change, declares: 'Thou art wise, Enkidu, art become like a god!'[54] Later, Enkidu voices bitter regret at his enlightenment. The dialogue in Genesis 3 about the forbidden fruit is used by the narrator to articulate a similar ambiguity. In that context the serpent enunciates the god-like potential of humanity to unlock the gate of knowledge:

> You will not die; for God knows that when
> you eat of it your eyes will be opened,
> and you will be like God,
> knowing good and evil. (Genesis 3:5)

Psalm 8 is positive and celebratory about the human potential:

Yet you have made them a little lower than God,
and crowned them with glory and honour. (Psalm 8:5)

The vision of Wisdom was glorious in its comprehensiveness and
in its articulation of a single, harmonious, logical, functioning
universe. Wise men could enjoy, probe and even enumerate
some of its wonders. There is a sense of fun in reading off a
collection of natural phenomena which share characteristics of
'industry and order':[55]

Four things on earth are small,
yet they are exceedingly wise:
the ants are a people without strength,
yet they provide their food in the summer;
the badgers are a people without power,
yet they make their homes in the rocks;
the locusts have no king,
yet all of them march in rank;
the lizard can be grasped in the hand,
yet it is found in kings' palaces. (Proverbs 30:24–28)

More seriously, it was claimed for Solomon, whom tradition
reckoned as the wise king *par excellence*, that,

he would speak of trees, from the cedar that is in the Lebanon to
the hyssop that grows in the wall; he would speak of animals, and
birds, and reptiles and fish. (1 Kings 4:33)

Botany and zoology were but two of his accomplishments.

It is Psalm 104 that most obviously witnesses from within the
biblical tradition to the reality of the claim made for Solomon.
There, the ability of the wise person or counsellor to 'conjugate
the universe' is exhibited; it is a bit like a grammarian setting
out the principal parts of a verb and so displaying knowledge of
its structure. The recounting of the securing of the waters of
creation and the laying of earth's foundations is followed by an
enumeration of creation's marvels and the niche which everything
occupies. The 'principal parts' of order set out include the fowls
of the air (v. 12), provision of food for cattle and people (v. 14)
and wine to gladden the human heart (v. 15), the world of
vegetation and trees (v. 16), the heavenly bodies marking the
seasons (v. 19), and the world of fish (v. 25). At night animals
creep from the forest (v. 20), during the day humans go to their
labours (v. 23). The psalmist exclaims:

> O Lord, how manifold are your works!
> In wisdom you have made them all. (v. 24)

The practical application of these insights, however, was where
theory could be applied, and where Wisdom engaged with daily
life. It was at this point that Wisdom's principles related directly
to human behaviour. Although the weight of humanistic concerns
must not be allowed to camouflage the principles upon which
Wisdom operated, yet those principles had significant
implications for every detail of human life. It has been expressed
by H. H. Schmid: 'The crux of original Wisdom is not humanity,
but the order of the world, its concern not anthropology, but
cosmology, however surely it may apply its cosmological interest
to anthropological material.'[56]

The insistence that the world is logical and consistent enabled
the Wisdom tradition to observe and predict outcomes of human
action. It accounts for Wisdom's most characteristic principle,
that of the act–consequence connection. Particular acts may be
observed to have specific outcomes. The insight that the world
operated as a cosmos, that is a single whole throughout all of its
parts, meant that consequences might be quite far apart from
the original acts or related in quite complex ways. If it can be
observed that particular actions consistently have specific
consequences, then human behaviour needs to be trained or
adjusted so that acts that result in positive outcomes are
encouraged, and acts that trigger negative outcomes are
discouraged. By keen observation and accumulated verification
the Wisdom tradition produced advice on patterns of behaviour
that recognized this basic insight. Because of the predictable and
ordered nature of the universe it was deemed possible to calculate
correct human responses to particular situations which would
result in success of one sort or another. Put positively the
conclusion of the research was:

> In the path of righteousness there is life,
> in walking its path there is no death. (Prov. 12:28)

The exact contents of a righteous life (ṣedāqâ) varied to some
extent in Wisdom's long history stretching over millennia, but
it always related to right order (ṣedeq); that is, life lived in
harmony with the order of the universe.[57] There is a grain to the

universe, and going with the grain leads to smooth and frictionless integration into world order, and consequently to health, wealth and the blessings of peace. Failure to recognize the grain of the universe leads the fool to calamity, to poverty, to discomfort and disgrace. Human behaviour has to take account of the providential nature of the cosmos as the work of a moral creator.

In respecting order, human beings are not simply performing a private good, they are playing their part in the continuing maintenance of an ordered universe. 'When it goes well with the righteous the city rejoices' (Proverbs 11:10). Human beings in wholesome relationship with order are part of a universal communion in which the thread of Wisdom's rationality binds all together. To depart from order is to disturb a cosmic harmony with dire results. It triggers the 'wrath of God' in a way that is not about arbitrary anger but is about the inner logic of the universe itself – 'the crookedness of the treacherous destroys them' (Proverbs 11:3b).

It is not always easy to see how some of the seemingly trivia of Proverbs have a cosmic significance. The lazy one turning on his bed like the creaking hinges on a door (Proverbs 26:14) hardly seems to shake the universe. Yet it is a single vision of order that unites the otherwise piecemeal items of advice in Proverbs and which is a feature of the Hebrew Wisdom literature. There are particular sayings which are transparent to the premise of the creator's order for their validity. For instance:

> Those who oppress the poor
> insult their Maker,
> but those who are kind to the needy
> honour him. (Proverbs 14:31)[58]

Again the concern of Proverbs for just weights and measures is a regular theme, but in Proverbs 16:11 it has a particular significance in the way it is expressed:

> Honest balances and scales are the Lord's:
> All the weights in the bag are his work.

It has been pointed out that it could be paraphrased:

> Who falsifies the balance offends against an order of corporate human life which was established and guaranteed by the creator.[59]

Crenshaw has noted that the doctrine of creation, always implicit in Wisdom, tends to surface explicitly at times when one part of the universal order is being called into question; that is at times of doubt or anxiety.[60] It is at times of calamity that the Wisdom tradition is driven back to first principles. It is at that point that the true significance of creation as the source of its vision is exposed. It is certainly true that not only does the fact that God is the creator ultimately have to satisfy Job's complaint, but also throughout the dialogue it is to the fact that God is the creator that the theme regularly returns.[61] The personal despair of Proverbs 30:1–3, that reminds the reader of Job, seems to be groping after its resolution by an appeal to creation in the following verse. The Wisdom passage in Isaiah 40:12–14 quoted earlier serves exactly the same function within Deutero-Isaiah's message of comfort to the exiles. Concern about the immediate and current chaotic world can be allayed by looking at the reliable operation of the great scheme of things. If the universe is operating properly across its length and breadth, then it brings reassurance to local anxieties that in some way the lesser is connected to the greater if one could but perceive it.

The fact that it was the single great order of the universe to which human behaviour had to relate meant that everything was relativized. The universe had no particular centre. There was no corner of the universe where valid observations about order were suspended. There could be no special pleading of place, of race or of religion. There was no navel of the universe, as in the Jerusalem traditions, where the graceful lines of order were 'bent' by encounter with its special gravitational field. Wisdom dealt with universally valid observations which enabled genuine scientific reflection on human beings within their environment. One of the reasons why Wisdom literature was exchanged throughout the Ancient Near East was that its principles were based on universal insights. Its traditions had the ability to rise above the prejudices, the claims and counter-claims, of nations and states in regular warfare or mutual deprecation. Neither pride in civic customs and conventions which myth traced to the gift of the gods, nor local insistence that their soil was the place of original creation, could be allowed to interfere with Wisdom's principles. There is no local label, for instance, on the basic human advice that: 'Those who do violence to their father and chase away their mother are children who cause shame and bring reproach' (Proverbs 19: 26). For Wisdom, all human beings are equidistant from God.

There is about Wisdom a feeling of secularism in that it refuses to allow that God intervenes to override the strict act–consequence structure of the universe. There is no special pleading, divine intervention or miraculous deliverance. Yet, a religious ambience permeates everything through the recognition of a moral grain integral to a universal divine order. It is a feature of Wisdom that its observations are not 'value-free'. It is of its essence that it includes human moral responsibility within the predictable order of act and consequence. Wisdom as it was applied to human behaviour was about ethics. There was envisaged to be a moral recoil of creation to immoral acts which was delivered in an appropriate way:

> Whoever digs a pit will fall into it,
> and a stone will come back on the one who starts it rolling. (Proverbs 26:27)

Conversely, there was a providential consequence to good deeds.

There was no distinction made between inevitability operating in the natural world and inevitability of a different order operating in the social and moral affairs of individuals. The Wisdom tradition, having observed the relentless operation of uninterrupted logic in the strictly natural world, extrapolated those same principles across into the unpredictable world of human affairs. The random interface, for instance, of nature's natural disasters and human endeavour, say, in building dwellings, homes and cities would not have been handled as morally neutral. An inner logic would have been searched out that might embrace the two and reveal an overarching meaning and order.

It was a brave and attractive feature of Wisdom that it attempted a theory of everything. It adopted the insight of the Ancient Near East that order was the single great miracle of the universe and treated it in a rigorous quasi-scientific fashion. Wisdom attempted, by observation of the way things are, to codify and articulate the principles upon which life operated in so far as they affected human behaviour. Of course, in the end there was bound to be

a void between prediction and actuality. Wisdom's assumption
that the moral order of the universe was an exact equivalent of
its natural order could not be sustained. Scientific scrutiny could
not be applied in an identical way to the human and moral as
to the strictly material and natural world. An apple always falls
to the ground. The good are not always and everywhere rewarded
– the wicked do prosper; blind chance does intervene. That
conflict of principle and observation was bound to lead to soul-
searching and, in the end, question the basic validity of Wisdom
as the guide for life.

Wisdom could not appeal to anything incomplete or
impermanent when its principles based on the order of creation
were perceived to be breaking down. It had a distinct perspective
on the significance of the Creator's work in contrast to the cultic
perspective reflected in the psalms uninfluenced by Wisdom.
Although these cultic psalms take their mythical narrative from
Yahweh's original triumph over the waters of Chaos, they present
it as immediate and present. Creation was something always
open and ever incomplete in the breathless 'now' of liturgy:

> More majestic than the thunders of mighty waters,
> more majestic than the waves of the sea,
> Majestic on high is the Lord! (Psalm 93:4)[62]

By contrast, for Wisdom the vigorous mythology is often subdued,
the confinement of Chaos is final and permanent with the
consequence that Order is established 'once and for all'. God
has said to personified Chaos:

> Thus far shall you come, and no farther,
> And here shall your proud waves be stopped. (Job 38:11)

Wisdom's vision was of a world of gleaming perfection founded
on primal universal order established once and for all by the
creator. There is no question of that good order being threatened
by anything impermanent or provisional about the original act
of creation.[63] Wisdom with Genesis 2:1 could say: 'Thus the
heavens and the earth were finished'. The only allowable reason
for the breakdown of order, therefore, had to be human error.
The threat according to Wisdom's analysis came from the 'fool',
the one who lacked wisdom:

God made human beings straightforward,
but they have devised many schemes. (Ecclesiastes 7:29)

The disconnection between prediction and reality became an increasingly difficult moral and philosophical objection to Wisdom's magnificent theory of the universe. Different times and different circumstances threw up varied manifestations of this struggle with the dark night of the soul. The classic disputation on the subject is to be found in the Book of Job. It was precisely Job's complaint that traditional explanations no longer adequately accounted for the breakdown of order; the old logic no longer held true. The moral dilemma posed by Wisdom is put from within its own circles. As we noted, the only solutions were either to accentuate the creatureliness of human beings or to point to the utter transcendence and unknowability of God, which also served to highlight the poverty and partiality of all human knowledge and understanding. As we gather from the Book of Ecclesiastes, inevitably, Wisdom's optimism was being replaced by a profound pessimism which could easily be exchanged for cynicism. Its days as an independent practitioner were numbered. The process already under way in Psalm 73, for instance, is confirmed at Ben Sira's Jerusalem school[64] where reason reaches for help from revelation. Instruction and Torah join hands. The current of Wisdom, always interactive, is not lost but defused within the general theological enterprise. It ceases to be a distinct alternative source.

Interestingly, contemporary thinking with its scientific tools more precisely tempered is in tune with Wisdom's endeavour. A theory of everything which relates the macro and micro is still the prize of science. The interface between natural catastrophe and human endeavour is not always as empty of moral consideration as earlier science would have predicted. The sense of the world of nature as an order of which human beings are both a part and for which they carry some responsibility is now axiomatic. Scientific knowledge is not 'value free', but it is unrestricted by artificial boundaries of race, religion and territorial disputes. Ultimate questions are being raised again at the boundaries of scientific knowledge. Wisdom's insights are very much reasserting themselves in the twenty-first century. Those insights are carried within the Hebrew Scriptures and are transparent to the broad horizon of creation theology which the Ancient Near Eastern context brought to the biblical tradition.

Points for Discussion

1. The Wisdom tradition enabled an international dialogue and a respect for a common humanity. How could that be achieved in the modern world, and can religious institutions be part of it?
2. Can the ordered world alone inspire contemporary human beings to a belief in God? How would you begin to answer the anxieties of a Job?
3. Wisdom teachers trained young people in the good life. One set of characteristics is identified from Proverbs 10:1 – 22:16 (first Solomonic collection) and another from the Egyptian work of Amenemope. How different or similar would be your list of the characteristics of the good life?
4. Wisdom literature enabled the civilizations of the Ancient Near East to pass on values and standards to a new generation. How does contemporary civilization pass on its values to a new generation?
5. If you had been responsible for deciding which books to include in the Bible would you have included Ecclesiastes (Qoheleth)?

Key Bible Passages

Proverbs 10:1 – 22:16 (first 'Solomonic' proverbial collection); Proverbs 22:17 – 23:11 (Instruction Genre connected with the wisdom of Amenemope); Job 31 (moral principles that have broken down); Job 38 and 42:1–6 (the Creator's response); Ecclesiastes 3 (the wisdom of pragmatism).

Further Reading

J. L. Crenshaw, *Old Testament Wisdom*, London (1982).
Stuart Weeks, *Early Israelite Wisdom*, Oxford (1994).
Katharine Dell, *Get Wisdom Get Insight*, London (2000).

Figure 4. A painted limestone statue of a seated scribe with papyrus, from Saqqara, Egyptian Old Kingdom 2658–2150 BCE. (Egyptian Museum, Cairo.)

Endnotes

[1] H. W. F. Saggs, *Babylonians*, London (2000), p. 152.

[2] For the distribution of the root ḥkm in the Hebrew scriptures see R. N. Whybray, *The Intellectual Tradition in the Old Testament*, Berlin and New York (1974), p. 4 and chapter 4.

[3] We may identify Simon, the High Priest adulated by Ben Sira (Ecclesiasticus 50:1 ff) as Simon II, and date the book's completion to around 180 BCE in Jerusalem.

[4] Written in the final pre-Christian century.

[5] Ecclus. 24:1–23.

[6] Ecclus. 50 vv. 25 and 26.

[7] S. N. Kramer, *The Sumerians*, Chicago and London (1963), pp. 237–8.

[8] G. Pettinato, 'The Royal Archives of Tell Mardikh-Ebla', *Biblical Archaeologist* 39/2 (May 1976).

[9] J. L. Crenshaw, *Studies in Ancient Israelite Wisdom*, New York (1976), p. 22.

[10] E. W. Heaton, *Solomon's New Men*, London (1974).

[11] Genesis 37–50.

[12] 2 Samuel 9 – 1 Kings 2.

[13] Genesis 1–11 (J).

[14] T. N. D. Mettinger, *Solomon's State Officials*, Lund (1971).

[15] D. W. Jamieson-Drake, *Scribes and Schools in Monarchic Judah*, Sheffield (1991), argues on socio-economic grounds that Judah is an 'extended chiefdom' until the eighth century, when it reaches definitive statehood which could warrant a scribal bureaucracy and associated educational institutions. The starkness of this conclusion has been challenged by G. I. Davies both on the grounds of exaggerated contrasts and of seriously underestimated archaeological evidence from the early monarchical period. (G. I. Davies, 'Were there Schools in Israel?', in ed. John Day *et al*, *Wisdom in Ancient Israel*, Cambridge (1995), pp. 199–211.)

[16] R. B. Y. Scott, 'Solomon and the Beginnings of Wisdom in Israel' in J. L. Crenshaw ed. *Studies in Ancient Israelite Wisdom*, p. 273.

[17] W. McKane, *Prophets and Wise Men*, London (1965), envisaged a confrontation between the wise men with their pragmatic advice on statecraft and the prophets with their Yahwistic perspective. He envisaged Wisdom as initially 'secular' and only later 'religious'. A similar development is assumed by J. Blenkinsopp, *Wisdom and Law in the Old Testament*, Oxford (1995), pp. 24ff.

[18] Isaiah 29:13–14,15–16; 30:1–5; 31:1–3.

[19] A possibility allowed by E. W. Heaton, *The School Tradition of the Old Testament*, Oxford (1994), p. 34.

[20] Fourteenth century BCE.

[21] F. W. Golka, *The Leopard's Spots: Biblical and African Wisdom in Proverbs,* Edinburgh (1993), using African examples stresses Proverbs as a universal phenomenon and the significance of their prior circulation in oral form before they find a literary context.

[22] Ecclesiasticus 51:23.

[23] F. W. Golka has argued that African folk-sayings suggest that king-sayings often arise outside of court circles. (*Vetus Testamentum* 36 (1986), pp. 13–36.) Conversely, G. von Rad suggests that the wise men of the court collected non-courtly material. (G. von Rad, *Wisdom in Israel,* London (1972), p. 17.)

[24] S. Weeks, *Early Israelite Wisdom,* Oxford (1994), p. 156.

[25] R. N. Whybray, *The Intellectual Tradition in the Old Testament,* Berlin (1974).

[26] J. Day, 'Foreign Semitic Influence on the Wisdom of Israel' in ed. J. Day *et al., Wisdom in Ancient Israel,* Cambridge (1995), p. 61.

[27] W. McKane, *Proverbs: A New Approach,* London (1970); C. Kayatz, *Studien zu Proverbien* 1–9, Neukirchen (1966).

[28] KUB iv No. 97 vv. 7–9; see J.B. Pritchard ed. *ANET,* p. 425.

[29] For instance Proverbs 13:12

Hope deferred – sickness of heart
and a tree of life – desire fulfilled.

[30] John Day, ('Foreign Semitic Influence on the Wisdom of Israel' in ed. J. Day *et al., Wisdom in Israel,* Cambridge (1995), p. 63') suggests that as the righteous/wicked contrast is to be found in the Aramaic Wisdom of Ahikar it is a feature of the West Semitic tradition of Wisdom.

[31] Proverbs 1:20–33; 8:1–36.

[32] Proverbs 9:13–18.

[33] It seems itself to divide into two parts with a preponderance of contrasting parallelisms in ch. 10:1–15:33 and a mixture in Proverbs 16:1–22:16.

[34] Published by E. A. W. Budge, *Hieratic Papyri in the British Museum,* Second Series, 1923, plates 1–14. The dependence of Proverbs 22:17–23: 10 on Amenemope was argued by A. Erman, 'Eine ägyptische Quelle der 'Sprüche Salomos', *SPAW* 15 (1924), pp. 86–92. A wide consensus for some sort of relationship of dependence of these verses of Proverbs on Amenemope has been challenged by R. N. Whybray, 'The Structure and Composition of Proverbs 22:17 – 24:22', in S. E. Porter *et al.* (eds). *Crossing the Boundaries: Essays in Biblical Interpretation in Honour of Michael D. Goulder,* Leiden, New York and Köln (1994), pp. 83–96. The relationship of dependence has been subsequently re-established by

J. A. Emerton, 'The Teaching of Amenemope and Proverbs 22:17 – 24:22: Further Reflections on a Long-Standing Problem', *Vetus Testamentum* 51 (2001), pp. 431–65.

[35] Translation and Text of Amenemope from W. Beyerlin (ed.), *Near Eastern Religious Texts Relating to the Old Testament*, London (1978), pp. 49–62.

[36] *The Instruction of Ani*, III 13–14. Translation, *Near Eastern Religious Texts*, p. 48.

[37] C. Kayatz, *Studien zur Proverbien 1–9*, Neukirchen-Vluyn (1966).

[38] Donn F. Morgan, *Wisdom in the Old Testament Traditions*, Oxford (1981); Joseph Blenkinsopp, *Wisdom and Law in the Old Testament*, Oxford (1995).

[39] John Day, 'Foreign Semitic Influence on the Wisdom of Israel', ed. John Day *et al.*, *Wisdom in Ancient Israel*, p. 56.

[40] See W. Beyerlin (ed.) *Near Eastern Religious Texts Relating to the Old Testament*, pp. 140–42.

[41] *Ibid*, pp. 137–40.

[42] Job 9:2.

[43] Job 38:2.

[44] The personification of Wisdom that we see already in the first section of the Book of Proverbs (chapter 8) may be partly a response to the crisis of the transcendence of God. 'She' was a way of relating the divine presence to human affairs.

[45] Usually dated on linguistic grounds. The book's style resembles the latest Hebrew in the Canon, but was known to Ecclesiasticus writing in the early second century.

[46] Frequently in Ecclesiastes 1–10.

[47] *ANET*, p. 438.

[48] *ANET*, pp. 405 ff.

[49] Ecclesiastes 3:1 and 7:14.

[50] Ecclesiastes 8:11.

[51] Ecclesiastes 3:18.

[52] Ecclesiastes 7:20. In an optimistic moment Qoheleth allows that one in a thousand males might be righteous, but even that optimism does not overflow to the female sex! See Ecclesiastes 7:28.

[53] Roy Melugin, 'Deutero-Isaiah and Form Criticism', *Vetus Testamentum* 21 (1971), pp. 326–27 identifies in Isaiah 40:12–17 the distinct form of a Wisdom disputation. See also H. E. von Waldow, 'The Message of Deutero-Isaiah', *Interpretation* 22 (1968), pp. 269 ff.; W. McKane, *Prophets and Wise Men*, London (1965), pp. 81f.

[54] Epic IV: 34; *ANET* p. 25.

[55] W. Zimmerli, *Old Testament Theology in Outline*, Edinburgh (1978), p. 157 [German original published Stuttgart (1972)].

[56] H. H. Schmid, *Wesen und Geschichte der Weisheit*, Berlin (1966), p. 197.

[57] The significance of the root ṣedeq for Wisdom is clear from a single chapter of Proverbs. In Proverbs 12 in addition to v. 28 the root ṣdq appears in vv. 3, 5, 7, 10, 12, 13, 21 and 26. 'The noun ṣedeq originally denotes the cosmic order which is manifest in wisdom, justice and so on and guaranteed by the king in the context of this earth, whilst ṣedāqâ correspondingly denotes behaviour or action which is in accordance with order or even creates order in this understanding of the concept.' H. H. Schmid, *Gerechtigkeit als Weltordnung*, Tübingen (1968), p. 67.

[58] See also Proverbs 16:4, 17:5 and 22:2.

[59] Hans-Jürgen Hermisson, 'Observations on the Creation Theology in Wisdom', in B. W. Anderson (ed.), *Creation in the Old Testament*, London (1984), p. 122.

[60] J. L. Crenshaw, Prolegomenon, in J. L. Crenshaw (ed.), *Studies in Ancient Israelite Wisdom*, New York (1976), p. 31ff.

[61] Job 26:1–14, 36:3 and *passim*.

[62] See Psalm 89:9–13. The waters are still personified in the chaos monster Rahab (v. 10), and the 'pride' of the sea speaks of rebellion and emphasizes the need for God to exercise his strong arm.

[63] H-J Hermisson contrasts the drama of creation within the Wisdom tradition as it occurs in Psalm 104 vv 1–9 and Job 38–41 with that of a representative sample of psalms including 89:9–13 and 93. He points out that within the Wisdom tradition the confinement of Chaos is final and permanent. For instance, in Ps. 104 Yahweh's care for the created order is continuous, and therefore calls for the imperfect tense or for participles to express it. By contrast the perfect is used in v. 5 'Thou *didst* set the earth on its foundations . . .' and again v. 19 'Thou *hast* made the moon to mark the seasons . . .' both making the point that order has been established and is decisive (H-J Hermisson, Observations on the Creation Theology in Wisdom, in ed. B. W. Anderson, *Creation in the Old Testament*, pp. 118–34). A further example of this feature of Wisdom may be found in Proverbs 8:29.

[64] The Book of Ecclesiasticus; see endnote 3, Ch. 4, above.

CHAPTER 5

Tutor-II

A. Wisdom's Wider Influence

The authentic tones of Wisdom reach us from beyond the 'Wisdom Canon' of Proverbs, Job and Ecclesiastes. Those three books, rather like the authenticating stamp of the Assayer's Office, provide us with a standard by which we may recognize the presence of Wisdom or its influence in other parts of the biblical tradition. It is unmistakable, for instance, in Psalm 49:

> Hear this, all you peoples;
> give ear, all inhabitants of the world,
> both low and high,
> rich and poor together.
> My mouth shall speak wisdom;
> the meditation of my heart shall be understanding. (vv. 1–3)

Not only does the key word 'wisdom' (ḥokmā) appear which presents an initial clue, but also the psalm contains no mention of Israel's ancestral faith. The inscription is universal, addressed to 'all peoples'. According to the summons no particular favour is shown to national or religious identity, nor is one's station in life relevant. The hallmark of Wisdom was its ability to study and reflect on human beings as human beings in almost 'laboratory conditions'; somehow its principles were sturdy enough to resist compromise and collusion. Given its probable home at the institutional centres of power this is especially remarkable. This particular psalm goes on to raise issues not dissimilar to those of Job and Ecclesiastes.

In a Wisdom way, Psalm 37 also reflects on the wicked and the righteous, and gives assurance that it is the righteous who will prosper. It operates within Wisdom's parameters and makes no reference to election. There are other psalms which are certainly 'Wisdom influenced', and it is a fine point as to when they become 'Wisdom Psalms'.[1]

Von Rad highlighted the Joseph Narrative[2] in Genesis and the Succession Narrative (2 Samuel 9–20, 1 Kings 1–2)[3] as key works representing his proposed 'Solomonic Enlightenment'. He saw both as Wisdom literature. Interestingly, using the number of the occurrences of the word wisdom (the root ḥkm) as an indicator, R. N. Whybray[4] concludes that the three references in Genesis 41 occur at a turning point of the Joseph Narrative and so are probably significant. He notes that there are eight occurrences of wisdom in fourteen chapters in the Succession Narrative. The significance is highlighted by the fact that the word does not otherwise occur in 1 and 2 Samuel.

There are some sound reasons for thinking that a further place where the hidden hand of Wisdom is to be discerned is the Primaeval Narrative in Genesis 1–11. If this is so then it is of some consequence. The word 'wisdom' is not to be found in Genesis 1–11. What, then, are the indicators that the authentic tones of Wisdom may be detected here? We may begin by noting the significant point that the Primaeval Narrative clearly shows a Hebrew work that is set in the context of international traditions.

Leaving aside the Genesis 1 creation account, all the indications are that Mesopotamian traditions are significant. The potential age and source of the traditions relating to the Garden of Eden are evident in the single suggestion of J. B. Pritchard relating to the story of woman made from the rib of Adam:

> in Sumerian there is established through a play upon words, a definite connection between the rib and 'the lady who makes live'.[5]

Behind the creation of woman is probably a traditional story about the creation of a goddess in ancient Sumer and based on wordplay operating in the Sumerian language. The story of the Flood is indisputably adapted from Babylonian traditions. It circulated in literary form as part of *The Epic of Gilgamesh*, and that version includes an episode parallel to the detail of the dove in the biblical version. The older Atrahasis epic witnesses to the story in independent form, as does the earliest witness known as the 'Sumerian Flood Narrative' from the opening of the second millennium BCE. The Tower of Babel narrative, despite some misgivings on account of its anti-Babylonian nature, is to be seen as originating in Mesopotamia. The bricks with their bitumen mortar, unknown in Israel, are authentic enough.[6]

It is true of the way all of these venerable traditions are handled throughout the Primaeval History that they are accorded enormous respect. The stories are treated as, in some sense, part of sacred tradition. They are clearly regarded as canonical and not simply a quarry of literature to be foraged and discarded. In view of the way Israel's literature later became closed to outside influence this is particularly remarkable. The fact that it is possible to identify the building blocks in the colourful stories contained in the Primaeval Narrative is due to this reverence for the received tradition. These international traditions might be skilfully assembled but could not be simply rewritten. Their collecting was certainly carried out in intellectual circles, and their probing of primaeval time and human origins suggests a connection with the circle and the activities of those who handled and transmitted international Wisdom.

Before we proceed further it is helpful to clarify the uses of the terms 'Priestly' and 'Yahwistic' in commenting on Genesis 1–11.[7] We noted above that, according to conventional analysis of sources, the Primaeval History contains two traditions which continue on into the subsequent 'salvation history'. One is the Yahwistic tradition which commences with the creation account relating to the Garden of Eden (Genesis 2–3) and continues with the colourful stories of the Cain narrative, the 'Angel Marriages' (Genesis 6:1–4), the story of the Flood, Noah the Vintner, genealogies and the Babel narrative. The parallel tradition is the Priestly tradition which commences with the Genesis 1 creation narrative and continues with a genealogical table that links the creation account to the Flood narrative. Subsequently, the family tree of the patriarch Noah becomes the 'family of humanity' or Table of Nations with three limbs. Apart from the sons of Noah none of the listings are names, they are nations. A connective thread of genealogy leads on from the line of Shem to Abraham.

The raw material of the Primaeval History within both traditions includes genealogies which create the continuity from

Adam to Abraham, and also a 'Table of the Nations' which we have mainly in the Priestly form, but something, probably somewhat simpler, appeared in the Yahwist's tradition also. The genealogies, like the literature, seem to have attained some sort of authoritative shape. This can be discerned from the fact that the Yahwistic and Priestly traditions use similar schemes but in different ways.[8] It seems likely that the wise would have been the custodians of these 'family trees' of humanity. The Table of the Nations in Genesis 11 is something of a 'Mappa Mundi'. The nations of the world known in the Middle East at a time similar to the prophet Ezekiel,[9] that is, towards the end of the monarchy, are listed under three limbs of genealogy. It is a piece of world geography that needed researching even if it has a certain conventionality. Again, surely that would have been the interest and task of the wise, perhaps collected through trading links, before it passed into Priestly hands.

We need now to consider the Yahwistic and Priestly traditions separately. Let us take first the Yahwistic tradition. It can be claimed that the whole structure of the Yahwist's work is the product of one who has been trained in Wisdom. A parallel can be drawn between the structure of the Yahwist's Primaeval Narrative and the structure of the Succession Narrative[10] which concludes with the throne of David firmly in the possession of Solomon. The latter is clearly a self-contained work, and it has been effectively argued by R. N. Whybray that it is a Wisdom work and indeed presents the doctrines of the Wisdom school in a dramatized way.[11] The narrative is constructed around the principle that the inevitable consequence of wrongdoing is to bring calamity upon one's own head. Although this is a general insight of the creation theology of the Ancient Near East it appears in intensified form in Wisdom with vivid clarity. The Succession Narrative almost appears to be history deliberately written up so as to illustrate the basic Wisdom principle that:

Misfortune pursues sinners:
but prosperity rewards the righteous. (Proverbs 13:21)

This principle can be illustrated time and time again in the text of the Succession Narrative. The child of David's adultery with Bathsheba has to die. Amnon receives, at the hand of Absalom, the consequences of his rape of Tamar. This relationship of sin and consequence is maintained in a more subtle way than mere punishment. Here we meet a familiar principle of the Book of Proverbs:

> Whoever digs a pit will fall into it,
> And a stone will come back on the one who starts it rolling. (Proverbs 26:27)

The consequence always logically seems to have an appropriate relationship with the sin. Thus one of the consequences announced by Nathan to David for stealing the wife of Uriah (2 Samuel 12:11) looks ahead to the act of rebellion whereby Absalom publicly takes over David's harem. This sin–consequence principle is told in a perfectly natural way. It does not require special divine intervention but is a moral principle that the creator has built into the world.

In the same way the clarity of the pattern of sin–consequence and the uninterrupted evolutionary process of development are both reflected in the Yahwist's Primaeval Narrative. The wages of human sin are always recorded. The trespass of proper human boundaries as presented in the narrative of the Garden of Eden by the tasting of the forbidden fruit leads to human toil, the pain of childbirth and, appropriately, expulsion from the garden. Cain's murder of Abel leads to his alienation from the ground that 'opened its mouth to receive your brother's blood' (Genesis 4:11). He is to be a fugitive and a vagabond. The Flood Narrative is presented by the Yahwist as the response of God to the evil of a whole generation; it is the appropriate consequence of human wickedness. The story of Babel concludes the Primaeval Narrative (Genesis 11). It is told once again as a story of human beings trying to scale the limits of creatureliness and refusing to recognize proper boundaries. There is a recoil of their environment, as a work of massive human co-operation is rewarded by its shadow in confused tongues and the scattering of the human population in disarray. Here, scattering is punishment, rather than blessing as it was presented in the Yahwistic elements of chapter 10. Interestingly, in chapter 10 it is told in a natural way, in chapter 11 at Babel the narrative involves divine intervention. This difference is not significant, in the sense that

Babel, too, recounts sin–consequence, but in a more primitive way.

Taking up the point of the way the Primaeval Narrative of the Yahwist develops, it is a matter of some significance that the development of arts and civilization is recorded without discontinuity. When comparing the Yahwistic narrative with its Mesopotamian counterparts this becomes a very noticeable contrast. It is a feature of the Yahwistic narrative that the author includes notes alongside his genealogy which record cultural developments. It brings to it a liveliness that is more than the recounting of dry lists. For instance:

> Adah bore Jabal; he was the ancestor
> of those who live in tents and have
> livestock. His brother's name was
> Jubal; he was the ancestor of all those who play the lyre and pipe.
> (Genesis 4:20–21)

There is a major departure here from the way the Sumerian myths of organization were presented. In ancient Sumer the gods were considered directly responsible for the way in which society was arranged and organized. When Yahweh himself shuts the door of the Ark (Genesis 7:16b) the Yahwist returns to a primitive feature of Mesopotamian myth in which the gods undertake things personally. It was they who set out the canals, established the cities and built the temples. For the Yahwist those developments are simply part of the normal process of human endeavour. The founding of the first city, or the establishment of a particular way of life, are credited quite straightforwardly to evolving human achievement.

A logical chain of cause and effect in which there is an invisible providential activity, without divine intervention and discontinuities, is characteristic of the Succession Narrative; it is characteristic of the way the Wisdom tradition as a whole articulated the course of history. It is a basic feature of the Yahwist's Primaeval History.

We must now turn to a more specific look at the narrative related to the Garden of Eden in Genesis 2–3. In particular we must note the themes which emerge in Genesis 3 with its mythical trees ('The Tree of Life' and 'The Tree of the Knowledge of Good and Evil') which take us into an unidentified but very present world of Mesopotamian Wisdom and speculation about the primal man.

In his analysis of the opening chapters of Genesis, R. N. Whybray notes that the familiar Wisdom vocabulary (root ḥkm) does not occur. This affords a strong contrast both with the Babylonian creation epic (*Enūma Elish*) and with the *Atrahasis Epic*, which recounts the story of the Flood where the wisdom of the gods is much in evidence. It is also a feature of the vocabulary associated with the creator-god El in the Ugaritic texts. Yet the themes associated with 'Wisdom' in Proverbs, Job and Ecclesiastes are certainly present. These are themes of human knowledge, of life and death, and their relationship to obedience and disobedience. Particular vocabulary is also evident. The word used of the serpent's cunning or subtlety is ᶜārūm, and the desirability of the fruit of the tree for making one wise is lᵉhaśkīl. The latter is closely associated with ḥkm in a number of passages.[12] Whybray concludes:

> While hiśkl, though it occurs more frequently in the 'Wisdom Books' than elsewhere, is by no means entirely confined to them, ᶜārūm is one of the few words in the vocabulary of Biblical Hebrew which occurs almost exclusively there, and therefore constitutes as effective a confirmation of the intellectual tradition in Genesis 3 as would the occurrence of the root ḥkm itself.[13]

This conclusion is confirmed by the study of Luis Alonso-Schôkel who identifies particular themes in Genesis 2 and 3 as of sapiential origin – the knowledge of good and evil, the shrewdness of the serpent, the sage-like qualities of Adam and the detailed discussion of the four rivers.[14]

The reason given for the expulsion of the human couple from the garden at the end of Genesis 3 is more closely related to the Mesopotamian Wisdom traditions upon which the Yahwist was drawing than his own theme of human disobedience. We read:

> Then the Lord God said, 'See, the man has become like one of us, knowing good and evil; and now, he might reach out his hand and take also from the tree of life, and eat, and live for ever' – therefore the Lord God sent him forth from the garden of Eden. (Genesis 3: 22–23a)

In particular, we perceive in these verses the ancient tradition of the wisdom of the primal man who misses divinity itself only by a whisker as well as the theme of the jealousy of the gods. Of the primal man it could truly be said that 'he was like God, knowing good and evil'. Associated with that god-like quality was the legend of his beauty and grace. Within the biblical tradition we meet a reference to him in the speech of Eliphaz in Job 15: 7–8. From that short reference we gather that knowledge and wisdom relating to the secret counsel of God are his.

The name Adam has been related to the celebrated Babylonian figure of Adapa.[15] Here we have a human being who is summoned before the high god Anu; his wisdom is catalogued and set forth.[16] His very word is capable of breaking the wing of the south wind. He is the creation of the god Ea (Enki), and we learn:

> To him he had given wisdom,
> eternal life he had not given him.
> In those days, in those years, the sage of
> Ea, created him as the model of a man.[17]

The condition is exactly that of humanity expelled from the Garden of Eden which has obtained wisdom ('knowing good and evil') but is denied eternal life.

We have already had cause to note the creation of Enkidu in *The Epic of Gilgamesh*. Enkidu's creation is as if he were the first man; he is a 'special creation'. As he becomes human we noted the words of the cult prostitute:

> Thou art (w)ise, Enkidu, art become like a god.[18]

It is in this context of the primal man that we may make sense of Ezekiel 28:11–19. A figure 'full of Wisdom, and perfect in beauty' that inhabits Eden, the garden of God, and who was created perfect, is expelled from the mountain of God for his sin. This being is semi-divine and likened to a cherub. Here we have a clear example outside Genesis of a story about the first human who dwelt in the company of God and whose sin leads to expulsion. The context is set in a more mythological setting than the Yahwist's account in Genesis 2 and 3. We are touching on a rich area of Wisdom speculation around an established canonical story which is probably of much greater antiquity than Ezekiel's adaptation of it.

We must make a further observation prompted by the primal man references in Ezekiel 28. There it is the King of Tyre who is the specific application of the figure who falls from grace, and who calls forth from Ezekiel these particular fragments of Epic tradition. It is well known that for both ancient Egypt and ancient Mesopotamia the king was a crucial figure for the whole of society, and for the welfare of the social, political and natural order. Whereas in Egypt the Pharaoh was divine, and at death became a god, that was not quite the case in Mesopotamia. The king remained human; certainly whatever of divinity he might claim fell short of the gift of eternal life.[19] But it does seem that around the king naturally clustered the ideas associated with the first man – his wisdom, his glory, his beauty, his god-like qualities. According to the relatively late witness of Ezekiel that was true for Canaanite kingship. That is confirmed for Israel in the thinking of the Succession Narrative. We have already considered it for its parallels with the Yahwist's Primaeval History as a whole. Characteristic of the Succession Narrative is its noting of the beauty of the royal family and the wisdom of the king.[20]

It may not be too far fetched to surmise that it was Wisdom's speculation about the primal man in the context of the Jerusalem court with its local manifestation of Canaanite kingship ideology which gave the Yahwist his insight into 'fallen humanity'. In that case, there is an earlier and independent but somewhat similar process operating to that which enabled Ezekiel to apply his oracle to the king of Tyre. Through the king a microcosm of humanity could be observed, as it were, thrown into high relief. It was the king who enabled the limelight to be concentrated on a single human being. The king lived with normal constraints removed; that is, constraints imposed by poverty, by preoccupation with survival and living under authority. Wealth, political power, adulation, reverence for the royal command – all gave the monarch the temptation to hubris. The abuse of royal power, narrated by a basic admirer of the royal house, is the burden of the Succession Narrative. It is hubris, overstepping his limits, the desire to snatch at equality with God which is Adam's sin in Genesis 3.[21] We would venture the suggestion that the portrait of Adam in Genesis 2 and 3 owes more than a little to a democratization of observations made on the royal house.

If this is the case then not only did speculation about the primal man influence the way thinking developed about the person of the monarch, but observations on the king's behaviour also influenced the Yahwist's thinking about humanity per se. This is perhaps the clue as to how at so early a stage of human history Genesis 2–3 could so perceptively interrogate human psychology. The Wisdom tradition had enabled the Yahwist to turn the royal court into a sort of learning laboratory which allowed the isolation and observation of the behaviour of a single human being under controlled circumstances.

The ambiguity of Wisdom in Genesis 2–3 is a particular feature of these chapters. The 'wise advice' of the serpent which leads to disaster has been compared to the wise advice of Ahitophel overturned by the false wisdom of Hushai which deceives Absalom in his rebellion against David.[22] The point is that the serpent is a genuine spokesman for Wisdom, but actually the advice does not lead to life. It is what Blenkinsopp has referred to as 'lethal wisdom'. The question arises as to whether this is a later, interpretive, even mocking development put about by a 'theological wisdom' suspicious of the older pragmatic wisdom of the counsellor which precisely received prophetic scorn (cf. Isaiah 29:14).

Against this, it has already been noted that Enkidu in *The Epic of Gilgamesh* already articulates an ambiguity about Wisdom. Mesopotamian Wisdom, in particular, explored human boundaries and the dilemmas they posed by means of myth. For instance, Gilgamesh enters the garden of paradise named Dilmun with its lush fruits and vines with foliage of lapis lazuli. He presses on and acquires the secret of the plant that brings eternal rejuvenation. He obtains it only for it to be carried off by a serpent which immediately demonstrates the effectiveness of the plant by sloughing its skin. The message is spelt out to Gilgamesh:

> When the gods created mankind,
> Death for mankind they set aside,
> Life in their own hands retaining.[23]

The story of wise Adapa is also one about the lost opportunity to seize the life of the gods. In contrast to Genesis it is Adapa's obedience to the god Ea (Enki) which means he forfeits the opportunity of eternal life that would come from imbibing the water of life and eating the bread of life.

Throughout Babylonian Wisdom myth there are effectively two gifts which human beings seek from the gods; one is knowledge, that is skill and insight relating to the very processes of the cosmos, and the other is eternal life. These are expressed graphically in the two trees of Genesis 3. The former gift is obtainable by humans under limited circumstances, but only serves to highlight more urgently the frustration that the second is not available to humankind. Further, the concern that humanity might be a threat to the gods is part of the reason for the closure of the gate of eternal life and is very ancient in Mesopotamian tradition. Consequently, the ambiguity of Wisdom delegated to humanity is a consistent theme and even leads to tension between the gods. The gods often use their wisdom to thwart the human quest for divine status, although there is always a divine ally (usually Ea) using his cunning to make sure humanity evades the ultimate consequences of the wrath of the council of heaven. That there should be 'lethal wisdom' is certainly in line with the Yahwist's own insight that it is the good things of God's creation, that contain a lurking ambiguity, which humanity constantly abuses and corrupts.

Before we leave Genesis 2 and 3, one more connection with Wisdom must be noted. The pain of the world, from human toil to childbirth, is put down to human sin. This analysis gives to humanity a cosmic significance, which itself tends towards hubris, and is a particular way of tracing the source of injustice and evil in the world. There are other ways that it could have been explained; in some traditions in ancient Mesopotamia the disruption of creation was pushed back to the world of the gods and to a rebellion before the advent of human beings at all. But it was a particular feature of the Wisdom tradition that envisaged the rupture of the world as being brought about by erratic human behaviour. According to the logic of the Wisdom tradition, human disobedience could rupture the fabric of the universe, and disturb it from within. The biblical Book of Ecclesiastes has close affinities with Genesis 2 and 3 in blaming humanity's 'many schemes' (Eccles. 7:29) for the state of the world.[24] In this analysis of the origin of disorder in the world we have a further indication of the presence of the Wisdom tradition in these two chapters of Genesis. Indeed, it extends also to all of the Yahwist's individual narrative units which, like pearls on a string, articulate different ways in which humans, as primal couple, as brothers, as a whole generation or in highly organized society, are responsible for creation's disorder.

The story of the Garden of Eden, and in particular Genesis 3, introduces us to a mass of threads in which connections to Wisdom lead in all directions. The presence of the Wisdom tradition in the Yahwist's Primaeval History could hardly be more authoritatively confirmed than in the Garden of Eden narrative. It is summed up by J. Blenkinsopp:

> Its learned use of mythological themes, skilful dialogue and profound exploration of the limits of human resources suggest a sapiential origin.[25]

It is necessary to give some consideration to the Priestly tradition. In particular, what remains to be discussed is the magnificent creation tradition in Genesis 1:1–2:4a. Here we are probably dealing with an Egyptian rather than a Mesopotamian tradition.[26] One of the clues to that identity is its close relationship with Psalm. 104 which displays similarities with Akenhaten's 'Hymn to Aten'.[27] The psalm itself could be classified within the biblical Wisdom corpus. We are once again moving in the world of international traditions, of universal observations and world order. Psalm 104 carries no resonance of Israel's election traditions. It identifies itself as an ambassador of Wisdom:

> O Lord, how manifold are your works!
> In wisdom you have made them all; (Psalm 104:24)

That verse from the psalm can serve as a commentary on the Genesis 1 creation narrative and identify its true nature.

There is no doubt that the orders of creation are presented in the Priestly creation narrative with the insights, the regularity and the categorization that Wisdom's vision of creation demands. The principal parts of creation are enunciated. The waters are separated, and three great environments established – the sky, the seas under the sky and the dry land. The great lights and the stars are to 'be for signs and seasons and for days and years'

(Genesis 1:14b). The narrative records the creation of vegetation and notes the difference between plants which scatter their seed and fruits which contain their seed (Genesis 1:12). It analyses the different species supported by the three environments, that is the birds of heaven, the fish of the sea (Genesis 1:20–21) and terrestrial beasts (Genesis 1:24–25).

At two particular points we may identify the hallmark of Wisdom. One is the way it refers to the human race:

> So God created humankind in his image,
> in the image of God he created them;
> male and female he created them. (Genesis 1:27)

Human beings are given a universal dignity which comes from being in the divine image. Beyond any advantages or disadvantages of race, culture, religion or geography is the single insistence that human beings share what is essential in common; they belong to one another and are God's handiwork. Here the vision of Genesis and the vision of Proverbs are one:

> Those who oppress the poor
> insult their Maker,
> but those who are kind to the needy
> honour him.[28]

We encounter a basic principle of the Wisdom tradition.

The other hallmark of Wisdom comes at the end of the Priestly creation account, when it states of God that:

> He rested on the seventh day from all
> the work that he had done. (Genesis 2:2b)

We have already had cause to note that it is a feature of the Wisdom tradition that creation is something complete and finished:[29]

> Thus far shall you come, and no farther;
> And here shall your proud waves be stopped. (Job 38:11)

This is in contrast to the liturgical celebration of creation as something contemporary and present as the waves of Chaos are stilled even as the worshippers celebrate the annual New Year Festival. It was the vision of Wisdom that a beautiful and ordered world had been called into being by God, and that there was nothing impermanent or unfinished about its gleaming perfection. To that world Genesis 1 gives witness.

One further point about the Primaeval Narrative taken as a whole concludes our investigation and seals Wisdom's vision. It is both evidence of Wisdom and the key consequence of its presence. The Primaeval Narrative in both its Yahwistic and Priestly forms carries great integrity. Passions never overcome impartiality or prevent a completely evenhanded survey of the origins of the world and the evolving complexities of civilization and human society. The creation of the world, the placing of human beings within an ecology, the development from families and clans to cities, nations and empires with all their cultural richness eventually takes us close to the edge of political history, but the boundary is never trespassed. No sinister threat of Assyria or bitterness about world empire is transmitted within Genesis 1–11. No numerical 666 is attached to the menace of imperial expansion. Empire is recorded as part of the order established in primaeval time; it is simply an expression of the growing sophistication and refinement of civilization which is part of human achievement. There is no special pleading of geography, race or religion. Nowhere in the Primaeval text does Israel intrude into the picture. Indeed, the Yahwist is happy to record Babylon as the navel of human empire (Genesis 10:10)[30] and does not find Jerusalem a place in his scheme of things. This integrity is surely the 'litmus test' of Wisdom. Wisdom may have had its own cultural baggage, it was at home with the power structures of the Ancient Near East, but it never compromised its working principles.

B. The Old Testament to the Hebrew Scriptures

The whole enterprise of constructing a Primaeval History which relates simply to universal order, human origins, the development of civilization and the fundamental contradictions of existence is startling in its context; it completely rises above cultural relativism. Only Wisdom could contribute such enlightenment and discipline. In accordance with the strict canons of Wisdom the Primaeval History, throughout its complex literary structure, exhibits an integrity on a par with a modern scientific discipline. World order is presented as genuinely universal without manipulation to serve limited local cultural and political interests. Human nature is analysed without fear or favour of race, religion, language or culture. It is a remarkable achievement, and brings its authority to the whole biblical legacy.

The Book of Genesis opens the biblical tradition with a profoundly significant statement of what it means that God is the creator and that human beings are his creatures. There are eleven chapters in which this is articulated. They are the bedrock of the Hebrew Scriptures.

They are a bedrock in as much as they set out the significance of God as creator as fundamental to biblical faith. So often faith in the order of the world in the Ancient Near East operated in a hidden way, as a sort of invisible organizing principle. Israel could not emerge in her context without something similar being true for her also. In the Genesis Primaeval Narrative the significance of creation and creator surfaces clearly and unequivocally. They are a bedrock, further, in that they articulate creation as an order dependent upon balance and harmony. It is captured helpfully by G. von Rad when he writes:

> This is, then, a concept of reality which realized that the behaviour of an individual was connected much more intensively, much more 'organically', with variations in his environment, of a concept of reality which was able to understand the effect of the environment on man as a challenge, but also as a response to his behaviour.[31]

But those initial chapters of Genesis are a real bedrock because of the integrity with which they speak of God as creator. He is no one's possession, but rather faith in God relativizes everything: God has no favourites. In a quite remarkable way the Primaeval Narrative states that all human beings are equidistant from God.

Chapters 1–11 of the Book of Genesis comprise what is effectively 'the Old Testament to the Hebrew Scriptures'.[32] Wisdom's hand, present in Genesis 1–11, has a potentially transforming impact upon the whole biblical tradition. The universalism of those opening chapters of the Bible cannot be surpassed. They need to be recognized as of immeasurable worth in setting out the moral significance of affirming faith in God the creator, maker of heaven and earth. They make a statement about God which honours the transcendence and goodness of God, and prevents faith being demeaned to become a badge of tribalism. All the partial schemes of human beings are relativized by reference to the one God who bestows a profound moral unity on the one universe and an equal dignity on all human beings. That is the necessary starting point of the whole theological enterprise if it is to be truly grounded in the Bible.

Points for Discussion

1. How can we raise awareness of the big questions relating to meaning, mystery and purpose for people today, as the Wisdom teachers could through myths and stories about the quest for wisdom and eternal life?
2. What are the strengths and weaknesses of trying to build a morality based on respect for creation as God's work and all human beings made in God's image?
3. If Genesis 1–11 is the 'Old Testament of the Hebrew Scriptures' and brings its authority to the whole biblical tradition, how should it impact on the way we read the Bible?
4. If Genesis 1–11 is conceived of as the 'Old Testament to the Hebrew Scriptures', how might that help us in dialogue with other world religions?

Key Bible Passages

Genesis 1:1–2:4a (Priestly creation account); Genesis 2:4b–3:24 (Yahwist's creation account).

Further Reading

J. Blenkinsopp, *Wisdom and Law in the Old Testament*, Oxford (1995).
Donn F. Morgan, *Wisdom in the Old Testament Traditions*, Oxford (1981),
especially chapter III, pp. 45–62.

Figure 5. A man is led into the presence of a god. Cylinder seal and image from the time of Ur-Nammu, King of Ur c. 2100 BCE (©British Museum).

Endnotes

[1] R. E. Murphy, A Consideration of the Classification 'Wisdom Psalms', SVT9 (1962), pp. 156–67 identifies 1; 32; 34; 37; 49; 112; 128.

[2] G. von Rad, 'The Joseph Narrative and Ancient Wisdom', *The Problem of the Hexateuch and other Essays*, Edinburgh & London (1966).

[3] G. von Rad, 'The Beginning of Historical Writing in Ancient Israel' in *The Problem of the Hexateuch and Other Essays*, Edinburgh & London, (1966).

[4] R. N. Whybray, *The Intellectual Tradition in the Old Testament*, pp. 87 ff.

[5] J. B. Pritchard, 'Man's Predicament in Eden', *Review of Religion* 13 (1948/9), p. 15.

[6] A. Parrott, *The Tower of Babel*, London (1955) p. 15.

[7] See Appendix I for a chart setting out the parallel Yahwistic and Priestly traditions in the Primaeval History which have been edited into the single narrative as we have it.

[8] Compare Genesis 5:1–27 (P) and Genesis 4:1, 17–18 and 25–26 (J).

[9] There is a remarkable correspondence between the knowledge of Ezekiel and the Japheth branch of the genealogy which suggests that it is fairly contemporaneous with P. See C. Westermann, *Genesis*, p. 509.

[10] 2 Sam. 9:1 – 1 Kings 2:46.

[11] R. N. Whybray, *The Succession Narrative*, London (1968).

[12] Deuteronomy 32:29; Ps. 119; 98ff.; Prov. 16:23; 21:11; Daniel 1:17.

[13] R. N. Whybray, *The Intellectual Tradition*, p. 107.

[14] L. Alonso-Schôkel, 'Sapiental and Covenant Themes in Genesis 2–3', in ed. J. Crenshaw, *Studies in Ancient Israelite Wisdom*, pp. 468–80.

[15] E. Ebeling, *Tod und Leben nach den Vorstellengen der Babylonier*, Berlin & Leipzig (1931), p. 27, note 'a': an unpublished syllabary equates a-da-ap with man (hence 'Adam').

[16] Baking, providing bread and water, setting the offering table, steering ships and fishing.

[17] The Story of Adapa, *ANET*, p. 101.

[18] *The Epic of Gilgamesh*, IV: 34; *ANET* p. 75.

[19] Gilgamesh is two-thirds divine but the burden of the Epic is about that one-third which condemns him to the consequences of his mortality (Tablet 1, *ANET*, p. 73).

[20] For instance, of the king's wisdom, we may quote the words on the lips of the woman of Tekoa: 'For my lord the king is like the angel of God discerning good and evil.' (2 Samuel 14:17b); and of the beauty of the royal family the narrator notes: 'Now in all Israel there was no one to be praised so much for his beauty as Absalom: from the sole of

his foot to the crown of his head there was no blemish in him.' (2 Samuel 14:25) see also Tamar (2 Samuel 13:1).

[21] It is recounted in terms of the breaking of a direct command laid upon Adam by the creator. The charge of hubris against the monarch is certainly as old as the Sumerian poem 'The curse on Agade' written (perhaps partly as priestly propaganda) against Naram-Sin (2291–2255 BCE).

[22] J. Blenkinsopp, *Wisdom and Law in the Old Testament*, Oxford (1995), p. 7. 'Yahweh had ordained to defeat the good counsel of Ahitophel, so that Yahweh might bring ruin on Absalom' (2 Samuel 17:14).

[23] *The Epic of Gilgamesh*, Tablet X (iii): 2–5. Translation: *ANET* p. 90.

[24] The resemblances between Genesis 1–11 and Ecclesiastes are not restricted to this single observation. C. C. Forman, 'Koheleth's Use of Genesis', *JSS* 5 (1960), pp. 256–63 enumerates a number of con-nections, for example, human beings return to dust, the need for companionship, life as toil, preoccupation with death.

[25] J. Blenkinsopp, *Wisdom and Law in the Old Testament*, p. 42.

[26] J. E. Atwell, 'An Egyptian Source for Genesis 1', *JTS* NS 51 (2000), pp. 443–77.

[27] For the relationship of Psalm 104 to Genesis 1 see *ibid*, pp. 460ff.

[28] Proverbs 14:31; cf; 16:4 17:5 and 22:2.

[29] See Chapter 4 endnote 63.

[30] With a different significance, that is perhaps true of Genesis 11 also.

[31] G. von Rad, *Wisdom in Israel*, p. 78.

[32] It has been pointed out to me that the term 'Old Testament' has been applied to the patriarchal narratives by Walter Moberly, *The Old Testament of the Old Testament*, Minneapolis (1992). It is used here rather differently, and without prior knowledge of Moberly's adaptation, to refer to the Primaeval History.

PART III

The Rolling Waters

The River Jordan is dependent upon the melting snow of the Hermon range. It is fed from three significant sources. It foams as the sources merge, and travels through a changing landscape creating two very different seas. On its way it generously sustains a great variety of life – aquatic, terrestrial and celestial. Unique features are created by the rift valley through which it flows. To comprehend it as a geographical feature a total perspective is necessary. The fragments do not comprise the whole. Our parable requires that we consider a total vista on the biblical perspective.

CHAPTER 6

The Foaming of the Sources

A. Prophecy in Israel

Prophecy in Israel became the distinctive ingredient which enabled the potential of its theological sources to be released. It is likely that without prophecy the unique potential of the Hebrew religious perspective to challenge the established conventions of the Ancient Near East would never have emerged. That potential would have remained latent and dormant. Prophecy was able to stir and activate that which was slumbering. Prophecy was the great enabler, the catalyst, the midwife of what was unique in Hebrew religion. However, it was always the servant. Viewed in the context of Israel's rich theological diversity:

> Prophecy is only one of several such forms, and it seems that its fate is to be always necessary but never by itself sufficient.[1]

The nature of prophecy, rather like mistletoe, is that it draws its life from another system. It lives by constant engagement, either in support or in controversy, with other institutions. It requires an environment: it is not in itself complete. Prophecy flourishes when its host environment needs it for its effective development.

To understand prophecy in Israel we need to be open to the big picture of its context in the Ancient Near East and of its diversity within Israel. However, we also need to encounter it in its particularity and engage with a specific tradition. For that particularity, which necessarily has an element of arbitrariness in its selection, we shall look to the Isaianic tradition.

B. The Big Picture

The phenomenon of prophecy in Israel is one of the great adventures of the Hebrew Scriptures, but we have to acknowledge that prophecy is not unique to the Bible. It is an activity shared with the rest of the Ancient Near East. It has a context, and that context may help us to understand its significance within Judah and Israel.

Discoveries from the city of Mari on the River Euphrates, dating back to the period just before Hammurabi and the time we have suggested for Abraham, that is the eighteenth century BCE, throw light on the history of prophecy in the Ancient Near East. The archives recovered from Mari include some clay tablets recording the activity of a number of prophets. One tablet records how a named person, Shelebum, who is located in the temple, uttered a prophecy while in a trance in the name of the goddess Annunitum. It commences: 'Thus spoke Annunitum'. It reassures the king, Zimri-Lim, that, so long as he is alert, a revolt will come to nothing. 'The Palace is safe and sound', which, no doubt, is what he wanted to hear. Already there is a recognizable formulaic introduction to the prophetic words which is parallel to the familiar biblical words a millennium later: 'Thus says the Lord'. Shelebum is recognized as one who could transmit revelations from the deity and these were connected with a particular psychological state. His ministry, we may note, was based at the temple.[2]

Some Assyrian prophecies which date from the seventh century, not long after the ministries of Isaiah and Micah, have been published by S. Parpola.[3] A collection of tablets record the words of a number of prophets, both male and female. Several oracles occur on each tablet carefully and deliberately arranged. One of the texts addresses the king:

> Fear not, Esarhaddon!
> I am Bel. (Even as) I speak to you,
> I watch over the beams of your heart.
> When your mother gave birth to you,
> Sixty great gods stood with me and protected you.[4]

These verses are reminiscent of the prophetic reapplication of Jerusalem Temple oracles to Jacob-Israel by Deutero-Isaiah:

But now thus says the Lord,
he who created you, O Jacob,
he who formed you, O Israel:
Do not fear, for I have redeemed you:
I have called you by name, you are mine. (Isaiah 43:1)

The family resemblance is distinct and convincing. The Ancient Near East shared its cultural norms which included the prophetic word of reassurance.

The central oracle of the third collection is from the lips of the state god Ashur. It refers to itself as 'the covenant tablet of Ashur': divine favour is pronounced upon the king. D. L. Petersen writes:

> The third collection commences with a prologue or introduction prior to the citation of the oracles, and the oracles themselves have been arranged in a temporal sequence. One might view this text as a primal form of a prophetic book.[5]

A similar oracle to the one delivered to Esarhaddon is recorded for Zakir, King of Hamath (c. 800 BCE) when the city is under siege. He seeks an oracle from the god Be'elshamayn (Baalshamen: 'Lord of Heaven') which is forthcoming:

> Be'elshamayn [spoke] to me through seers and through diviners. Be'elshamayn [said to me]: 'Do not fear, for I have made you king, and I shall stand by you and deliver you from all [these kings who] set up a siege against you!'[6]

The direct speech of the god is recorded. The spokesmen are plural, suggesting several confirmatory oracles, and described as seers. The oracle commences with the, by now familiar form, 'Fear not'.

An example of a prophet outside of Israel is provided for us within the Bible. The story is told in Numbers 22–24 of Balak, King of Moab, summoning Balaam, son of Beor to curse the Israelites. The prophetic word is regarded as having a powerful effect once uttered. However, according to the biblical narrative, Balaam is divinely restrained from cursing the Israelites and instead pronounces blessings. Another example of the prophetic activity of Balaam, son of Beor, was committed to writing to be discovered in excavations at Tell Deir 'Alla (in the east Jordan valley) in 1967.[7] Although fragmentary, the early seventh century inscription is prefaced by lamentation and reveals how the 'seer' has a divinely inspired vision (dream) in the night and is privy to a decision of the council of the gods to plan disaster ensuing in a chaotic world in which order is breaking up. The similarity, for instance, with the call of the prophet Isaiah in Isaiah 6 and his commissioning from the very council of Yahweh is striking. Balaam in the biblical witness is evidence of a 'freelance' prophet, who, although he makes sacrifices, is not restricted to a specific temple but travels to meet the King of Moab.

All of the examples of prophetic activity from the Ancient Near East cited above involve a king seeking reassurance about state security. All but one, Balak, receive the reassurance that they are looking for. The oracles that have survived in the record are overwhelmingly those of temple prophets and typically reassure with the words 'fear not'. They are examples of prophecy as part of a pattern of the way religion operated in the Ancient Near East. It was expected of religion that it would underwrite the status quo, and that the deity would provide security and protection for the state political structures focused in the person of the king. The priority of the apparatus of religion was to provide comfort and reassurance in an uncertain and often brutal world. It is clear that prophecy could operate effectively within that structure.

The rhythm of normality in the Ancient Near East was conceived to be safeguarded by the priest and the cult, with the temple as the symbol of cosmic stability and divine control. Nevertheless, there remained the moments of sudden unexpected crises to be dealt with. A palace revolt, a siege or perhaps a plague might pose an immediate threat which needed to be resolved. The prophet was able to provide instant divine guidance as to the outcome. It was normally reassurance that the state deity could be relied upon to bring resolution. The very uttering of the reassurance was conceived to help to bring it about.

Prophecy in ancient Israel was very diverse. There were bands of prophets, such as the group King Saul famously fell in with, as they came from a shrine with harp, tambourine, flute and lyre exhibiting a prophetic frenzy (1 Samuel 10:5ff.). There was Samuel the seer, Nathan who seems to be part of the court retinue and the independent figures of Elijah and Elisha. There must have been temple prophets responsible for 'The

Proclamation of Salvation' form which Deutero-Isaiah could imitate. This is confirmed by the prophecy of Jeremiah (cf. Jeremiah 23:11). Then there are the lone prophets who have bequeathed the biblical books that bear their names. Of these, some claimed to prophesy but were reluctant to adopt the title of prophet. For instance, Amos declares:

> I am no prophet, nor a prophet's son: but I am a herdsman and a dresser of sycamore trees, and the Lord took me from following the flock, and the Lord said to me: 'Go, prophesy to my people Israel.' (Amos 7:14–15)

The perplexing diversity of prophecy in Israel is tacitly acknowledged by the note in 1 Samuel 9:9:

> Formerly in Israel, anyone who went to inquire of God would say, 'Come let us go to the seer (ḥōzeh)'; for the one who is now called a prophet (nābī) was formerly called a seer.

To what extent could all of these diverse expressions of the phenomenon of Israelite prophecy find typical representation in prophecy as we have encountered it in the surviving texts from the Ancient Near East? Is prophecy, in origin, characteristic of the settled land in the context of state security? Or should we perhaps look for more diverse origins? Could the individual seer have roots in the nomadic way of life in contrast to the cultic prophets of the settled land?[9] Is there a phenomenon of 'War Prophecy' that accompanied Israel's arrival in Canaan, and even has roots in the wilderness period?[10]

Two facts may be significant. The first is that prophecy in Israel directly correlates with the monarchy. It is a phenomenon of 500 years. Although in retrospect Moses may be described as a prophet,[11] prophecy actually appears with Samuel and the formation of the Israelite state with Saul as the first king. It languishes soon after the exile when the monarchy is extinguished. Clearly, the monarchy provided an environment in which prophecy thrived. Something symbiotic is going on. Prophecy and monarchy are in an interdependent relationship. That is true of Israel for prophecy in all its forms.

Secondly, prophecy in Israel does seem to be particularly associated with times of crisis. Samuel has to handle the emergence of the state and the development of new institutions,

Nathan has the challenge of coping with David's wish to build a temple and secure a new religious model, Elijah is faced with state syncretism in the northern kingdom and the possible extinction of a distinctive Yahwistic faith. Amos and Hosea have a ministry against emerging Assyrian imperial expansion which by the time of Isaiah and Micah claims the kingdom of Israel and is at Jerusalem's walls. Jeremiah and Ezekiel have to interpret Babylonian aggression and the final extinction of the state of Judah. The crisis of exile raises up Deutero-Isaiah. Whatever the different responses of prophecy to these crises certainly it is vigorous at those moments when both king and commoner are looking for that reassurance: 'fear not'.

These twin facts tend to associate prophecy in Israel with the profile established by the examples from the Ancient Near East that have been discussed above. That is, its relationship with the royal house and state security, as well as its ability to bring rapid reassurance at times of specific crisis. If we can press that case then it is likely that prophecy was not a product of the nomadic inheritance of Israel's past. It was something encountered in the settled land. The religious experience of the nomad was more to do with adoption by the deity. The key person was the father of the clan in whom was vested religious as well as other authority. The religion of the settled land looked for reassurance, sources of confidence and divine legitimization for its ruling house. Just as we discovered that Wisdom is often close to the royal court but not exclusively practised there, so perhaps similarly, prophecy flourished under royal patronage as part of official religion but also raised up independent practitioners such as Balaam.

It seems that the diffuse nature of Israelite prophecy has to be sought within the immediate environment of the city states of Canaan as representative of the perspective of the Ancient Near East. We have already noted that the Temple prophets with their hallmark utterance 'fear not', typical of the ancient Near East, were mirrored in the life of the Jerusalem Temple. Certainly bands of prophets, such as those encountered by Elijah on Mount Carmel, were a feature of the religion of Ba'al. They exhibited ecstatic behaviour and, in performing a limping dance and cutting themselves until the blood gushed,[12] enacted prophetic symbolism which was intended to precipitate divine action – in this instance bringing about rain. We are aware from the Ugaritic texts of the significance of dream communication between humans and the divine world; this is particularly associated with El, the Canaanite deity who is understood as father and creator. Within the Bible there are episodes that involve dream communication, such as the story of Jacob's ladder, and they are associated with the fixed sanctuaries of the settled land. That is specifically the case for the boy Samuel who is apprenticed to Eli, the hereditary priest of Shiloh. Samuel is lying down in the temple and hears God's call. It was that sort of communication that meant he 'knew the Lord' (cf. 1 Samuel 3:7). The settled land certainly exhibits the potential for nurturing temple prophet, seer and ecstatic prophet. They were all examples of human beings who were reckoned to be channels of divine power with reliable insight into the plan and purpose of the divine. Inevitably, no doubt, observed boundaries between the different activities became blurred in the course of time and this was reflected in the inclusive use of the word 'prophet'.

If this analysis is correct and prophecy as we encounter it in Israel is primarily to be understood in terms of the need for stability and security in a monarchical setting, then it serves to throw into high relief the achievement of the Hebrew prophets. They were responsible for a mutation of considerable significance in the nature of prophecy. As practised by them, prophecy challenged a false sense of security. A crisis became a moment to proclaim God's judgement rather than to give assurance of his peace. They re-formed the familiar in new ways, turned reassurance into goading, recast old truths and articulated new ones. Indeed, it could be said that the classical prophets of the eighth century, that is Amos and Hosea, Isaiah and Micah, were the midwives of Yahwistic faith. They brought to birth that which had remained embryonic and largely latent from the moment Mosaic Yahwism entered Canaan. The seeds of controversy reach back to the period of the Judges,[13] but it was the prophets who recognized and relentlessly proclaimed the challenge that Yahwistic faith brought to the religious conventions of the settled land. They were the ones to whom it fell to administer a little grit to the system.

In particular, the eighth-century prophets were a watershed in that they articulated the inner controversy that 'Yahweh only' demanded of the Hebrews. For Amos there was a radical moral demand contained in the stark theological insight of the Exodus: 'You only have I known of all the families of the earth'. (Amos 3:2a.) For Hosea there was an unwillingness to live with the compromise of syncretism which he regarded as utterly unfaithful:

> Yet I have been the Lord your God
> ever since the land of Egypt;
> You know no God but me,
> and besides me there is no saviour. (Hosea 13:4)

Already the clouds are gathering and the storm anticipated with Elijah on Mount Carmel:

> How long will you go limping with two different opinions? If the Lord is God, follow him; but if Ba'al, then follow him. (1 Kings 18:21)[14]

It was the eighth-century prophets who realized and publicly presented the profound religious insight that the holiness of God was bigger than the fortunes of the state. Yahweh could not be subordinated to a function of state security. His identity did not depend upon Israel's existence. Rather, Israel's existence was based upon the reality and goodness of God. If his people had claims on him, it was only so long as the claims were mutual and reciprocated in loyalty and moral integrity. Otherwise the holiness of God would mean judgement and not security. The concept of covenant with mutual obligations now emerges as the defining feature of God's relationship with his people. With the prophet Hosea we are aware that the new ground has been broken (Hosea 6:7).[15] There are commitments and responsibilities upon both parties if trust is not to break down and the relationship collapse.

The eighth-century prophets looked at the darkening international scene and the threat of extinction that the super-power Assyria posed to the kingdoms of Syria and Palestine. They recognized in the threat the hand of the one God who was lord of history and author of unfolding events. They saw not a threat from which God would protect them, but judgement being brought by Yahweh upon his people. It was not simply that he was chastising them, but the very unthinkable according to conventional logic was looming: 'The end has come upon my people Israel' (Amos 8:2). The transcendence of God could not be expressed more radically than that. The potentially new in Israel's faith is released at great cost. Divinity challenges the status quo absolutely. There is a fracture between God and the created order. The boundaries of Ancient Near Eastern faith are pushed beyond their limits – the skins have burst. That message was carried forward by the classical prophets who had to interpret the Babylonian threat.

Such birth is not without its birth-pangs. The great writing prophets were located in the very crucible of creativity. To be the ones who initiated controversy, confronted the nation in the name of God and predicted unparalleled judgement made the prophets very exposed. They found themselves paying in their own person the price of their controversial ministry necessitated by their faithfulness to God. Amos is told by the priest of Bethel:

> O seer, go, flee away to the land of Judah,
> earn your bread there, and prophesy there;
> but never again prophesy at Bethel, for
> it is the king's sanctuary, and it is a
> temple of the kingdom. (Amos 7:12–13)

Hosea, in the ultimate act of prophetic symbolism had to model an unfaithful marriage as a parable of Yahweh's treatment by unfaithful Israel (Hosea 1:2–3). Similarly, as an act of prophetic symbolism Isaiah has to walk around naked predicting Assyrian victory (Isaiah 20). Jeremiah laments his own predicament:

> But I was like a gentle lamb
> led to the slaughter.
> And I did not know it was against me
> that they had devised schemes, saying,
> 'Let us destroy the tree with its fruit,
> let us cut him off from the land of the living,
> so that his name will no longer be remembered!' (Jeremiah 11:19)

The prophets were certainly 'forthtellers'; they had to speak hard and unpopular words at considerable personal cost. To what extent were they 'foretellers'? It is clear that prophecy from at least the eighteenth century BCE in the Ancient Near East was about the prediction of specific and fairly immediate outcomes. Similarly, Samuel as a seer is able to tell Saul details of the encounters about to unfold on the day of his anointing as a sign of its authenticity (1 Samuel 10:2–7).

The prophets of the Assyrian and Babylonian threats also predicted outcomes. Again, they were relatively short term predictions; for the most part they were of judgement and the relentless advance of imperial appetite as the instrument of God's providence:

> Hear this, you rulers of the house of Jacob
> and chiefs of the house of Israel,
> who abhor justice
> and pervert all equity,
> who build Zion with blood
> and Jerusalem with wrong!
> Its rulers give judgement for a bribe,
> its priests teach for a price,
> its prophets give oracles for money;
> yet they lean upon the Lord and say,
> 'Surely the Lord is with us!
> No harm shall come upon us'.
> Therefore because of you
> Zion shall be ploughed as a field;
> Jerusalem shall become a heap of ruins,
> and the mountain of the house a wooded height. (Micah 3:9–12)

There may have been a certain amount of political acumen and shrewd judgement involved. For the most part it was about living in an act–consequence world. There was a connectedness to things which meant that cosmic moral equilibrium had to be satisfied and that the perceived unfaithfulness and reckless behaviour of God's people would reap its inevitable consequence.

According to the understanding of the Ancient Near East there was what has been described as a cosmic covenant[16] operating universally. The world was so ordered that an equilibrium must be respected. There were defined limits to and responsibilities required of human behaviour. This was intensified with the preaching of the eighth-century prophets into a conditional covenant between God and his people. They had reformed the insights of the Ancient Near East relating to creation's order to apply to the structure of God's relationship with his people. The prophets knew that with dire consequences the intensified covenant had been broken. They could but warn of the outcome; actions had inevitable consequences in a divinely ordered world and most especially in a model corner of it.

The Hebrew prophets were not much concerned with long-term predictions. Yet the disciples of these prophets collected their oracles, sometimes commented upon them, and reapplied them to developing historical circumstances. They were cherished through generations until they became canonical. They attained a dignity which their authors could hardly have imagined. Yet there is a validity to this process.

Hebrew prophecy was the instrument which broke through the boundary decreed by Ancient Near Eastern philosophy, theology and sociology. In so doing not only did it challenge the status quo, but its corollary was the fracture of divinity from the given order of the universe. The world could no longer be perceived as a single continuum between the material and the divine. The consequent expression of real transcendence liberated theology to contemplate and expect God's new thing. The creator could act not simply to maintain but to transform. The poor were to be lifted up; the world might be redeemed. The new theology, secured by the activity of the Hebrew prophets, articulated a radical hope based on God's sovereign freedom: there can be a new divine act that truly makes a difference. That new perspective carries a hope that is true for every generation and in the end stands at the summation of all history. What these prophets had to say and to predict about God is valid to the furthest horizon:

> They shall beat their swords into ploughshares,
> and their spears into pruning hooks;
> nation shall not lift up sword against nation,
> neither shall they learn war any more. (Micah 4:3)

C. Isaiah of Jerusalem

Any study that claims to be about sources cannot refer to the Isaianic tradition without paying attention to the eighth-century prophet Isaiah, son of Amoz, without whose distinctive ministry there could have been no 'Book of Isaiah'. We cannot hope to understand the stream of tradition which bears the prophet's name if we have not first encountered its well-spring; that is, the prophet himself. The whole is not less than the sum of its parts. His record is within chapters 1–39 of the Book of Isaiah, but intermingled in a complex way with layers of subsequent redaction and editorial activity over several centuries.

Isaiah is well-named Isaiah of Jerusalem. He is not an interpreter of the Tent traditions but of the Temple traditions. Unlike Amos and Hosea, for whom the wilderness wanderings are Israel's honeymoon with her God, Isaiah does not take the Exodus as his point of departure. Indeed, he makes no mention of it.[17] The traditions that relate to Jerusalem, its Temple, its king, its people and its security captured his heart. It is in that context that he speaks of and for God. It is in that context that the people of God are constituted in loyalty to 'the Holy One of Israel'.[18]

The significance of the Temple and its worship, and therefore the cluster of traditions which it nurtures, is clear from Isaiah's call. The Temple at Jerusalem cradled the cherubim throne and was the place where the coronation of God Most High over a universe ordered in righteousness and peace was celebrated and acknowledged. Precisely that is the inspiration of Isaiah's call. The prophet has a vision of the heavenly king enthroned in all of his majesty and awesome glory with the choir of seraphim in worshipful attendance. The incense billowed, the earthly Temple seemed to tremble and Isaiah was overcome with a sense of the loftiness[19] and transcendence of God and of his own unworthiness in the presence of absolute righteousness. His sense of total moral inadequacy is purged by a burning coal seemingly placed upon his lips. He is able to respond to the divine voice: 'Here am I, send me!'. (Isaiah 6:8b)

Isaiah's sense of radical transcendence, which is captured in the description of God as the 'Holy One of Israel', is from the moment of his call the driving force of his proclamation. With burning passion he disturbs any sense of ease in the presence of holiness. As we noted above,[20] the Jerusalem cult in its witness to divine transcendence may have been an example of the religion of the Ancient Near East pushing near the boundaries of the normally permissible even before the arrival of David. The identification of Yahweh with the creator El Elyon (God Most High) brought to Jerusalem the imagery of the Ark, which symbolized the presence of the deity who could not be represented in an image, powerfully affirming the priority of transcendence. The significance of a deity who could not be captured or localized in an image[21] but whose presence could be indicated by Temple and Ark enabled a tension to be held between touching the skirts of mystery but honouring transcendence. In Isaiah's estimation, living at the source of holiness carried awesome responsibility for 'the house of Israel and the people of Judah' (Isaiah 5:7).

The call of Isaiah already identifies the dimension of conflict between the demands of the holiness of God and the dulled awareness of Israel of whom it could be said:

> The ox knows its owner,
> and the donkey its master's crib;
> but Israel does not know,
> my people do not understand. (Isaiah 1:3)

There is a terrible incongruity. The prognosis is desperate. The prophet is sent to the uncomprehending and the deaf:

> Until cities lie waste
> without inhabitant,
> and houses without people,
> and the land is utterly desolate. (Isaiah 6:11b)

It seems that Isaiah is not sent to call to repentance so much as to proclaim and interpret a growing conviction that the plan and purpose of God in judgement is set. If Isaiah was once a royal counsellor, as is quite possible given the ease with which he enters the king's presence and the wisdom vocabulary he uses, he no longer contributes to shaping human schemes. The action has moved on. The strategy of the wise has been overtaken and consequently wisdom taken away from the decision makers:

> The wisdom of their wise shall perish,
> and the discernment of the discerning shall be hidden. (Isaiah 29:
> 14b)

It is now the turn of God to devise his plan, for it is he who is wonderful in counsel and excellent in wisdom.[22] The people may scoff:

> Let him make haste,
> let him speed his work

> that we may see it;
> let the plan of the Holy One of Israel hasten to fulfilment,
> that we may know it! (Isaiah 5:19)

It remains inevitable that the Lord will rise up:

> to do his deed – strange is his deed! –
> and to work his work – alien is his work! (Isaiah 28:21b)

It is the turning of the righteousness of God against his people which is so strange and alien, and which Isaiah has to interpret.

The Temple of the Lord, according to the prophet's understanding, is not just about assurance. Those who interpreted God's choice of Zion as his dwelling and Israel as his people as without condition and without the need for moral or spiritual discernment were terribly wrong. The inviolability of Zion was not a blank cheque. It was not enough, as Jeremiah was to proclaim in different circumstances over a century later, to chant 'The Temple of the Lord' as a mantra that would stay all threat.[23]

The psalms celebrate the impregnability of Zion, probably articulating traditions lost in the mists of time. Psalms 46 and 48 are robust in their assertion of the divine protection bestowed upon the city. Prophecy in the Book of Isaiah itself gives assurance of Zion's security:

> Like birds hovering overhead,
> so the Lord of Hosts will protect Jerusalem;
> he will protect and deliver it,
> he will spare and rescue it. (Isaiah 31:5)[24]

Such non-Isaianic oracles gathered into the Isaianic collection relocate Isaiah of Jerusalem within the wider prophetic tradition of the Jerusalem Temple and were part of the assurance expected from the apparatus of state religion. Within those parameters the primary duty of religion was to bestow stability on the ordered world. Isaiah himself, in a sea change of Ancient Near Eastern theology, emphasizes the transcendence of God, the independent identity of God over against the state, and the judgement that can sacrifice state security in the name of holiness. The ministry of Isaiah is one of the very moments when the wineskins of Ancient Near Eastern religion are burst and potentially a new understanding of God is released. It is an uncomfortable time for prophet and people, a boundary moment, but a moment of enormous significance. The status quo is challenged in the name of God.

A key concept of the Jerusalem theology is one that reflects the creator's order and is usually translated as 'righteousness' (ṣedeq). The word is best rendered as 'right order' with the related form ṣedāqâ signifying 'right conduct' in keeping with the creator's good order. We noted above that ṣedeq is in many ways the local equivalent of the Egyptian concept of Ma'at which signifies the delicate equilibrium of universal order including, specifically, justice and social cohesion.[25] It is that latter emphasis which is picked up by Isaiah when he regularly uses the term 'justice' (mišpāṭ) as the balancing concept for right order (ṣedeq). Justice is an associated concept to right order within the Jerusalem traditions, and was the particular prerogative of the king. His championing of justice was crucial for guaranteeing ordered community life understood as contributing to an ordered cosmos.

The perspective of Isaiah on the Jerusalem traditions high-lighted moral responsibility and integrity in social relationships. He was an interpreter of righteousness and justice as nothing less than the character and will of the high and lofty one who inhabits eternity. They were concepts to be handled with reverence and cautious awe.

In the estimation of the prophet Isaiah, as a man takes a line and plummet to a wall to see if it is truly vertical, so righteousness and justice were the very line and plummet by which the God of Zion measured the uprightness of his people (Isaiah 28:17). If Israel was close to the Holy One then that was a presence that could not be lightly entertained. Isaiah's call had personally convinced him of that. Transcendence made a radical claim upon those whose allegiance was to Zion:

> But the Lord of hosts is exalted by justice,
> and the Holy God shows himself holy by righteousness. (Isaiah 5:16)

Isaiah's famous Song of the Vineyard recorded in Isaiah 5:1–7 presents the special significance of the relationship between God and the 'inhabitants of Jerusalem and the people of Judah'. The prophet refers to 'my beloved' and his vineyard. Everything had

been done that agricultural science and careful husbandry could
demand in care for the vineyard. Then came the enormous
disappointment when the vineyard harvested only wild grapes.
What was left but to neglect it, to break down the hedges and
let in the wild beasts and the wilderness? The parable ends:

> For the vineyard of the Lord of Hosts
> is the house of Israel,
> and the people of Judah
> are his pleasant planting;
> he expected justice
> but saw bloodshed;
> righteousness,
> but heard a cry! (Isaiah 5:7)

Isaiah of Jerusalem's indictment of Israel for her lack of social
morality is based on the divine call for righteousness and justice
conceived of as part of the fabric of the created order, and is of
the essence of the Jerusalem traditions. The clutch of concepts
native to the Jerusalem traditions, related to the right ordering
of the world and centred on the honouring of righteousness and
justice, alone accounts for the observation of J. Barton:

> Commentators have for a long time noticed that Isaiah offers a more
> integrated, less piecemeal approach to human sin than the other
> prophets, and have looked for some unifying theme.[26]

Clearly, those who pervert the course of legal justice most
obviously betray the traditions of Zion. Like many other
misdemeanours which incur the wrath of Isaiah, these are
perpetrated by the ruling élite:

> Your princes are rebels
> and companions of thieves.
> Everyone loves a bribe
> and runs after gifts. (Isaiah 1:23)[27]

Isaiah attacks vices legislated against in the decalogue including
theft and murder.[28] Concerns familiar from the Wisdom tradition
are also his preoccupation including the protection of land
belonging to the vulnerable[29] and the responsible care of widows
and orphans:

> Cease to do evil,
> learn to do good;
> seek justice,
> rescue the oppressed,
> defend the orphan,
> plead for the widow. (Isaiah 1:16b–17)[30]

Isaiah also criticizes those whose lifestyle is contrary to the values of the kingdom as defined by righteousness and justice; this includes excessive luxury and indulgence[31] as well as using high office for personal aggrandizement.[32] Those who are regularly drunken are also included in this catalogue of inappropriate behaviour.[33] In common with other prophets and the Wisdom tradition, Isaiah is critical of the cult and its sacrifices. Given his own vocation was in the context of temple worship, and perhaps, one wonders, the Enthronement Festival itself, it may be inner motivation which is his concern. Worship which is not genuine and bathed in moral integrity is obscene in the presence of the Holy One of Israel. His articulation of the deity's frustration is radical:

> What to me is the multitude of your sacrifices? says the Lord;
> I have had enough of burnt-offerings of rams
> and the fat of fed beasts;
> I do not delight in the blood of bulls,
> or of lambs, or of goats. (Isaiah 1:11)

The consequence of the neglect of righteousness and justice is the languishing of order in distress. The finality of that distress is a feature of Isaiah. In his series of 'woes' that are to be found in chapter 5:8–23 with the probable addition of chapter 10: 1–4, each one has a curse attached to it. For instance:

> Therefore my people go into exile
> without knowledge;
> their nobles are dying of hunger,
> and their multitude is parched with thirst. (Isaiah 5:13)

The sense of 'more to come' is expressed in a salutary way in the refrain:

> For all this, his anger has not turned away,
> and his hand is stretched out still. (Isaiah 5:25b cf. 10:4b)

The implications are that evident localized distress cannot compensate for the scale of cosmic justice that has been offended. This message hardened as political reality took hold and Isaiah saw no change in God's people. It seems that Isaiah reached the conclusion that there could be no word of comfort until Jerusalem were razed to the ground:

> I will besiege you with towers
> and raise siege-works against you.
> Then deep from the earth you shall speak,
> from low in the dust your words shall come;
> your voice shall come from the ground
> like the voice of a ghost,
> and your speech shall whisper out of the dust. (Isaiah 29:3b–4)

The opening decades of the eighth century saw the final run of prosperity and independence for the modest states of Syria–Palestine. With the accession to the throne of Assyria by Tiglath-Pileser III in 744 BCE the situation changed dramatically. There was a super-power who would devour the independence and sap the economic prosperity of the smaller states of the Ancient Near East. There was no effective balance of power, with Egypt a broken reed. The prophet Isaiah was an alert observer of international affairs. For him, close to the creation traditions of Zion, Yahweh was sole lord of history. The gathering clouds were his work. He had whistled to summon a people at the ends of the earth.[34] The sinister international situation was his strange work. Assyria was his tool:

> The Lord spoke to me again:
> Because this people has refused
> the waters of Shiloah that flow gently,
> and melt in fear before Rezin
> and the son of Remaliah;
> therefore the Lord is bringing up
> against it the mighty flood of the River,
> the king of Assyria and all his glory. (Isaiah 8:5–7a)

The oracle that threatens the mighty flood of Assyria expresses a development in Isaiah's perspective. He is becoming secure in the vision of the finality of God's judgement. To what extent the words associated with the original call of Isaiah represent an element of retrospective reflection on what God had called him to do is not possible to assess at this distance. However, it is possible to relate his ministry to particular developing historical circumstances.

H. G. M. Williamson has drawn attention to the significance of two notes in the text of Isaiah 1–39 which anchor his ministry in terms of the date of the death of the reigning monarch. The first are the familiar cadences of Isaiah 6:1 'In the year that King Uzziah died . . .' and clearly of the utmost significance in identifying the prophet's call and the commencement of his ministry. The second comes at Isaiah 14: 28 'In the year that King Ahaz died . . .' Williamson suggests that this also had an equivalent significance and was initially intended to introduce the original oracles against the nations as well as the early material in chapters 28–32. He sums up:

> In the earliest version of the book to which we have access . . . we find the form 'In the year that King X died' at 6:1 and 14:28. And this was intended to distinguish between two main periods in which Isaiah himself was active.'[35]

The year that King Uzziah died was probably 740 BCE.[36] Already Tiglath-Pileser was secure upon the throne of Assyria. However, the impending crisis exploded in the reign of Uzziah's grandson Ahaz (735–715). The advance of Assyria in Syria and Palestine led to a fruitless attempt to establish a coalition to resist the inevitable. The northern kingdom of Israel, ruled by Pekah ben Remaliah, and Rezin, King of Damascus, established an alliance; they sought to involve Ahaz of Judah and, if necessary, to replace him by force if he did not co-operate. Chapters 7 and 8 of the Book of Isaiah relate to this period. The alarm that the 'Syro-Ephraimite Coalition' caused in Judah is vividly portrayed:

> When the house of David heard that Aram had allied itself with Ephraim, the heart of Ahaz and the heart of his people shook as the trees of the forest shake before the wind. (Isaiah 7:2)

Isaiah is sent by Yahweh to meet King Ahaz 'at the end of the conduit of the upper pool on the highway to the Fuller's Field' (Isaiah 7:3b). He is accompanied by his son Shear-jashub whose name is heavy with prophetic symbolism and translates as 'A remnant shall return'. On this occasion Isaiah offers, at least partly, a typical prophetic oracle of reassurance commencing 'Do not fear'. He announces:

> It shall not stand,
> and it shall not come to pass. (Isaiah 7:7)

But it is qualified with a further statement demanding faith and not political tactics:

> If you do not stand firm in faith,
> you shall not stand at all. (Isaiah 7:9b)

The consistent message of Isaiah was that scurrying around attempting to find security in alliances, political manoeuvring or even enhanced security of the water system was not only futile but an act of faithlessness. Such activity was simply an indication that Israel did not trust her God or understand true religion. It was itself a symptom of the desperate condition of God's people. They were called simply to stand firm in faith. Such advice was not what those who dealt in practical statecraft could easily accept or adopt, but it was Isaiah's unyielding and profoundly held conviction.

It appears that Isaiah did not envisage Ephraim or Damascus to be part of the divine strategy, or, at least, as any more than a divine shock tactic for Judah. The famous Immanuel prophecy promises the threat will be short-lived (Isaiah 7:10–16). However, underlying the reassurance remains a more realistic and fundamental threat. It is contained in the name of Isaiah's oldest son, perhaps conceived and named in association with his call, which perceives the threat of decimation. It is also contained in the name of the younger son named and conceived within the episode recounted. Maher-shalal-hash-baz translates as 'The spoil speeds, the prey hastens'. Its immediate application is the demise of Samaria and Damascus at the hands of Assyria, but the implications for Judah at the fate of her twin were not sanguine.

Isaiah stayed his prophesying for a time at this point while he awaited its outcome. He, perhaps, consciously modelled for Judah and Jerusalem his call for trust in God and human inactivity. At the conclusion of chapters 6–8 there are two instances of his prophecy being recorded so that it can be verified in the course of time. In Isaiah 8:1ff. the name of Maher-shalal-hash-baz is to be written on a tablet and verified by the witness of two public figures. In the same chapter at v. 16 the instruction is given: 'Bind up the testimony, seal the teaching among my disciples.' It is suggested by Clements that these refer to a single act of the sealing up of prophecy and that a consecutive text has become separated.[37] H. G. M. Williamson denies this; he points out that the children are plural on the second occasion and that something more substantial than a name seems to be envisaged for the written document.[38] It would have been sufficient to encapsulate Isaiah's prophetic ministry up to this point. Clements envisages a substantial memoir written by the prophet himself soon after the predicted events were confirmed.[39] We must note as significant both the reference to disciples (8:16b), and the assumption of Isaiah, signified in the use of the first person (8:17a), that he will be alive when the fairly immediate circumstances are fulfilled. The act of recording prophecy and waiting contains both threat and promise. What the prophet has announced in the name of God must unfold, but beyond the prophecy is new opportunity as yet undeclared and unwritten.

Isaiah's ministry is certainly active again 'in the year that King Ahaz died' (Isaiah 14:28) with the succession of Hezekiah (715–687 BCE).[40] We may suppose that the waiting was over. Samaria had been sacked by Shalmaneser V of Assyria in 722. The word of God had fallen upon Ephraim.

Shalmaneser's was a short reign and he was succeeded by Sargon II (721–705) whose credentials as legitimate heir had to be established at home, and consequently perceived instability fermented rebellion at the extremities of empire including its western reaches. It was the second wave of resistence to Sargon (c. 714) led by the Philistine city of Ashdod, encouraged by Pharaoh Shabaka of Egypt and involving Edom, Moab and Judah in the diplomatic frenzy which called for Isaiah's prophetic denunciation.[41] In 711 BCE Sargon sent his general to put down the rebellion. Ashdod was quenched and its king who had taken refuge in Egypt, far from being protected by a secure ally, was handed over by them to the Assyrians.[42] For the three years leading up to the events of 711, Isaiah walked barefoot and naked around Jerusalem like a humiliated captive being marched into exile (Isaiah 20). His dramatic prophetic warning was true in as much as Egypt did not protect Ashdod from the consequences of its rebellion against Assyria, but if it was a warning directed against Judah on that occasion she escaped unblemished.

The son and successor of Sargon was Sennacherib (704–681). His accession to the throne was the signal for another bid for freedom. Perhaps encouraged by diplomatic awareness of the revolt of the lion-hearted Merodach-baladan (then King of Babylon) against Assyria, Hezekiah along with the kings of certain Philistine cities withheld tribute. The hollow encouragement of Egypt was again significant and resisted, as ever, by Isaiah as a 'covenant with death' (28:15). Isaiah contrasts the human plans for alliance and resistance against Assyria with the strategy of God:

> Oh rebellious children, says the Lord,
> who carry out a plan, but not mine;
> who make an alliance, but against my will,
> adding sin to sin. (30:1)

This second phase of Isaiah's ministry, as recorded in the Book of Isaiah, is a mirror of the first in ending with another prophetic sealing:

> Go now, write it before them on a tablet,
> and inscribe it in a book,
> so that it may be for the time to come
> as a witness for ever. (30:8)

Isaiah knows the die is cast – 'they are a rebellious people' (30:9). There is no applying the brakes before the buffers are reached. The written word bears witness to the inevitability of the prophetic word. It is also a testimony, when the time comes, that the calamity foreseen is judgement. The people have not comprehended what it means to be under the protection of the holy God. They 'honour me with their lips, while their hearts are far from me' (29:13). The essence of Isaiah's message is distilled in a few verses which must encapsulate what was written down on the tablet:

> For thus said the Lord God, the Holy One of Israel:
> In returning and rest you shall be saved;
> in quietness and in trust shall be your strength.
> But you refused and said,

'No! We will flee upon horses' –
therefore you shall flee!
And, 'We will ride upon swift steeds' –
therefore your pursuers shall be swift! . . .
until you are left like a flagstaff on the top of a mountain,
like a signal on a hill. (Isaiah 30:15–17)

The flagstaff and the signal were indeed how Jerusalem was left. In 701, having dealt with Babylon only with some difficulty, Sennacherib was ready to turn westwards. His own annals record how he laid siege to forty-six Judaean cities and tied up Hezekiah in Jerusalem 'like a bird in a cage'.[43] The devastation, the toll in human life and the deportations add up to a terrible trail of misery:

Your country lies desolate,
your cities are burned with fire;
in your very presence
aliens devour your land . . . (Isaiah 1:7)

Thanks to Hezekiah's swift action in capitulation Jerusalem was saved.[44] A price was paid in tribute, including the gold plate from the Temple doors, as well as in territory and in the king's own daughters as concubines for the Assyrian king. Nevertheless, there was great relief in Jerusalem; the event seems to have fed the tradition of the inviolability of Zion and even been recast in legendary form.[45] Isaiah's own reflections, and bitter disappointment that even this close to the abyss there had been no spiritual reformation, may be contained in a specific oracle:

On that day the Lord God of Hosts
called to weeping and mourning,
to baldness and putting on sackcloth;
but instead there was joy and festivity,
killing oxen and slaughtering sheep,
eating meat and drinking wine.
'Let us eat and drink,
for tomorrow we die.'
The Lord of Hosts has revealed himself in my ears:
Surely this iniquity will not be forgiven
you until you die,
says the Lord God of Hosts. (Isaiah 22:12–14)

Isaiah never shares his emotions in an oracle or confronts God about the burden of his office, as does Jeremiah over a century later. Yet the pressure that his task put upon him is clear. From his very call, in the year that King Uzziah died, there is woven into his ministry the distress of labouring 'until cities lie waste without inhabitant' (Isaiah 6:11). That is taken to a crescendo in what must have been one of Isaiah's final oracles. The bitter condemnation of the popular celebration of Jerusalem's lone survival of the wrath of Sennacherib is charged with emotion. It is difficult to encounter his utter disdain at the festivity and feasting, or read the final denunciation 'until you die', without sensing the tears behind the tirade. The Zion traditions were Isaiah's pearl of great price; the truth of the holiness of God inhabiting Jerusalem and the consequent demand for righteousness and justice thrust enormous responsibility and significance upon Judah and Jerusalem. If Judah was broken so must have been Isaiah's heart. Managing the moment at which the wineskins of transcendence burst for the Ancient Near East involved profound travail of soul for the prophet.

The material of Isaiah, son of Amoz, ends on a terrifying note. Even after the devastation of the cities of Judah the final consequence of the holiness of God remains outstanding; 'His hand is outstretched yet.' The significance of his righteousness and justice have still not been vindicated. The absolute end is still awaited. But we have to note a further element relating to the recording of prophecy in Isaiah 30:8. This time the witness is 'for the time to come' and paralleled with 'as a witness for ever'. It is pointed out by Williamson:

> The text's function as a witness is cast into the indefinite future . . .
> and the likelihood that this will be remote from Isaiah's life time is
> suggested by the further qualification 'for ever'.[46]

The prophecy of Isaiah of Jerusalem is not quenched in hopelessness but waiting for the time when holiness shall be satisfied and the prophetic word can be renewed. It could not be read or cherished without a sense of waiting and anticipation. There will be a further story to be told. The possibility of something beyond devastation is coming very close to the concept of radical renewal and new creation. It bears the seeds of the concept of creation out of nothing, and eventually will nurture the possibility of God's justice vindicated in a personal life beyond death. It is an indication of Isaiah's ministry on the very frontiers of theology.

Points for Discussion

1. How far should society receive support and encouragement from religion, or to what extent should religion shock and disturb complacency?
2. To what extent is the presence of a worshipping community in its locality similar to the prophetic presence in Israel in being an enabler and midwife? What can it bring to birth that might otherwise not have happened?
3. Could a concept of the 'absolute end' beyond which God can work renewal have developed without the experience of devastation and total destruction by Israel and Judah? What are the implications of considerable human suffering for a new understanding of God to emerge?
4. Future generations would relate the lesson of God's ability to bring renewal from the other side of total destruction to creation out of nothing, and a renewed existence beyond death. Do you find this a helpful approach to these two ideas?
5. Have you had an experience you could recount that is similar (if less vivid!) to Isaiah of Jerusalem's sense of the holiness of God which he felt in the Temple and which has given the 'sanctus' to the Christian Eucharistic celebration?

Key Bible Passages

1 Samuel 3:1–4:1 (the call of Samuel); Isaiah 6 (Isaiah's call); Isaiah 5:1–7 (the Parable of the Vineyard); Isaiah 22 (a final oracle).

Further Reading

J. Blenkinsopp, *A History of Prophecy in Israel*, Philadelphia (1983). D. L. Petersen, *The Prophetic Literature*, Louisville & London (2002). J. Barton, *Isaiah 1–39*, Old Testament Guides, Sheffield (1995).

Figure 6.   Reconstruction of the entrance to the Tell Ta'yinat Temple in Syria. It has great similarity with the description of Solomon's Temple in the Bible. (Taken from the *Illustrated Atlas of Jerusalem*, ed. Dan Bahat, reconstruction L. Ritmeyer.)

Endnotes

[1] J. Blenkinsopp, *A History of Prophecy in Israel*, p. 18.

[2] W. L. Moran, 'New Evidence from Mari on the History of Prophecy', *Biblica* 50 (1969), pp. 15–56. See especially pp. 29–31, and p. 26: "The speaker is not a messenger, he is the mouthpiece of the deity. The most striking expression of this is found in (f): 'Šelebum went into a trance and thus (spoke) Annunitum'."

[3] S. Parpola, *Assyrian Prophecies*, State Archives of Assyria 9, Helsinki (1997).

[4] S. Parpola, *Assyrian Prophecies*, p. 6 (Oracle 1.3). Bel is one of the names of Marduk, later in the prophecy identified with Ištar. The significance of Ištar for the texts is emphasized by Parpola; the state god Aššur speaks in the collection once only (Oracle 3.3), pp. 23ff.

[5] D. L. Petersen, *The Prophetic Literature*, Louisville and London (2002), p. 18.

[6] J. B. Pritchard, *ANET* (with supplement), pp. 655f.

[7] J. Hackett, *The Balaam Text from Deir 'Alla*, Harvard Semitic Monographs 31 (1980). Hackett concludes (p. 125): 'This new inscription serves to authenticate the Balaam traditions in the Hebrew Bible to the extent that the bare facts of his existence are the same in each case'. There are two sets of fragments (Combination I and II): the first relates to the decision of the council of heaven and the second obscurely to a ritual connected with death which Hackett relates to child sacrifice.

[8] 'This term comes from outside Israel. It is most probably derived from the Akkadian word 'call' (nabû), but does not mean in the active the 'caller' who passes on the divine message, but rather in the passive 'the man called', who is appointed for a task by a revelation.' W. H. Schmidt, *The Faith of the Old Testament*, p. 225. The Akkadian origin of the word for prophet itself locates prophecy within mainstream Ancient Near Eastern custom and practice for which Akkadian became the international diplomatic language.

[9] G. Fohrer, *History of Israelite Religion*, London and Nashville (1972), pp. 223–9 makes a clear distinction between nomadic seers and ecstatic prophecy.

[10] J. Blenkinsopp, *A History of Prophecy in Israel*, p. 64: 'One possible approach is by way of Deuteronomy and Hosea to Ephraimite traditions preserved in the Pentateuch, one of which provides fascinating if obscure glimpses of the oracle tent and its resident seer. Miriam, sister of Moses and member of the Levi clan, is called a prophetess (n^{e}bî'āh, Exodus 15:20), in which capacity she provided encouragement in battle by singing, dancing and music. During the conquest another prophetess,

Deborah, issued a call to arms, accompanied the tribal levy into battle, gave instruction on when to attack, and also took part in singing and playing musical instruments (Judges 4–5).'

[11] J. Blenkinsopp, *A History of Prophecy in Israel,* p. 63: 'Hosea seems to have been the first to describe Moses as a prophet (Hosea 12:13).'

[12] 1 Kings 18:26–29.

[13] Gideon (Judges 6:25) is reported as tearing down the altar of Ba'al with its Asherah.

[14] The use of the concept 'limping' rather neatly picks up the practice of the prophets of Ba'al in their dance.

[15] E. W. Nicholson, *God and His People,* chapter 9, pp. 179–188.

[16] R. Murray, *The Cosmic Covenant,* London (1992).

[17] Deutero-Isaiah appeals to the Patriarchal and Exodus (Tent) traditions in addition to the Temple traditions of Jerusalem.

[18] 'Ephraim' is Isaiah's preferred designation for the northern kingdom. Israel captures Judah and Ephraim as together one people under God.

[19] This vision of God is reflected in the oracle in Isaiah 2:11ff.

[20] Chapter 3: *Temple,* pp. 77, 87.

[21] The impossibility of representing Israel's God by an image is later used as polemic against gods represented by idols, for example, Isaiah 40:18–20; 44:9–20; 46:5–7.

[22] Isaiah 28:29.

[23] See Jeremiah 7:4.

[24] See Isaiah 29:8; Isaiah 37:22,29.

[25] See Chapter 3, pp. 75ff. for a discussion of ṣedek within the Temple traditions.

[26] J. Barton, *Isaiah 139,* Old Testament Guides, Sheffield (1995), p. 49.

[27] See also Isaiah 3:9; 5:23; 10:1–2; 29:21.

[28] Isaiah 1:21–23a.

[29] Isaiah 5:8.

[30] Cf. also Isaiah 1:23b.

[31] Isaiah 3:16–4:1; 32:9–14.

[32] Isaiah 22:15–19.

[33] Isaiah 5:11–13, 22.

[34] Isaiah 5:26.

[35] H. G. M. Williamson, *The Book Called Isaiah,* Oxford (1994), p. 164.

[36] The dates follow those of G. Leick, *Who's Who in the Ancient Near East,* London & New York (1999).

[37] R. E. Clements, *Isaiah 1–39,* Grand Rapids and London (1980), p. 100.

[38] H. G. M. Williamson, *The Book Called Isaiah,* pp. 101 ff.

[39] Isaiah 6:1–8:18 without the later redactional elements. See R. E.

Clements, *Isaiah 1–39*, p. 4. Cf. K. Budde, *Jesajas Erleben: Eine gemeinverstandliche Auslegung der Denkschrift des Propheten*, Gotha (1928).

[40] This interpretation of the dating would mean that Ahaz, not Hezekiah, was on the throne when Samaria was sacked. The chronology adopted by R. E. Clements in his commentary, however, places Hezekiah's dates as 725–697.

[41] Isaiah 18; 19:1–5; 20 seem to refer to this period.

[42] See *ANET*, p. 286.

[43] *ANET*, p. 288.

[44] 2 Kings 18:14: 'King Hezekiah of Judah sent to the King of Assyria at Lachish, saying 'I have done wrong: withdraw from me; whatever you impose on me I will bear.' This version of events is confirmed by the Assyrian records.

[45] Three sources or possibly layers of tradition have been distinguished of the sparing of Jerusalem. (i) 2 Kings 18:14–16. The pragmatic political action of Hezekiah who sues for peace and offers tribute. (ii) Isaiah 36:1–37:9a and 37:37–38 = 2 Kings 18:17–19:9a and 19:36–37. The Assyrian official, the Rabshakeh, dialogues publicly with Hezekiah's ministers of state. Hezekiah sends to Isaiah for an oracle who in the context of 'fear not' gives assurance that a rumour will entice Sennacherib back to his own land where he will die by the sword. (iii) Isaiah 37:9b–36 = 2 Kings 19:9b–35. Hezekiah receives a letter from the King of Assyria warning him not to trust in his God. Isaiah volunteers a complex oracle of assurance. The Angel of God strikes down the camp of the Assyrians. R. E. Clements, *Isaiah and the Deliverance of Jerusalem*, JSOT Sup. 13, Sheffield (1980) argues for a developing Midrash on the basic tradition of (i). B. S. Childs, *Isaiah*, Louisville (2001), pp. 259ff. argues for a core of pre-exilic historical memory in (ii) and stresses the theological perspective of (iii) and an overall witness of chapters 36–37 as 'a truthful witness to God's deliverance of Israel' (p. 277). John Bright, *A History of Israel*, London (1960), pp. 269ff. argues for two campaigns against Jerusalem in which (701) Hezekiah pays tribute, and subsequently (688) a further bid for freedom leads to another siege in which Jerusalem is saved by one or a combination of (ii) and (iii). The difficulty with this hypothesis is that there is no evidence for two campaigns either in the Bible or in Sennacherib's annals.

[46] H. G. M. Williamson, *The Book Called Isaiah*, p. 105.

CHAPTER 7

The Healing Flow

A. Deutero-Isaiah

A second major figure emerges from the Book of Isaiah. The record is contained in chapters 40–55 of a prophet to the exiles in Babylon. These chapters are evidence of a ministry which commences almost a biblical generation after Nebuchadnezzar's devastation of Jerusalem with its Temple and the deportation of many of the population in 587 BCE. One and a half centuries have elapsed since the ministry of Isaiah of Jerusalem.

Deutero-Isaiah, like Isaiah of Jerusalem before him, receives his commission from the council of heaven. He eavesdrops a voice[1] that commissions the heavenly messengers who are to announce the establishment of a grand processional way through the desert leading from Babylon to Jerusalem. The divine glory is to return to Jerusalem. The image of the hills threshed and the valleys raised is almost a blueprint for a piece of exquisite Victorian railway engineering. It is none other than the highway of God along which the Holy One may make a royal progress, gently cherishing the accompanying exiles in their return to Zion as a shepherd would his flock.

Cosmic justice has been satisfied; universal equilibrium can now be restored. The position of Jerusalem at the fulcrum of things can be re-established: 'she has served her term, her penalty is paid.' (Isaiah 40:2b) God's relationship with his people can flourish again. The same voice that ordered the messengers commissions the prophet: 'Cry out' (Isaiah 40:6). He has the task of going to the captives languishing in exile to proclaim, despite the immediate evidence to the contrary, that their release is already secure because the decision has been made in heaven. This mood of exultant celebration for liberation which has happened even although it is not yet evident is celebrated by Deutero-Isaiah in his hymns. They would have communicated vividly with those he addressed. They are genuine psalm-type pieces which praise God for his acts and invite creation itself to rejoice. They are close to those biblical (enthronement) psalms which celebrate the Kingship of God. It is the presence of hymnic and liturgical pieces, so typical of Deutero-Isaiah, which gives the impression that his proclamation sings and rings out with a sense of festivity:

> Sing, O heavens, for the Lord has done it;
> shout, O depths of the earth;
> break forth into singing, O mountains,
> O forest, and every tree in it!
> For the Lord has redeemed Jacob,
> and will be glorified in Israel. (Isaiah 44:23)[2]

The musical score that characterizes Deutero-Isaiah should not camouflage from our understanding the toughness of his task. Just as the classical prophets paid in their own person the price of being forthtellers of bad news, so Deutero-Isaiah paid the price of being a proclaimer of good news. Rather than feeling uplifted by his words it seems that the exilic refugees felt taunted by false hope. The state of mind of the exiles has to be understood in the context of the theological norms of the Ancient Near East. The destruction of the state, the state capital and the Temple were, according to all the prevailing canons, evidence of the powerlessness of the state god. The Temple, the very beacon of security and evidence of divine rule over an ordered cosmos, was rubble. Its witness was reversed; it spoke of Yahweh's inability to vanquish disorder and protect his own. There was a double crisis of politics and faith.[3]

Rather than any supposed grand processional way stretching to Jerusalem, the exiles were witnesses of the reality of a vigorous intellectual and liturgical life centred on the great ziggurats of Babylon under the patronage of Marduk and Nabu. Babylon had its impressive processional way along which the decorated idols were carried on public festivals. The exiles were confronted with a religious life that seemed to undergird the success of a great empire, and perhaps with some credibility the New Year Festival could claim to validate Marduk's credentials to be the creator of the entire universe.

Deutero-Isaiah's oracles harnessed types or analogies from specific areas of common usage to the primary task of commending his message of liberation and contradicting both the malaise of the exiles and the claims of Babylonian religion. These types fall into various different classifications known as 'forms'. Certain forms reveal the prophet either dealing with low morale or in fervent and contradictory dialogue with his audience. These include the gentler 'Oracles of Salvation' and the more argumentative 'Polemic Genres'.

The original home of an Oracle of Salvation[4] is at the temple. It is not unlike the use of the confessional as practised in some contemporary Churches. It consisted of a message of reassurance commencing 'Fear not' spoken to a named individual, often a royal figure, in response to a psalm of lament. Begrich, who identified the form, envisaged it as spoken by a priest, but in the light of Ancient Near Eastern parallels discussed above, perhaps it was the prerogative of a temple prophet. Once the word of reassurance is spoken the dramatic change of state that is hoped for is assured. The psalm therefore changes mood.[5] The form as adapted by Deutero-Isaiah addresses 'Jacob-Israel' as a community by name, proclaims definitive reassurance and then spells out future positive consequences.[6] Very often, when Deutero-Isaiah uses this form in the process of naming Jacob-Israel, he picks up the wording of the psalm of lament. The spiritual condition with which he is dealing is laid bare:

> Do not fear, you worm Jacob,
> you insect Israel! (Isaiah 41:14a)

Related to the Oracle of Salvation is the 'Proclamation of Salvation'.[7] The form omits the words 'fear not' with the specific named addressee; in origin it may have been a prophetic response to a communal lament. The positive consequences within Deutero-Isaiah are spelt out in terms of the blooming desert. Again it often takes up and contradicts the lament:

> When the poor and needy seek water,
> and there is none,

and their tongue is parched with thirst. (Isaiah 41:17)

The psychology of the exiles is revealed. Both types of the words of salvation are spoken to a community *in extremis*, vulnerable and sapped of confidence.

The Polemic Genres have a more irascible tone; they reveal the prophet taking on a combative context. These include 'Trial Speeches' and some of the category known as 'Disputations'. In the trial speeches there is a summons to attend. The proceedings are analogous to civil justice in which there are disputed claims put forward and a decision is made. There are two sorts of trial speech: one involves Israel and the other the nations and their gods.[8] The first seeks to establish that Israel's exile was due to Israel's sin and not Yahweh's failure. Clearly this was a sensitive issue. Deutero-Isaiah stands in the tradition of the pre-exilic prophets including Isaiah of Jerusalem. However, the point here is not to indict Israel but to justify the exile. The second challenges the nations to acknowledge the validity of the predictions made by Israel's prophets which they cannot match. In this context, Israel is a passive witness who knows her story corroborates Deutero-Isaiah's claims. These include the prediction of the success of Cyrus the liberator, about which the idols were silent, and the predictions of the exile itself.[9] Does this prediction of exile refer to the prophets as a whole, or could he have specifically Isaiah of Jerusalem in mind? The Disputations within the Polemic Genres press and argue the same two cases but not in courtroom circumstances.[10]

Although Israel is the object of only one type of the Polemic Genres, it must be remembered that the oracles cast in the setting of a universal summons of the nations with their ardent argument were actually delivered in the presence of, and for the benefit of, the exiles. It is to them that the energy is directed. Typical of the sense of controversy of this whole category is Isaiah's passion in the dismissal of the validity of the Babylonian gods.[11] It is contained within a Trial Speech relating to the prophet's prediction of the victory of Cyrus in Isaiah 41:23–24:

Tell us what is to come hereafter,
that we may know that you are gods;
do good or do harm,

that we may be afraid and terrified.
You, indeed, are nothing
and your work is nothing at all;
Whoever chooses you is an abomination.

Clearly we have already assembled substantial evidence that an analysis of the forms used by Deutero-Isaiah gives significant insight into his historical context. These forms represent the basic building blocks of the prophet's oracles. They seem to be oral forms. Here we encounter the prophet at the 'coal face', at the moment of the delivery of his message as he interacts with the exiles. This analysis of structure can give the impression of the fragmentation of the prophet's unity of delivery. It has been captured by Barnabas Lindars:

> The grand sweep of Deutero-Isaiah's vision begins to disappear, as the prophet's work disintegrates into a mass of short pieces.[12]

However, it is likely that a number of individual units or forms that make up the text of Deutero-Isaiah were already combined by the prophet within a single oracle. The debate as to the length of the individual compositions delivered by the prophet continues among scholars.[13]

Although Deutero-Isaiah is part of the Book of Isaiah, it responds, in a way outstanding among biblical books, to careful analysis. This is a valid reason, despite the significant trend of current scholarship for giving the different parts of the Book of Isaiah independent attention. This response to careful analysis is true not only at the level of individual forms, but also in its literary structure. At this point we probably encounter the work of a disciple-editor rather than the prophet himself.

Isaiah 40–55 divides neatly into two halves comprising chapters 40–48 and 49–55. It has even been argued that they should be treated quite distinctly alongside Isaiah 56–66.[14] However, the two parts are tightly bound together by a prologue (40:1–11) and an epilogue (55:6–13).

In the first of these two sections there is a concentration of the Oracles of Salvation and the Polemic Genres. The address is to Jacob-Israel, with the assurance that the elective love of Yahweh still holds good. The case is pressed home by engagement with the disparagement and faltering faith of the exiles, and carried through to the point of dismissal of the Babylonian gods. The political transformation being achieved by Cyrus, foreign king and yet Yahweh's anointed, is proclaimed as the 'new thing' which God is doing. The prophet looks to the fall of Babylon and the liberation and return of the exiles.

In the second section the emphasis has moved from the captivity to the Holy City. The text is completely silent about Cyrus, and there is no more engagement with the spiritual malaise of the exile. Now it is no longer as Jacob-Israel, but as Zion-Jerusalem that the redeemed community is addressed. There is a personification of Zion so strong that it must have roots in ancient mythological traditions. She is envisaged as once again the bride of Yahweh, and mother of burgeoning offspring. The proclamation goes out to depart from Babylon.

Chapters 49–55 of Deutero-Isaiah are further given a distinctive quality because they contain all but the first of what are known as the 'servant songs'.[15] These passages have a particular spiritual intensity to which we shall return; their distinctiveness has often led commentators to set them apart.[16] T. N. D. Mettinger is one of those who has found an overall interpretative pattern which includes the 'so-called' servant songs.[17] He argues that the use of contrasts is a deliberate feature of the work. Thus he maintains that just as in chapters 40–48 the victories of Cyrus lead to the downfall of Babylon, so intentionally, as a sort of mirror image, in chapters 49–55 the sufferings of the servant lead to the re-established glory of Zion. The two sections, therefore, exhibit a balance of contrasts between hero and anti-hero; that is, Cyrus in the first and the Man of Sorrows in the second. There is a deliberate contrast in the destined reversal of fortunes between Babylon in the first section and Zion in the second. Mettinger is able to maintain that the second servant song (in its 'long form', that is, Isaiah 49:1–12), far from being extraneous to the whole, is actually the central 'bridge passage' of the complete Deutero-Isaiah work.

A brief excursus is necessary relating to Cyrus, who figures significantly in the analysis of the literary structure of Deutero-Isaiah. A foreign king, he is declared not simply 'my shepherd' (Isaiah 44:28), but the Lord's 'anointed' (Isaiah 45:1) by Deutero-Isaiah. Cyrus is responsible for a complete change in the international order comparable with the surprise of the restructuring of the contemporary international order under President Gorbachev and the opening up of the Berlin Wall in November 1989. The enlightened policy of Cyrus allowed for a general repatriation from which the Jews benefited, and even the vessels were restored to the Jerusalem Temple (Ezra 6:3–5, cf. Isaiah 52:11).

Vassal King of Anshan in southern Iran, Cyrus succeeded, in 550 BCE, in dethroning the Median King Astyages who ruled from Ecbatana. At that point Deutero-Isaiah, with astute political insight, seems to have identified him as a potential liberator of the captives in Babylon. It is probably reflected in the Trial Speech which summons the nations to admit the validity of Deutero-Isaiah's early predictions regarding Cyrus in Isaiah 41: 21–29. The rapidly ensuing pace of events culminating in the defeat of Croesus of Lydia at Sardis in 546 BCE is probably reflected in the further Trial Speech of Isaiah 41:1–5. The absentee Nabonidus, King of Babylon, who had neglected the cult of Marduk and alienated the powerful Babylonian priesthood, returned to the capital too late. Gobryas, now one of the generals of Cyrus, entered the city of Babylon in 539 BCE without any resistance whatsoever. When Cyrus himself entered the city shortly afterwards, according to the evidence of the Cyrus Cylinder,[18] he was hailed as the chosen of Marduk and liberator of Babylon. His victory was credited, in terms reminiscent of Isaiah 45:1–4, not to Yahweh, but to Lord Marduk.

The identification of some of the different forms used by Deutero-Isaiah in his oracles has further significant evidence that must now be considered. The various forms actually reveal two quite different bases for undertaking the theological enterprise. Some proceed from the basis of what we have identified as Temple traditions and others from the basis of Tent traditions. Temple traditions are clearly indicated in the presence of hymns and lament psalms as well as in the adaptation of Oracles of Salvation and Proclamations of Salvation. Tent is associated with history, events and predictions. Precisely the arguments in the Polemic Genres about the prediction of Israel's exile and God's ownership of the sweep of history in the anticipation of the victories of Cyrus lead us in that direction.

The significance of these two sources handled by a single prophet
need further consideration.

The major key for the prophet Deutero-Isaiah lies in the
Temple traditions. In this source is the dominant inspiration of
his proclamation. Temple traditions relate to right order and
universal harmony and have to do with creation theology.
Creation traditions are of the utmost significance for Deutero-
Isaiah to the extent that it is often difficult to discern whether
the good news he proclaims is the liberation of the exiles or that
God is the creator. The two facts are substantially interwoven.
Perhaps the most persistent indicator of the gospel of the creator
is the way he expands the prophetic messenger formula with
hymnic participles extolling the fact that God is creator.[19]
Deutero-Isaiah borrows balanced hymnic forms from the Temple
environment and accentuates them. He gathers a whole arsenal
of creation language and heaps them together. An example from
Isaiah 45:18 is wonderfully typical:

> For thus says the Lord,
> who **created** the heavens; he is God;
> who **formed** the earth and **made** it;
> he **established** it; he did not **create** it a chaos,
> he **formed** it to be inhabited:
> I am the Lord, and there is no other.

The clue to understanding the significance of God as creator for
Deutero-Isaiah is announced in the prologue in the form of 'a
highway for our God' (Isaiah 40:3b). The purpose of the
processional way identified is developed in the report of heralds
proclaiming 'Here is your God' to the waiting Jerusalem (Isaiah
40:9). The scene is taken up again vividly at the heart of Isaiah
49–55 with its emphasis on the exaltation of Zion. In Isaiah 52:
7–10 the feet of the messengers are in evidence, the message of
comfort is given, but all is in the service of the great proclamation:
'Your God reigns.'[20] The oracle paints those who hear it into the
picture of the very Enthronement Festival as it had been
celebrated each autumnal New Year at the Jerusalem Temple. The
herald-runners are proclaiming their news to the sentinels and
the excited crowd straining to catch a first view of the Ark as it
is borne along the processional way to the Temple:

> Listen! Your sentinels lift up their voices,
> together they sing for joy;
> for in plain sight they see
> the return of the Lord to Zion. (Isaiah 52:8)[21]

The previous chapter has already prepared the way for this moment. Isaiah 51:9–10 has rehearsed the divine victory of Order over the threat of Chaos and disintegration. The form is that of a traditional psalm in the lament mode which calls upon 'the arm of the Lord' to awake and remember the great victory over the dragon and the deep:

> Was it not you who cut Rahab in pieces,
> who pierced the dragon?
> Was it not you who dried up the sea,
> the waters of the great deep? (Isaiah 51:9b–10a)

We are familiar with Deutero-Isaiah reapplying Oracles of Salvation and Proclamations of Salvation from their original temple context to serve the purpose of his message of liberation. But, by far his most daring and most programmatic prophetic initiative is to take the New Year Festival as it had been celebrated in the Jerusalem Temple before its destruction and reapply it to the condition of the exiles. He announces a rekindled festival of sabbatical proportions. This festal celebration is carried through into the blooming desert spelt out in the Oracles of Salvation and also in the divine victor's triumphal progress.[22]

Before peace (šālôm) can be announced to Jerusalem (Isaiah 52:7), right order (ṣedeq) must be established. The champion of that right order is, of course, the king. It is precisely that which Cyrus is called to undertake in the first half of Deutero-Isaiah's record. In giving Cyrus the responsibility of being champion of order within the context of the Jerusalem traditions Deutero-Isaiah is passing beyond the very boundaries of every established convention. So it is that Cyrus meets 'right order' at every step (Isaiah 41:2). The world falls into place before him: 'I have aroused Cyrus in righteousness' (Isaiah 45:13). He is called to restore the correct order of things. For Isaiah of Jerusalem right order corresponded to justice and related very specifically to the human moral sphere.[23] Whereas for Deutero-Isaiah, in the words of H. H. Schmid, the concept:

denotes the order of Yahweh, which, corresponding to the order of creation, will break through in the time of salvation.[24]

According to the Jerusalem traditions the return of the cosmos to its proper equilibrium involves the exaltation of Zion. It is for that reason that news of liberation and the news that Yahweh is the creator are one. That also explains why in the proclamation of Deutero-Isaiah the right order of creation and salvation are parallel concepts:

> My righteousness (ṣedeq) is near,
> my salvation (yᵉšûʿā) is gone forth. (Isaiah 51:5a R.V. translation)

The creation traditions of the Temple applied to the exile spell out salvation.

The Tent traditions may provide the minor key of Deutero-Isaiah's score, but nonetheless, they are present and must be fully taken into account. A sense of God's purpose in history, the effectiveness of the prophetic word and, unlike Isaiah of Jerusalem, familiarity with the Exodus traditions are all evident. Deutero-Isaiah is party to the recovery of the traditions relating to Noah (Isaiah 54:9) and the patriarchs (Isaiah 41:8) going on at the time of the Exile. In exploring the latter two traditions Israel's historical faith, and in particular the Priestly tradition, casts around for a basis for divine reliability beyond what had come to be regarded as the broken promises of the Mosaic traditions.

The historical perspective is most vigorously articulated within the Polemic Genres. The trial speeches and the related Disputations base their reasoning on the 'Salvation history' approach of the prophetic and Deuteronomistic traditions. The case against Israel is precisely that argued by the pre-exilic prophets that has shaped the record of Israel's history from Deuteronomy through to II Kings. Israel's exile is due to her sins and was Yahweh's legitimate judgement. It was deserved, it was Yahweh's deliberate act and not a sign of his inadequacy:

> Who gave up Jacob to the spoiler, and Israel to the robbers?
> Was it not the Lord, against whom we have sinned,
> in whose ways they would not walk,
> and whose law they would not obey? (Isaiah 42:24)

The efficacy of the prophetic word in announcing events, including the exile, before they happen is the preoccupation of the other type within the Polemic Genres. It argues that foretelling the future is the test of deity, because only such a deity owns the sweep of history and therefore is truly God. Included within the evidence is the fact that Yahweh, through Deutero-Isaiah, has foretold the coming of Cyrus (Isaiah 41:21–29).

A favourite device of Deutero-Isaiah is to contrast the 'former things' with the 'new things' or 'things to come'.[25] These concepts relate directly to the prophetic word. The 'first things' cover the sweep of Israel's history which is viewed as totally encompassed within the broad principle of prediction and fulfilment.[26] In Isaiah 43:16–17 these events include specifically the Exodus, and in 41:25–26 the initial prophecies concerning Cyrus. The 'new things' or 'things to come' which we might paraphrase as 'latest things' are still open-ended. The prophetic word in Israel's history is brought right to the present where it is poised between annunciation and fulfilment. This coming event is focused on Cyrus, but involves the fall of Babylon, the liberation of the exiles and the return.

Israel has to admit that her story witnesses to the truth of the prophet's claim. There is no parallel in the gods of the nations foretelling the future. The verdict in favour of Israel's historical faith therefore has the further consequence of exposing the other deities as 'a delusion' and 'nothing' (Isaiah 41:29b). They are the butt of Deutero-Isaiah's disdain and of no consequence. The 'Yahweh only' dimension of Israel's Tent traditions is worked by Deutero-Isaiah within these particular forms into a clear monotheism. The gods of the nations, including the tantalizingly attractive idols of Babylon, may have a shadowy identity but, similar to the nations, they are 'like a drop in a bucket' or 'as the dust on the scales' before Yahweh who is God.

To what extent do the sources foam? There is a coming together of the Temple and the Tent, of the Festal celebration of New Year and the historic witness of Israel's faith in the ministry of Deutero-Isaiah. For his proclamation it is not normally 'the sea' that can link the Festal traditions with those of Exodus,[27] but rather the parallel between the divine victor's triumphal progress along the processional way and the journey of the redeemed through the desert. The Proclamation of Salvation in its consequences for the future regularly uses festal themes, and often combines these with Exodus traditions. Isaiah 43:16–21 unmistakeably refers to the Exodus with a 'way in the sea' (v. 16) and mention of 'chariot and horse' (v. 17). Yet later on 'a way in the wilderness' (v. 19) is ambiguous, whereas 'I give waters in the wilderness, rivers in the desert' (v. 20) is definitely festal. When there is emphasis on God accompanying the return journey of the exiles or leading them, this too is probably influenced by a festal theme (see Isaiah 42:14–17).

The epilogue which closes the oracles of Deutero-Isaiah clearly combines the festal traditions of prodigious fertility with the efficacy of the word of God spoken through the prophet into a single form. It is a fitting conclusion to the dual inspriation of the prophet:

> For as the rain and the snow come down from heaven,
> and do not return there until they have watered the earth,
> making it bring forth and sprout,
> giving seed to the sower and bread to the eater,
> so shall my word be that goes out from my mouth,
> it shall not return to me empty,
> but it shall accomplish that which I purpose,
> and succeed in the thing for which I sent it. (Isaiah 55:10–11)

The combined sources of Temple and Tent in Deutero-Isaiah bring to maturity the hallmark of Israel's faith and present to the world a vibrant monotheism. There is one God who is creator and saviour – 'I have made, and I will bear' (Isaiah 46:4b). That which we noted was evident in the work of the Yahwist and exhibited in his Primæval History is secured once and for all by the ministry of Deutero-Isaiah. It is, as it were, newly minted and still untested; it has yet to grow and flourish. However, the watershed has taken place: 'Yahweh only' has now passed over into 'Only Yahweh'. Monolatry has become monotheism.

Deutero-Isaiah manages to work out parallel visions of the only God through Temple and Tent which complement and strengthen each other. The Jerusalem Temple traditions provided a mighty witness to the significance of creation traditions. They brought to Israel's faith a universal perspective which encompassed all the nations. Creation was presented in the context of an ordered world understood to operate in equilibrium and relationship. The burgeoning historical consciousness of the Tent tradition develops through the ministry of the classical prophets to encompass God's ownership of the sweep of history. International events, often contrary to immediate perception, do not cause random casualties, but represent the plan and purpose of God. This perspective, evident in Isaiah of Jerusalem, is brought into sharp focus in the trial speeches and related disputations of Deutero-Isaiah.

The exalted nature of the creator in the Ancient Near East, specifically worked out in the context of the Temple traditions at Jerusalem, is evident in Deutero-Isaiah's proclamation. Also evident is the strong insistence of 'Yahweh only' as the author of historical events which is a feature of prophetic-Deuteronomistic traditions, with its priority accorded to the active word of God in history. In the workshop of Deutero-Isaiah the two traditions become a single dynamic monotheism. Classic expression of this achievement is given by Deutero-Isaiah himself in an oracle of God:

> I form light and create darkness,
> I make weal and create woe;
> I the Lord do all these things. (Isaiah 45:7)

A further priority question remains to be put to Deutero-Isaiah: how far is he able to develop the crucial insight of the pre-exilic prophets who coped with the devastation of first Samaria and then Jerusalem by developing a profoundly new theological understanding of the transcendence of God? The canons of the religious thought of the Ancient Near East exercised a grip that valued sameness and prevented the development of the concept of a radically new act of God. However, we were able to identify Isaiah of Jerusalem as a particular instance of a prophet on the threshold of a breakthrough when he envisages further divine initiative beyond total devastation. God could act even after 'the end has come upon my people Israel'. To what extent could it be said of Deutero-Isaiah that in his proclamation the absolute end is reached and breached?

Interestingly, as we discuss the 'foaming of the sources' the breakthrough seems to be made by him only within the forms representative of the Tent tradition, and not the Temple or creation forms. It is almost as if he is still carefully and gingerly handling two powerful ingredients that cannot be mixed without enormous consequences. It is evidence, too, of Deutero-Isaiah's ministry at a moment of formation – theological developments are in process.

In terms of the creation traditions, it seems that the canons of the Ancient Near East prevail. The liberation of the exiles is presented as the restoring of creation to its original and primal state. What is necessary for salvation is for the proper order of creation to break through. That order, which necessarily involves the exaltation of Jerusalem, is a restored order not a new order. Yahweh did not divorce Zion, otherwise there would be legal evidence (Isaiah 50:1–3). The covenant with David remains valid (Isaiah 55:1–5). The buffers were not reached in Zion's destruction.

Given the prophetic proclamation of the rejection of Israel and the demise of the monarchy at the exile, it could be thought that Deutero-Isaiah is not being sufficiently radical in his reapplication of the Jerusalem traditions. In fact, he is only a whisker away from the breakthrough to a 'new creation'. He has taken a timeless liturgical festival and applied it to the concrete circumstances of history and specific events. Indeed, anyone coming upon his use of the verb create (bārā')[28] from the Priestly tradition, where its use is restricted to primæval time, would instantly understand a radically new act of God to be involved. In fact the breakthrough is made by the time of Trito-Isaiah when he proclaims:

> For I am about to create new heavens and a new earth;
> the former things shall not be remembered or come to mind. (Isaiah 65:17)[29]

One area where it is difficult for Deutero-Isaiah's message to shun novelty is in the commissioning of Cyrus, a foreign ruler, as Yahweh's shepherd and anointed one. It certainly tests the Jerusalem creation traditions to their utmost. It is this circumstance that provokes the breakthrough in the Tent traditions, specifically in the Disputation in Isaiah 48:3 –11. The context within the Polemic Genre seems to refer the form to a

Cyrus prediction. The relevant lines are as follows:

> From this time forward I make you hear new things,
> hidden things that you have not known.
> They are created (bārā') now, not long ago;
> before today you have never heard of them,
> so that you could not say, 'I already knew them'. (Isaiah 48:6b–7)

Of this passage it has been said:

> The really 'new' thing is the fact that the salvific events for Israel are
> brought about by a pagan, Cyrus.[30]

The wineskins of the old order are in the process of breaking
up in the ministry of Deutero-Isaiah.[31]

B. The Unity of the Book of Isaiah

The founding father of modern Isaiah studies is B. Duhm, a status
he achieved with his commentary *Das Buch Jesaia*, published in
1892.[32] In that commentary he unveiled the thesis of a third
Isaiah. He limited Deutero-Isaiah to chapters 40–55, and assigned
chapters 56–66 to a different author of the time of Ezra. It was
also in that commentary that he identified and separated out from
the body of Deutero-Isaiah the Servant Songs. In his view these
poems relate only loosely to their contexts. They form a
connected series from a hand other than the prophet and portray
the career of an historical person, a leprous teacher of the law,
conceived of as other than the prophet.

Since Duhm, priority in Isaiah studies has largely been given
to understanding the integrity of the separate parts of the Book
of Isaiah and rather less effort has been devoted to understanding
its unity. In recent scholarship that priority has been reversed;
the unity of the Book of Isaiah is being reasserted. Although there
is no unanimity about what constitutes the book's unity, there is
a growing conviction that the integrity of the book is undermined
if it is not taken as a whole.

An earlier generation led by S. Mowinckel[33] grounded the unity
of Isaiah in the assumption of a continuing school of disciples.
R. E. Clements[34] questions the existence of a school of disciples

surviving in any meaningful way over a period of two centuries, but does see Deutero-Isaiah consciously carrying forward the message of Isaiah of Jerusalem. He does not rule out access by the exilic prophet to a written collection of oracles emanating from the eighth-century prophet. He draws attention particularly to the theme of the blind and the deaf in Isaiah 42–43, and the resonance there to the call of Isaiah of Jerusalem (Isaiah 6: 9–10).

J. Vermeylen[35] regards the combination of Deutero-Isaiah's oracles with the tradition of Isaiah of Jerusalem as happening at a relatively late stage. But he suggests that a modest original core of Deutero-Isaiah's oracles received a substantial redaction in order to link it with the initial thirty-nine chapters. The redactor was Trito-Isaiah, active at the time of Nehemiah; the three parts of the Book of Isaiah therefore have a strong redactional unity. R. Coggins, by contrast, emphasizes the final literary shape of the Book of Isaiah which brings its own perspective and needs to be properly acknowledged: 'we may be wiser to read Isaiah as a structured collection of religious verse'.[36] B. S. Childs[37] takes the final literary form a stage further in championing the notion of 'canonical shaping'. He argues that it is the final form of scripture which is authoritative. It is not the complex path of tradition through which scripture has evolved, but its final theological shape which must be addressed. This approach is developing into something doctrinal rather than strictly critical.

The perspective of this work is that sources often reveal crucial insight into understanding the final form. It is, therefore, important that in the contemporary recovery of the unity of the Book of Isaiah we do not simultaneously lose a grip on the sources or their significance. Indeed, there may well be an interconnectedness at that fundamental level. That possibility is allowed for in what H. G. M. Williamson identifies as the crucial question for assessing the unity of Isaiah as 'the extent to which, if at all, Deutero-Isaiah may have written in conscious dependence on and in elaboration of the work of Proto-Isaiah'.[38] He argues that Deutero-Isaiah himself was responsible for combining his prophecies with those of Isaiah of Jerusalem and editing them in a single work. However, his major insight into the potential relationship between the two parts is not dependent on the particular editorial linkage. The crux is contained in Williamson's claim that Deutero-Isaiah 'regarded the earlier work as in some sense a book that had been sealed up until the time when judgement should be passed and the day of salvation had arrived'.[39] Deutero-Isaiah believed that time to have come.

Trito-Isaiah can be bound into the whole by recognizing the particular historical circumstances of that section of the book:

> Those who returned to Zion sadly did not experience the fulfilment of Second Isaiah's brilliant promises of prosperity and peace and joy.[40]

If the time had come for the unsealing of prophecy why was God silent? Chapters 60–62[41] reaffirm the promises of Deutero-Isaiah as still valid despite the hardships experienced by the first returnees. The other chapters of Trito-Isaiah accept postponement of the prophetic promise as reality, and begin to search for reasons to account for the delay.[42] In the process of contemplating further purgatory the final breakthrough is made to the articulation of a 'new creation'.[43] Arguably, in that achievement Trito-Isaiah names the theological potential for the whole Book of Isaiah.[44]

There may be a further clue to the unity of the Book of Isaiah in the themes which carry right through the total book. The role of the nations both in judgement and salvation for God's people is played out with enormous variety even within the distinct layers of the Isaianic material. The phrase 'the Holy One of Israel' is characteristic of all three parts of the book. Zion/Jerusalem, the concepts associated with righteousness (ṣedeq) and its championing by a royal figure, or an anointed one, are also of central concern to all three sections. These indicators point to the single unifying factor of the Jerusalem temple traditions. It has been summed up by G. I. Davies:

> The primary focus of unity in Isaiah is, I suggest, the tradition which underlies it, and that means above all the Jerusalem cult tradition with its cosmic and universal perspective. Isaiah is above all the book of the prophetic reinterpretation of the Jerusalem cult traditions, one might say, the fall-out from the explosive encounter between the spirit of classical prophecy and the Jerusalem community's developing pattern of worship over a period of several centuries.[45]

It does seem that the Book of Isaiah is united by the single phenomenon of prophecy associated with the Jerusalem Temple.

There is no doubt that Deutero-Isaiah, inheritor of the Jerusalem prophetic traditions, takes up a dialogue with his prophetic predecessors. H. G. M. Williamson has identified the sense of expectancy with which Isaiah of Jerusalem seals his prophecy. Whilst recognizing Deutero-Isaiah's debt to the total prophetic movement[46] and his ability to work with Tent as well as Temple traditions, it does seem likely that as a practitioner of the Jerusalem prophetic traditions he consciously awoke the dormant prophecy of Isaiah of Jerusalem. In that case the reference includes the Son of Amoz when the trial speeches refer to the 'former things'. Trito-Isaiah circles had to live with and interpret the consequences of unsealed prophecy in the face of the raw reality of the returning few to challenging circumstances.

C. The Soul of a Prophet

For the Ancient Near East only one human story was of real significance and affected the processes of the cosmos. That was the story of the king. It was the king's administration of justice, according to the Jerusalem traditions, upon which rested the integrity of creation. Throughout the Ancient Near East the involvement of the king in the temple liturgy, and particularly in the ceremonies associated with the New Year, was of the utmost significance. In Canaan the royal stature equated with that of the primal man. In the person of the king one human being was writ large.

The Tent tradition, by contrast, emphasized the value of the human story and could articulate emotions, achievements and subterfuge within the human context. But it was in the person of the prophet that this rich potential was most intensely manifest. A human being was thrown into high relief with a record of conflicting emotions, the pain of integrity, the drama of events and the transparency of the soul. History for the first time included a personal journal: 'We are shown men who have become persons because God has addressed them and they have had to make a decision in his presence'.[47] In the circumstances of the prophet the received wisdom of the Ancient Near East that the good always prospered was radically challenged. Closeness to God was often demonstrably shown to involve ridicule and even humiliation. The prophet emerged as a counterpoint to the king.

Near the end of Israel's prophetic period and after monarchy had ceased to be a contemporary reality, the royal and the prophetic insights merge in a single collage of 'the Suffering Servant'. The foaming of the sources converge in an unsurpassed mingling. The witness is in the text of Deutero-Isaiah.[48]

In maintaining that the Servant Songs were secondary to the primary text of Deutero-Isaiah, Duhm had failed to recognize the significance of tension in the structure of the presentation of the prophet's oracles. The contrast between the servant 'Jacob-Israel' of the first part of the book who is drained of initiative and self-confidence, suffering on account of sin, needing to be stirred to life, and the servant of the poems, three of which are in the second half of the book, who is full of initiative, obedient and suffering on account of faithfulness to Yahweh is deliberate. Further, it has become clear that the poems belong with the primary text on grounds of both linguistic form and theological content. For instance, in terms of linguistic form C. Westermann has pointed out the typical Deutero-Isaianic expansion of the prophetic messenger formula in the second Song (Isaiah 49:5).[49] As regards theological content, Westermann has also highlighted the significance of 'servant' for the prophet's thinking, reflected in the oracle of God in chapter 43 verses 23b and 24b. The argument runs: 'You did not really serve me. In actual fact you made me into a servant'.[50]

The first of the Servant Songs (Isaiah 42:1–4) breaks into the middle of a trial speech for which Cyrus is of central significance.[51] This suggests that the primary editor related the servant of this particular 'Song' to Cyrus. He understood Cyrus, in these verses, to be designated servant, a typical royal title in the context of the Zion traditions, as well as elsewhere shepherd or anointed one. This identification removes the anomaly of a poem relating to the Suffering Servant in the first half of Deutero-Isaiah's oracles where prominence is accorded to the career of Cyrus. The most natural interpretation of 'a bruised reed' and 'a dimly burning wick' (v. 3) becomes Israel languishing in her exile. In that case, this oracle, as a royal commissioning, has the best claim to be one of Deutero-Isaiah's early pronouncements referred to as already fulfilled within the trial speech of Isaiah 41:26. The world 'mission' is the restored universal order which Cyrus meets at every step. Here it is represented by the concept justice (mišpāṭ) and is reminiscent of the usage in Isaiah 1–39.

We next turn to the third Servant Song (Isaiah 50:4–9). Although the word 'servant' is not mentioned in this passage, we encounter an individual whose words are similar to the outpouring of the soul found in the prophet Jeremiah.[52] They have been called 'pure prophetic confession'.[53] It is quite logical to take this passage as from the lips of Deutero-Isaiah, and a window into his soul. Every morning he is awakened by the 'word of God', and he is given words to sustain the weary exiles. He has not been rebellious, he has willingly accepted the prophetic commission although it has cost him suffering and pain. The latter part of the confession (vv. 7 ff.) is typical of Deutero-Isaiah in having the shape of a psalm of confidence.

Next for consideration is the second Servant Song (Isaiah 49:1–6) placed at the turning point of the literary structure of Deutero-Isaiah's oracles. We may interpret it in the context of Isaiah 50:4–9. It certainly includes prophetic confession:

> But I said, I have laboured in vain,
> I have spent my strength for nothing and vanity. (Isaiah 49:4a)

This is met with a now familiar expansion of the messenger formula (v.5), followed by a recommissioning (v.6). The messenger formula includes the repeated reference to the prophet as 'called from the womb'. It picks up a phrase that elsewhere applies to Jacob-Israel, and also echoes the prophetic vocabulary of Jeremiah (Jeremiah 1:5). The recommissioning expands the prophet's brief, he is called not only 'to raise up the tribes of Jacob' but also as 'a light to the nations'. At his low-point of seeming failure Deutero-Isaiah is nourished by the thought that Israel's return has universal significance. This, as we have seen, is well within the framework of the cosmic perspective of restored world order as the prophet understood it. It underlines the fact that the significance of Israel's return for the Gentiles (cf. Isaiah 45:22) was indeed far more than window-dressing for his message. The opening of this poem, which refers to the initial call of the prophet and describes him as protected and equipped by God for adversity, goes on to name him not only as 'my servant' but also as 'Israel'. The significance of that designation will be taken up later.

We turn now to the final Servant Song (Isaiah 52:13–53:12). This is clearly a very complex piece that can be taken at many levels. The starting point must be the straightforward line of continuity it exhibits with the two immediately previous servant passages. It takes forward the 'prophetic confession' and the element of biography that we have noted as characteristic of them both. The ingredient of confession brings to a crescendo the resistance met by the prophet and his consequent sufferings. The language that expresses it is again reminiscent of the outpourings of Jeremiah:

> He was oppressed, and he was afflicted,
> yet he did not open his mouth;
> like a lamb that is led to the slaughter,
> and like a sheep that before its shearers is silent.
> (Isaiah 53:7, cf. Jeremiah 11:18ff)

A specific individual encounters us through the complexities of the poetry.

The three Servant Songs of Isaiah 49–55 exhibit a unity and enable the articulation of the prophet's spiritual journey. A personal journal follows them through. However, there remains one major difference between the final servant passage and its two predecessors even at the level of confession and biography. The final Servant Song is in the third person and not the first; it is a report. This is noted by Whybray in the context of identifying the nature of the final poem:

> The basic form of this chapter is that of the thanksgiving of the individual for deliverance from trouble, with the unusual feature that it is not the former sufferer himself but his friends who give thanks.[54]

The assumption must be that the element of biography in the passage includes the prophet's death. That alone accounts for the third person. It is confirmed by the fact that Deutero-Isaiah nowhere shows awareness of the peaceful possession of Babylon by Cyrus. His predictions are all stereotyped anticipations envisaging the lumbering of idols into captivity (Isaiah 46:1–2) and the survival of a remnant (Isaiah 45:20). Given the communal resistance to the prophet and the evidence of the sufferings precipitated by his ministry, both embedded in the Servant Songs, as well as the indications from the Polemic Genres, it is most likely that his death was by the hands of his own people rather than Babylonian justice. That story, which takes the prophet from the call in the womb to death, brings to the whole drama of the Suffering Servant the reality of a genuine life, of human dilemmas writ large and of the cost of discipleship and faithfulness.

Two notable features indicate that the biographical interpretation is at this point exhausted and that we must look elsewhere for further understanding of the passage. One is the atoning nature of the servant's suffering. The other is the reference to the servant's resurrection. Both need to exercise our attention.

We commence with the challenge of atonement. The sufferings of the servant as a life-giving and healing source are integral to the whole presentation of the final Servant Song. Indeed it starkly claims: 'Yet it was the will of the Lord to crush him with pain' (Isaiah 53:10a). Not only does the servant bear the guilt of many (53:11), but in Isaiah 53:10 he is described as a 'sacrifice for sin' (āšām). The whole adds up to a remarkable claim: what could have generated it? John Day directs our attention towards the psalms and the nature of kingship within the liturgical custom and practice of the pre-exilic Jerusalem Temple. He states:

> There are good reasons for supposing that the description of the suffering and vindicated king of the psalms in part underlines the suffering servant.[55]

Day draws attention to the potential significance of Zechariah 13:1 as evidence for the atoning effect of royal suffering.

Confirmation of the appropriateness of linking themes from the Temple liturgy and in particular the New Year Festival with Isaiah 53 is evident in the vocabulary of 53:1 which mentions 'the arm of the Lord'. It is a common phrase extolling the power of God associated with the primæval battle drama and typically occurs in the ancient cultic psalm reproduced by Deutero-Isaiah in Isaiah 51:9–10. It seems, then, that elements of the pattern of the Suffering Servant in Isaiah 53 are drawn within the umbrella of the general significance of the New Year Festival for the inspiration of Deutero-Isaiah's proclamation. That fact, and the significance of the king in the Festival, reveals to us some of the underlying logic for contrasting the Suffering Servant of the second half of Deutero-Isaiah's recorded oracles with Cyrus the King in the first half. It would further explain the liturgical feel that pervades Isaiah 53 and might bring an additional significance to the resurrection symbolism we must now discuss.

How are we to understand the death (53:8b) and burial (53:9) of the servant and then the subsequent change of mood? The change is captured in chapter 53 verse 10b:

> he shall see his offspring, and shall prolong his days;
> through him the will of the Lord shall prosper.

Whybray gives a poetic interpretation to this sense of death and resurrection by suggesting it celebrates the release of the prophet from a Babylonian jail.[56] However, the evidence forces us to take the death seriously and literally.

It is likely that the liturgical resonances of the royal suffering and vindication have influenced the way that the servant's change of fortune has been presented. If the atonement imagery was inspired by analogy with the understanding of the significance of the role of the king in the temple liturgy, then the rhythm of fall and rise would also commend itself. It must be acknowledged that our information about practice and interpretation relating to Ancient Near Eastern cultic conventions generally, and the Jerusalem Temple in particular, remains obscure. The contention of the Myth and Ritual School that a single pattern extended across the Ancient Near East has not found supporting evidence.[57] In the specific case of the Jerusalem cult it is possible that Canaanite conventions relating to Ba'al's death and resurrection, inappropriate to God Most High (El Elyon), may have found some sort of resolution in the part played by the king in suffering and vindication within the cultic drama.

If the articulation of death and resurrection in Isaiah 53 involves the dramatic colours of cultic influence, it still remains to ask what was the trigger that established the relevance of the analogy? In all probability, parallel to the vision of Ezekiel in the valley of Dry Bones (Ezekiel 37:1–14), we should be looking for a communal renewal of life within the exiles. The resurrection referred to in the context of Isaiah 53 would be the first group of exiles setting out from Babylon to initiate the long haul to the rebuilding of the walls of Jerusalem. Subsequent to the prophet's violent rejection events confirmed his preaching. Cyrus did indeed enter Babylon, the smouldering wick was not quenched and the exiles were free to return. The ultimate prediction-proof of Deutero-Isaiah's oracle was given. His ministry generated the momentum for the restoration of Zion/Jerusalem.

As the resurrection of the servant melts into the community of the restored Israel a whole new dimension is introduced into the symbolism. In as much as this community is representative of Israel proper, so the servant becomes identified with Israel.[58] Israel, too, is to be included in the imagery of the servant in the fourth Servant Song. That, in particular, is the significance of Isaiah 52:13–15, a passage which should be regarded as inalienably part of the structure of the whole song.[59] The verses refer clearly to Israel whose change of fortune is to 'startle' the nations.

In the identification of the servant with Israel two tides meet. The weak and demoralized servant drained of initiative and suffering on account of sin evident in Isaiah 40–48 encounters the servant of the Songs from Isaiah 49–55 who is vigorous, faithful and suffering on account of the prophetic office. It is that identification which has resulted in the description of the servant as 'Israel' in Isaiah 49:3. It is a very early 'touching up' in the light of the association of the final servant passage with the previous ones. The identification of the two servants relating to the two halves of Deutero-Isaiah's record potentially provides a whole new theological context for the Exile. The alternative perspective to the community of Israel paying the price of their sins becomes Israel witnessing to the persistence of faith, tenaciously holding on in adversity, offering suffering as in some way atoning and life-giving for the world: 'by his bruises we are healed' (Isaiah 53:5b).

There is presented in the identification of the servant with Israel a whole new template for the relationship between the people of God and the nations. Just as the prophet stands in relation to his people, so is Israel to the nations. As the prophet's faithfulness and tenacity to the point of suffering is life-giving for the nation, so Israel's presence among the nations as a servant, even to the point of the Exile's humiliation, brings life. It has taken the promise made to Abraham 'and in you all the families of the earth shall be blessed' (Genesis 12:3b) to a quite unexpected place. From being a spectator of the servant's suffering and indeed its cause, the fluidity of the final servant poem allows Israel to be dressed in the mantle of the servant.

The disciple who edited the oracles of Deutero-Isaiah shared the master's creativity and delight in contrasts and juxtapositions when he had the inspiration to unite the whole work by presenting king and prophet in counterpoint. He brought together festal and prophetic traditions, Temple and Tent, in a totally new and explosive way to the extent that, in the final servant song, allusions to royal destiny are absorbed into prophetic biography. He realized that the person of the prophet had implications that might match the words he had delivered.

Deutero-Isaiah's relationship as a prophet to exiled Israel becomes the type of Israel's relationship with the Gentiles. In him, the prophetic vocation to bear suffering and persecution on account of faithfulness to God's call, and so become a source of healing, is translated to describe Israel's life in relationship to the nations. His biography triggered the figure of the Suffering Servant with its myriad of mysterious resonances. The verdict once passed upon Jeremiah is the only accolade fitting for the prophet to the exiles:

In typical Hebrew fashion the word was made flesh.[60]

Points for Discussion

1. We are told by modern science that we live in a space-time continuum. Deutero-Isaiah brings together reflections about God as creator (space) and God as responsible for the sweep of history (time). Which of these is more real for your own faith?

2. What are the main positive developments between a 'Yahweh only' faith and Deutero-Isaiah's articulation of 'Only Yahweh'.

3. In your experience can suffering ever be atoning?

4. Does the final Servant Song provide a helpful model for understanding the relationship between the community of faith and the world?

5. How do you explain the persistence of faith in the face of so much suffering and disappointment?

Key Bible Passages

Isaiah 48:3–11 (Polemic Genre disputation: Cyrus as God's new thing); Isaiah 52:7–10 (Prophetic reapplication of the New Year Festival); Isaiah 52:13–53:12 (Suffering Servant).

Further Reading

R. N. Whybray, *The Second Isaiah*, Old Testament Guides, Sheffield (1983).

Walter Brueggemann, *Hopeful Imagination*, London (1992).

H. G. M. Williamson, *Variations on a Theme: King, Messiah and Servant in the Book of Isaiah*, Carlisle (1998).

Figure 7. Reconstruction of a section of King Nebuchadnezzar's Processional Way in Babylon. (Vorderasiatisches Museum, Berlin.)

Endnotes

[1] Isaiah 40:3.

[2] Other examples include: Isaiah 42:10–13; 45:8; 48:20f. 49:13; 52:9f. and 54: 1f. 'This is a form of psalm found only in the prophecy of Deutero-Isaiah and is the product of his prophecy. It is an "eschatological" hymn of praise, since Israel's answering exultation assumes that God's final act has already taken place.' C. Westermann, *Isaiah 40–66*, London (1968), p. 205.

[3] See H. H. Schmid, *Altorientalische Welt in der alttestamentlichen Theologie*, pp. 54–5.

[4] Examples of this form include: Isaiah 41:8–13, 14–16; 43:1–4, 5–7; 44:1–5.

[5] Compare the change at Ps 22:22 or Lamentations 3:57 which actually includes an oracular 'Do not fear!'.

[6] J. Begrich, 'Das priesterliche Heilsorakel', *ZAW* 52 (1934), pp. 81–92 identified the form of an oracle and its connection with the lament. He regarded the form as used by Deutero-Isaiah as a literary imitation. H. E. Von Waldow, *Anlass und Hintergrund der Verkündigung des Deuterojesaja*, Dissertation, Bonn (1953) taking up the closeness of Deutero-Isaiah's

oracles to the lament form, has suggested that they are not imitations but were actually delivered as part of worship. However, the fact that a personal oracle is applied to the collective 'Jacob-Israel' already distances it from its original setting.

[7] Examples of this form include Isaiah 41:17–20; 42:14–17; 43:16–21; 49:7–12. See J. Begrich, *Studien zu Deuterojesaja*, Stuttgart (1938) and C. Westermann, *Isaiah 40–66*, pp. 13ff.

[8] Examples of this form include (i) Against Israel: Isaiah 43:22–28; 50:1–3; (ii) Against the nations and their gods: 41:1–5; 41:21–29; 43:8–13; 44:6–8; 45:20–25.

[9] Isaiah 44:7b: 'who has announced from of old the things to come' cannot refer to the recent rise of Cyrus but could refer to the exile.

[10] Disputations that are part of the Polemic Genres include Isaiah 42:18–25; 46:5–11; 48:1–11. These are to be differentiated from a 'creation type' found in 40:12–26; 20:27–31; 44:24–28; 45:9–13.

[11] Various passages in Deutero-Isaiah ridicule the Babylonian idols. C. Westermann argues for these as a specific layer of secondary editing: 'The polemic against the manufacture of idols in 40:19f and 41:6f; 42:17; 44:9–20; 45:16f, 20b and 46:5–8 forms a group of homogenous additions.' C. Westermann, *Isaiah 40–66*, p. 29.

[12] B. Lindars, 'Tidings to Zion', *BJRL* 68 (1985/6), p. 47.

[13] For a specific example of the combination of forms in Isaiah 49:14–26 see C. Westermann, *Isaiah 40–66*, p. 14. For an older view of continuity see J. Muilenburg, *Interpreters Bible*, vol. V, New York (1956), 'Introduction to Isaiah 40–66'.

[14] J. Blenkinsopp, 'Second Isaiah – Prophet of Universalism', *JSOT* 41 (1988), p. 84: 'The break between 40–48 and 49–55 is also at least as clear as between 40–55 and 56–66.'

[15] (Isaiah 42:1–4); 49:1–6; 50:4–9; 52:13–53:12.

[16] C. Westermann, *Isaiah 40–66*, p. 20. P. E. Dion, 'L'Universalisme religieux dans les différentes couches rédactionelles d'Isaïe 40–55', *Biblica* 51 (1970), pp. 161–182.

[17] T. N. D. Mettinger, *A Farewell to the Servant Songs*, Scripta Minora, Lund (1983), pp. 18ff. Another supporter of the Servant Songs as part of the primary editing of Deutero-Isaiah's oracle is R. Rendtorff, *The Old Testament, An Introduction*, London (1985), pp. 193ff.

[18] *ANET*, pp. 315–316.

[19] Deutero-Isaiah also uses a very similar device when on occasion he expands the 'I' in an oracle that includes the form of the 'self-praise of deity'. Examples of this include Isaiah 45:7; 48:12–13; 51:13,15 and 16. These are the only identifiable forms which the prophet seems to have taken over directly from the environment of the exile rather than from the traditions of Zion or Jacob-Israel. See P. E. Dion, 'Le genre littéraire

Sumérien de l' 'hymne à soi-même' et quelques passages du Deutéro-Isaïe', *Revue Biblique* 74 (1967), pp. 215–34.

[20] Compare with the 'enthronement psalms', for instance, Ps 47; 93; 96–99.

[21] This is the reversal of the prophetic vision of Ezekiel 10–11 who sees the glory depart from the Temple to be with the exiles.

[22] For instance Isaiah 42:14–17.

[23] In the trial speeches of Deutero-Isaiah ṣdq often carries a forensic significance relating to the one vindicated or 'declared in the right', for example, Isaiah 41:26; 43:9; 43:26.

[24] H. H. Schmid, *Gerechtigkeit als Weltordnung*, p. 133.

[25] Isaiah 41:21–29; 43:8–13; 44:6–8; 46:9–11; 48:3–11. Cf. 42:8–9; 43:16–21.

[26] The use of the adverb mē'ôlām (literally 'from eternity') in Isaiah 46:9 clearly identifies the total sweep of Israel's history and not just recent events.

[27] An exception is the conclusion of the oracle referring to God's conflict with the dragon and the deep, Isaiah 51:10.

[28] J. Scullion, *Isaiah 40–66*, p. 30 notes that bārā' occurs in Deutero-Isaiah (17 times), in *P* (10 times), in Trito-Isaiah (3 times), in Psalms (4 times) and elsewhere in the Old Testament (15 times). Deutero-Isaiah contains 17 instances out of 49 of its occurrences in the Bible.

[29] Compare also Isaiah 66:22.

[30] A. Schoors, *I am God your Saviour*, p. 289.

[31] Similarly, the court speech in Isaiah 45:20–25 presents the possibility of the 'goal' of history, beyond the demise of Babylon, when the survivors are gathered and there is universal recognition and worship of the one true God.

[32] B. Duhm, *Das Buch Jesaia*, Göttingen (1892). The medieval Jewish commentator Ibn Ezra is usually credited as the first to raise doubts about the unity of the Book of Isaiah. It was not until the eigthteenth century that the second part of the Book of Isaiah was clearly linked with an anonymous prophet at the end of the Babylonian exile in the works of J.C. Döderlein, Altdorf (1755) and J. G. Eichhorn, Leipzig (1783).

[33] S. Mowinckel, *Jesaja-disiplene. Profeten fra Jesaja til Jeremiah*, Oslo (1925). See also, J. H. Eaton, 'The Origin of the Book of Isaiah', *VT* 9 (1959), pp. 138–157; D. Jones, 'The Traditio of the Oracles of Isaiah of Jerusalem', *ZAW* 67 (1955), pp. 226–46.

[34] R. E. Clements, 'The Unity of the Book of Isaiah', *Interpretation* 36 (1982), pp. 117–129; 'Beyond Tradition History, Deutero-Isaianic development of First Isaiah's Themes', *JSOT* 31 (1985), pp. 95–113.

[35] J. Vermeylen, 'L'Unité du livre d'Isaïe', in ed. J. Vermeylen, *The Book of Isaiah*, Leuven (1989), pp. 11–53.

[36] R. Coggins, *Isaiah*, The Oxford Bible Commentary, ed. John Barton and John Muddiman, Oxford (2001), p. 436.

[37] B. S. Childs, *Introduction to the Old Testament as Scripture*, London (1979) and *Old Testament Theology in a Canonical Context*, London (1985). R. F. Melugin seems to be arguing for something similar at the end of his form-critical work when he writes: 'We should not abandon historical scholarship, but we should recognise that the authority of the scriptures is rooted primarily in the completed Biblical texts.' (*The Formation of Isaiah 40–55*, p. 85.) W. Bruggemann, 'Unity and Dynamic in the Isaiah Tradition', *JSOT* 29 (1984), pp. 89–107 is concerned to interpret the final stage of the text, but as a sort of sociological pattern.

[38] H. G. M. Williamson, *The Book called Isaiah*, p. 18.

[39] *Op. cit.* p. 240.

[40] Paul D. Hanson, *Isaiah 40–66*, Interpretation, Louisville (1995), p. 187.

[41] 'On one point, however, there seems to be a measure of convergence which may prove to be of help to us, and this is that Chapters 60–62 are closest to the outlook of Deutero-Isaiah. As such, they are generally agreed to provide the earliest core of this material (and so, if anything does, to justify the title Trito-Isaiah), with the other chapters arranged around them having been written either in extension of them or in debate with them.' H. G. M. Williamson, *Variations on a Theme*, Carlisle (1998), p. 169.

[42] The postponement was related to unrighteous behaviour. The growing significance of a community defined by the keeping of regulations (see 56:2, keeping the sabbath) or 'law' is evident. 'But there is a subtle shift in emphasis from an announcement of what God is about to do to an admonition concentrating on what the community is to do.' (Paul D. Hanson, *Isaiah 40–66*, p. 193.)

[43] Isaiah 65:17 and 66:22. Travail followed by new creation anticipates later apocalyptic literature. If Isaiah 24–27 is an example of the latter it witnesses to the complex and lengthy editing which the Isaianic corpus underwent.

[44] The first verse of Trito-Isaiah neatly sums up the theology of the whole of the Isaianic corpus. The first couplet uses the concepts familiar from Isaiah of Jerusalem and the second those characteristic of Deutero-Isaiah:

> Thus says the Lord:
> Maintain justice (mišpāṭ), and do what is right (ṣedāqâ),
> for soon my salvation (yᵉšûʿā) will come,
> and my deliverance (ṣedāqâ) be revealed. (Isaiah 56:1)

[45] G. I. Davies, 'The Destiny of the Nations in the Book of Isaiah' in ed. J. Vermeylen, *The Book of Isaiah*, pp. 119–120.

[46] P. Bonnard, *Le Second Isaïe*, p. 75: 'Plus encore que Isaïe, c'est Jérémie qui a été le maître de notre prophète'. There is reason, too, to compare Ezekiel with Deutero-Isaiah.

[47] G. von Rad, *The Message of the Prophets*, London (1968), p. 57.

[48] The royal (anoint, v. 1) and the prophetic (proclaim, vv. 1 and 2) also converge in the text of Trito-Isaiah in the commission reported in Isaiah 61:1–3a. The passage further reflects, very specifically, the language of the prologue of Deutero-Isaiah. The 'servant' commissioned clearly claims to carry on the task of Deutero-Isaiah in the new circumstances of the return. It is a further witness to the interplay of prophet and king at the end of the exile. It is not part of the series in Deutero-Isaiah which may be reckoned to mark the high-tide of prophecy in the Hebrew Scriptures.

[49] C. Westermann, *Isaiah 40–66*, p. 211.

[50] C. Westermann, *Isaiah 40–66*, p. 131.

[51] A. Schoors, *ETL* 40 (1964). pp. 35ff. analyses 42:6–7 as an oracle relating to Cyrus.

[52] Cf. Jeremiah 10:19.

[53] P. E. Dion, *Biblica* 51 (1970), p. 172: '. . . le troisième <<chant>>, pure <<confession>> prophétique d'un caractère éminemment personnel . . .'. The mention in Isaiah 50:7b 'therefore I have set my face like flint' is reminiscent of the assurance given to the prophet Ezekiel (Ezekiel 3:8–9).

[54] R. N. Whybray, *Isaiah 40–66*, p. 172.

[55] J. Day, *God's Conflict with the Dragon and the Sea*, Cambridge (1985), p. 124. He identifies Psalm 22 'where the suffering and vindication of a figure is explicitly associated with the coming of the Kingdom of God (cf. vv. 28ff., ET 27ff.), a juxtaposition most easily understood if the figure is that of the king'. See also Psalm 18 and Psalm 144.

[56] R. N. Whybray, *Isaiah 40–66*, p. 172.

[57] A balanced 'Myth and Ritual' approach to the issues under discussion is to be found in I. Engnell, 'The Ebed Yahweh Songs and the Suffering Messiah in Deutero-Isaiah', *BJRL* 31 (1948), pp. 54–93. Engnell's approach is commended by J. Eaton, *Festal Drama in Deutero-Isaiah*, London (1979), p. 4.

[58] In Trito-Isaiah 'servants' used in the plural rather than the collective becomes the name for those who number amongst the faithful minority as opposed to the addressed majority (Isaiah 65:13–15).

[59] R. N. Whybray, *Isaiah 40–66*, p. 169 writes: 'But the minority view, held by Coppens, Snaith, and Orlinsky among others, that 52:13–15

constitute a separate piece, has much to commend it.' However, the opening verses of the passage (Isaiah 52:13–15) correspond to the closing verses (Isaiah 53:11b–12) which are both in the direct speech of Yahweh.

[60] J. Peterson, 'Jeremiah', in Matthew Black (ed.), *Peake's Commentary*, London (1962), p. 539, paragraph 466ff.

CHAPTER 8

The Single Stream: Hebrew Monotheism

The overwhelming significance of Creator and creation emerges from a study of the sources of the Hebrew Scriptures in the light of their Ancient Near Eastern context. For the world in which Israel's faith took shape, creation theology formed the 'broad horizon' of all reflection on the nature of divinity and the significance of human beings within their environment. Emerging Hebrew identity was inside, not outside that world. What we have discovered is a dynamic process through which the distinctive faith of the Hebrews evolved within that environment, rather than an original deposit of truth which simply had to be guarded and passed on.

It is unlikely that Yahweh was himself in origin a creator deity. He was of the 'God of the Fathers' type, but with specific features, such as association with a holy mountain, which his connection with Sinai brought with it. However, if biblical theology begins with Abraham, and therefore at a moment of transition, then it begins with the leavening by the Tent tradition of the faith of the settled land. The early identification of the God of the Father with the Canaanite creator-god El marks the very beginning of biblical religion and already identifies the significance of creation-faith. From its very inception biblical faith has a universal dimension and the call of the Hebrews is set within the plan and purpose of God for his whole creation.

In all probability Moses was the founder of distinct Hebrew Yahwism. He established its monolatry, exclusive commitment to a single deity which was the hallmark of the God of the Fathers tradition, as the characteristic of Hebrew faith. The route to monotheism was via monolatry. This emphasizes the significance of the tenacity of the bond between the Hebrews and their God in making the breakthrough. Moses was responsible for the bond rather than for handing monotheism to the Hebrews. It was the reality of the Exodus experience, for which Moses was the interpreter, which established a deeply rooted sense of adoption and a genuine thanksgiving for rescue directed towards Yahweh, that was the foundation of the exclusive relationship.[1] At heart it was a genuine religious experience as a result of rescue at the Sea which imprinted itself on the consciousness of a community. Its survival through subsequent generations required the tenacity of the minority who held on to the significance of 'Yahweh only'; it necessitated the tireless dedication of their lives by the classical prophets to confront the nation in the name of Israel's God. Real loyalty, real sacrifice, genuine historical risk, shared religious experience were all ingredients of Israel's faith.

Canaanite civilization was a particular manifestation of the cultural sophistication of the Ancient Near East. It had significant political structures based on kingship, developed agriculture, complex commercial activity, the differentiation of occupations necessary for city life, literary and artistic achievements as well as a vibrant polytheistic religious tradition which interpreted the processes of creation. It was the interaction of the Hebrews' Tent-identity, as an agent and ingredient, with that world that was potentially fruitful. This was possible because the memory and the force for the Hebrews of living at a boundary was never snuffed out, though the wick sometimes smouldered. It meant that the potential of Yahwism to be uncomfortable and confronter of the status quo was there from the very beginning.

That potential had to be awakened and nurtured, otherwise it might have simply been neutralized and overwhelmed by the custom and practice of the settled land. It was the ministry of the classical prophets which provoked Israel into a fresh awareness of the potential of her boundary faith and insisted that she live with its uncomfortableness. They recalled Israel to 'Yahweh only' and related the holiness of God to moral integrity. They brought a seriousness and sense of purpose to being the people of God. The eighth-century prophets, in particular, were responsible for a defining moment in Israel's development. With them the reciprocal nature of covenant is established. The framework of interdependence and responsibility that was conceived to operate across creation is applied with a greater intensity to the relationship between God and his people insomuch that it can be pushed to breaking point.

The fact that absolute loyalty was, in the circumstances of the settled land, directed towards the creator was of considerable significance. It was exclusive commitment to the creator which in the end passed over into monotheism. A synthesis of ingredients of both the steppe and the settled land is involved. Of this monotheism it has been said:

> it is arguably monotheism (at first monolatry), rather than God's mighty acts in history as used to be argued, that most distinguishes the Old Testament from the religions of the other nations of the Ancient Near East.[2]

The Hebrews did not come at monotheism as a philosophical concept. Hebrew monotheism grows out of experience, relationship and loyalty in the context of Canaanite civilization.

It is no coincidence that Deutero-Isaiah's strong monotheism is linked to faith in the creator:

> For thus says the Lord, who created the heavens: he is God; who formed who earth and made it; he established it; he did not create it a chaos, he formed it to be inhabited: I am the Lord, and there is no other. (Isaiah 45:18)

Already, the theology of the Ancient Near East had exalted the creator to a status of his own. In Canaanite mythology he presided over the council of the gods, and nothing – including the building of a palace for Ba'al – happened without his consent. In ancient Egypt the high god was the author of creation, and the other gods were simply, like human beings, servants of order. In ancient Mesopotamia, Marduk in the creation epic becomes 'King of the gods' by virtue of his victory over Tiāmat, which enables the creation of the ordered world. That combination of creator and combat deity was true also at Jerusalem where El Elyon achieved a unique and exalted position. The witness of the Wisdom tradition within Israel's own religious territory had also identified the creator as author of providence and the only god that truly mattered. He was God. Exclusive worship of the creator within the context of the Ancient Near East, therefore, had the effect of further marginalizing the significance of the other deities to a shadowy or eventually angelic identity. It accentuated a process already under way.

Reflection on the life of heaven in the Ancient Near East assumed that the emotions experienced by humans were also part of the divine world. Love, jealousy, intrigue, anger, compassion were also part of the nature of the gods. Indeed, they had priority over human emotions. As we noted, once the theatre for divine emotions is removed in heaven by emerging monotheism, then the relationship between God and creation, and in particular, God and human creatures, takes on a quite new significance. Divine emotion is redirected. The human creature is now the recipient of the divine love, anger and compassion. In other words, there is a corollary to developing monotheism and that is the heightened significance of the human story. It is no longer marginal; it is the object of the divine emotions. Monotheism is highly compatible with a significant characteristic of the religion of the God of the Fathers, that is the emphasis on the human story.

A very important conclusion must be drawn. Although God's occasional and episodic 'mighty acts in history' may not characterize that which constitutes Israel's identity, yet the significance of history as the place where God is encountered is indeed distinctive. It is the fact that the only God is the creator which enables a new axis of relationship and a heightened awareness of God's responsibility to and for his creation. In that relationship God is not simply interested in maintaining the cyclical processes but is also intimately involved in each unique human story; here we encounter a particularly distinctive feature of the Hebrew Scriptures. It is intimately bound up with Hebrew monotheistic faith and the distinctive epic literature it generated. A specific and early example of that is the Yahwistic account of Israel's history and God's involvement, which included the primaeval, patriarchal and Mosaic periods in a connected narrative.

It was in the Jerusalem traditions that Israel had the implications of Yahweh as creator most emphatically spelt out.

Yahweh-Elyon[3] was enthroned over world order. The implications of the creation theology of the settled land were clearly acknowledged within Israel's own religious institutions. We have noted how the Jerusalem Temple traditions enabled both the Yahwistic and Priestly traditions to reflect on the significance of God as creator within the Primaeval History. They were also the major inspiration of the prophet Deutero-Isaiah.

Both the Yahwistic and Priestly traditions assume that God as creator involves him also in an ongoing responsibility for, and relationship with, his creation. God not only creates but also carries his creation, such is his emotional involvement. For the Yahwist it is expressed in primaeval time with such touches as Yahweh himself making clothes for Adam and Eve on their expulsion from the Garden, and a mark put upon Cain to protect him from human rough justice. It is further focused in the blessing of Abraham set in a universal context and is worked out in a lively relationship between Yahweh and Abraham's often wayward offspring. For the Priestly tradition God is bound to the created order and to the People of God by a series of solemn covenants. He commits himself to his creation. His commitment to the Hebrews is a simple intensification of his commitment to the welfare of the whole created order.

We must also note the reverse perspective in the Primaeval History. Not only is it true that God is emotionally attached to his creation, but for both the Yahwistic and the Priestly traditions creation is presented as needing God as helper. It confirms as image to negative the understanding of the complexity of Hebrew monotheism.

A brief excursus into the parallel but different understandings of the Yahwistic and Priestly traditions on the reason why creation needs to be carried is helpful. For the Yahwistic tradition the Wisdom analysis of creation's predicament is dominant. That is to say, 'human inventions' are mainly responsible for the state of things. The presence of Wisdom's hand suggests that human responsibility is to be taken seriously, and that the stories are not just a literary device for expressing the way the world is, without really being concerned about human culpability. The Yahwistic Primaeval History ends with the jarring chord of Babel. It has to be so; the human creatures disrupt the good order of creation and cannot on their own survive the consequences of their action. Creation needs the sustaining and transforming activity of God. God is, therefore, both the one who creates and the one who calls Abraham.

The Priestly tradition is something of a contrast; it allows that human wickedness is part of the picture, but not the total story. Taken independently, it is commonly noted that for the Priestly tradition human wickedness appears in primaeval time and is reflected throughout Israel's history but there is no moment of fall or explanation of its arrival. However, the Priestly Flood Narrative is presented as a cosmic catastrophe and as the shadow to the Genesis 1 creation narrative. The Flood Narrative is made to correspond to the creation account. The deep,[4] the 'wind of God',[5] the description of the animals central to both stories,[6] the creation blessings pronounced over animals and human beings,[7] all bond the two accounts firmly together. This suggests that the Priestly tradition is presenting 'creation' and 'fall' not as two events but one; inevitably creation has a 'shadow side'. The cost of creation is creatureliness. The moment that God creates a world that is truly other than himself and genuinely free, then contingency, estrangement and sin are inevitable. The act of creation therefore involves God in nurture, in responsibility for what he has made and in drawing it back to himself in such a way that its freedom is respected. If creation involves the necessity of fall, then being creator involves being helper.

For the prophet Deutero-Isaiah the condition of the exiles presented only too pathetically the need for a saviour:

> But this is a people robbed and plundered,
> all of them trapped in holes and hidden in prisons;
> they have become a prey with no one to rescue,
> a spoil with no one to say, 'Restore!' (Isaiah 42:22)

The condition of the exile was a symptom not only of erring Israel, but also of creation's languishing. Nothing less than renewed world order heralded by Cyrus was needed. In bringing about this 'new thing' God was both creator and saviour. The divine responsibility for creation is an inalienable consequence of being the creator. The theology of the servant is transferred to God:

'I have made, and I will bear;
I will carry and will save.' (Isaiah 46:4b)

Hebrew monotheism is far from being a scientific, calculated, mechanistic theism. It emerges as a result of a dynamic encounter enabled by the leavening effect of the Tent tradition and its monolatry mixing with the creation-faith of the settled land. It developed as a result of passion, loyalty, commitment and relationship which is particularly evident in the ministry of the classical prophets. God himelf is never conceived to be devoid of relationship. As the sole occupant of heaven his emotions are directed towards his creation. That new axis affirmed the insight of the God of the Fathers tradition that told and re-told the human story. 'God loves stories' as the Jewish tradition insists. God is encountered in the human story and in the events of history. God's intimate involvement with his creation inevitably involves him in being saviour.

What do we mean by saying God is saviour and that he carries his creation? The significance of that statement is tied up with Israel's unique sense of God as judge which gave theological expression to the fracture between divinity and the created order. The hard-won acknowledgement of the transcendence of God, his being other than and separate from his creation, means that his presence can transform, change and renew his creation. It brings to the sense of God carrying his creation the significance of redemption. God is both creator and redeemer. If that is so then it is characterisitic of Hebrew monotheism that it articulates complexity in the Godhead. Precisely God's emotional involvement with what he has made means his responsibility for it is not exhausted simply by being the creator. The dynamic of the evolution of Hebrew faith is reflected in the being of God himself.

When did Hebrew monotheism with its rich web of connections emerge? We may quote J. Day again:

> I would argue that it is clear that there was indeed a monolatrous party already in the pre-exilic period . . ., and absolute monotheism was first given explicit expression by the prophet Deutero-Isaiah in the exile and became fully operative in the post-exilic period.[8]

According to Day, the dynamic process from which monotheism emerged needed the whole of the period of the Hebrew Kings as its gestation period. Certainly, the prophet Deutero-Isaiah clearly articulates the sole presence of Yahweh in heaven and the principle that all things are resolved in a single divine personality:

> I form light and create darkness,
> I make weal and create woe;
> I the Lord do all these things. (Isaiah 45:7)

Further, monotheism as we have encountered it in Israel required the prophetic vision of God's activity in history, of the articulation of God's judgement as a consequence of his transcendence and of the radical break between divinity and the natural order. This clutch of developments, latent in Israel's boundary faith, were emphasized as a consequence of the threat of Assyria in the eighth century and of Babylon by the end of the seventh century. Throughout that period, articulated by the great prophets, theology was adjusting to the newly crystalizing conviction of Yahweh's sole control of history to be understood in the context of the menace of world empire. It has been captured by G. Von Rad:

> The prophets were therefore the first men in Israel to proclaim over and over again and on an ever-widening basis that salvation comes in the shadow of judgement.[9]

Isaiah of Jerusalem had to deal with a low ebb in that he witnessed the demise of Samaria, and the destruction of all the fortified cities of Judah apart from Jerusalem. He had to manage a crisis in theology at considerable personal cost. He did so not by maintaining hope despite the terrible events that had taken place, but by maintaining that there could be no hope until the finality of God's judgement had worked itself out. We were able to comment at the conclusion of Chapter 6:

> The possibility of something beyond devastation is coming very close to the concept of radical renewal and new creation.

For the prophets Jeremiah and Ezekiel who managed the tiller of faith through the destruction of Jerusalem and the consequent Exile, the circumstances were even bleaker. The absolute end was reached. The theology of the Ancient Near East allowed for the articulation of the point of absolute finality. According to all the canons of the governing conventions of the Ancient Near East, the destruction of the state was the end of the theological structure which undergirded it. The special relationship with the state god had been shown to be terminated. It was no longer of any consequence or validity; the evidence was in the rubble of the devastated ruins of the state Temple. The classical prophets did not shrink from turning this concept around. They proclaimed that the honour of God himself might demand that he initiate the end of the relationship with his people. Devastation might be evidence not of God's powerlessness, but of his holiness. When the end is decreed by the sole-creator there can be no mitigating circumstances.

It was the fact that the point of finality had been reached that enabled Deutero-Isaiah to awaken the dormant prophecy of Isaiah of Jerusalem and to take up an answering dialogue with the classical prophets who had also predicted the devastation of Jerusalem. They had insisted that the absolute end must be reached before any hope could be presented again. Israel's faith had to think the unthinkable. There might be hope not in the revival of a remnant but beyond the end. The absolute end was, in the misery of devastation and exile, reached and breached. There was presented not a hope based on the renewal of nature's cycles but grounded in real corporate resurrection.

A radical hope emerged from the womb of exilic darkness. Deutero-Isaiah is breaking new ground and stands as the forerunner in this process. Ultimately, that hope required nothing less than the articulation of a clean break with the old order, the honouring of transcendence and the concept of a totally new act of God the equivalent of nothing less than a 'new creation'.

It was the setting forth of a fresh divine initiative beyond the end that enabled theological reflection to develop first the possibility of creation out of nothing and ultimately the possibility of personal life beyond death. The Exile truly was a moment of birth, a theological breakthrough, a quantum leap. Something unique in the Ancient Near East, which we have expressed in terms of the exploding of the wineskins, had broken through in Hebrew religion. All the evidence points to John Day's assessment that absolute monotheism was first given explicit expression in the Exile and became fully operative only in the post-exilic period.

Yet there remains one illogicality. It can be claimed that we see clearly in the Yahwist's Primaeval History the breakthrough to monotheism already made. Rather as, in the words of Wellhausen, the prophet Elijah stands in relationship to the classical prophets 'like a bird whose song heralds the coming of morning'[10] so the Yahwist anticipates in a remarkable way the vision of Deutero-Isaiah. The Yahwist's monotheistic faith is still youthful and its vibrance carries some as yet untamed borderlands. The episode of the 'sons of God and the daughters of men' in Genesis 6:1–4 is the most obvious of these 'borderlands'. Yet those verses are arguably unique and an exception in the Yahwist's Primaeval History.[11] Apart from that there are the plural imperatives which reflect the existence of the divine council. Yahweh God says: 'See, the man has become like one of us, knowing good and evil' (Genesis 3:22a), and in the episode of the Tower of Babel the divine reflection is reported 'Come, let us go down, and confuse their language there' (Genesis 11:7a). But these elements are simply evidence of the pre-history of the traditions with which the Yahwist is working, his respect for those traditions and the fact that he stands early in Israel's harnessing of them. They witness to a time past when the divine conversation was between the gods rather than with human creatures.

There are two crucial indicators that the threshold of monotheism has been crossed by the Yahwist. One relates to the structure of the narrative, the other to a more specific point. Firstly, we must note again the significance of the blessing upon Abraham in Genesis 12:1–3. It exhibits a close relationship with the Primaeval History not only because it mentions 'all nations', but also because creator and blessing go together. A blessing was one of those channels that linked the stability of primaeval order to the present. It connects with the patriarchs and subsequent Hebrew history because the recipient of the blessing is Abraham. But clearly the disruption of creation has been spelt out in the Primaeval History, and Abraham is called precisely as God's response to primaeval instability. In other words, against all convention and Ancient Near Eastern religious logic the 'lifeline' is working backwards from Abraham to creation. There is a real breakthrough to a concept of redemption; the full implications of what he had achieved may well have escaped the Yahwist. The significance is that the fracture between the divine and the stability of the created order has taken place. God is other than the created order and potentially the agent of its transformation. The stability of the eternal hills is no longer creation's reason to hope. Rather, hope is grounded in the redemptive presence of God over against any latent hope within creation itself.

Secondly, we must focus on the specific instance of the Flood Narrative. As we noted above, clearly the tensions generated by the competing gods of Mesopotamia working on the one hand for the destruction of humankind and on the other for the preservation of humankind are resolved in the single personality of Yahweh. The words of C. Westermann are worth repeating: 'dissension between the gods becomes dissension within God'.[12] The Yahwist even opens the door to the consequent suffering of God. Certainly, God as judge as well as sustainer and helper has breached the barriers of Ancient Near Eastern religion which prevented the development of the concept of divine transcendence. Hebrew monotheism is clearly already encapsulated in the Yahwist's prologue (Genesis 6:5–8) to the Flood Narrative.

There do seem to be anticipatory influences at work that enabled the Yahwist's breakthrough. We have recognized the similarity between the ministry of the eighth-century prophets and God's direct confrontation of his creatures in the Primaeval History. Interestingly, the Flood Narrative in the hands of the Yahwist expresses a judgement as radical as that faced by Isaiah or Jeremiah. The Yahwist had the resources that gave expression to raw judgement in the Flood Narrative that may have enabled him to articulate radical transcendence. Whether the Flood Narrative as adapted by the Yahwist is truly shrewd insight into human corporate moral breakdown or in any way generated by and reflective of threatening contemporary political circumstances is a question raised by our conclusions. Any decision on the evidence has to take seriously the optimistic theology of the overflow of Israel's prosperity to the nations: 'in you all the families of the earth shall be blessed' (Genesis 12: 3b). That perspective does not yet seem to be aware of any imperial menace on the horizon that threatens the termination of Israel's and Judah's existence.

Our conclusion is that with the Yahwist's work we meet the first overture of true Hebrew monotheism. All of the basic characteristics have been presented and the rich associations have already been made. He anticipates Deutero-Isaiah:

'I form light and create darkness',
'I have made and I will bear'.

Monotheistic faith as it is presented in the context of Hebrew religion has further major insights that it has been possible to identify. We may simply take in turn the Temple and Tutor traditions and reflect on the major issues which they marshal.

The Jerusalem Traditions that cluster around the image of 'Temple' present human beings as part of cosmic order and are able to articulate the world as a single total environment in which no area is disconnected from the whole. The different boundaries which define human life and make it manageable such as kingship, justice, commerce, agriculture, war or worship are not isolated, separate, fragmentary areas. All interact, affect one another and create a total picture. There is, in the end, a single environment, and only by living as a healthy part of that whole is there real health, or shālôm. The contemporary awareness of the environment, the growing sense that animals have to be reared in a healthy and wholesome way, for their own sake as well as to prevent their malfunctioning affecting human health and welfare, could be a straight deduction from biblical monotheism. The world operates throughout its length and breadth with a balance and with a harmony which need to be understood and respected. There is a total ecology which must be handled carefully if a healthy equilibrium is to be maintained.

Human dominion was part of that picture; it is celebrated in Psalm 8 as well as in Genesis 1. But it is in the context of the presentation of the divine order and the spelling out of the distinction between Creator and creature. It cannot be overstated that the dominion was not a blank cheque without responsibility. Dominion was given within the framework of an ecology. There were checks and balances by reason of living as part of a balanced environment where all the parts affect one another. For the ancient world it was evident and axiomatic that human beings were part of creation and consequently part of order and not separate from it. Biblical theology therefore takes that for granted. The Primaeval History speaks about the consequences of human beings refusing to recognize their creaturely limits. The abuse of the human environment triggers a moral recoil which damages the equilibrium of the delicate relationships within which creation operates.

Order was given a strong moral element, in that justice (mišpāṭ) in the Jerusalem traditions was intimately connected with right order (ṣedeq). In the hands of the prophet Isaiah of Jerusalem, justice becomes the major governing priority. Justice, including the wholesome functioning of society so that it does not exploit the poor, is critical for the well-being of total order. The neglect of justice in the human realm will have a detrimental impact on the functioning of the natural environment. The interconnectedness of things meant, for instance, that neglect of justice might produce a change in the climatic conditions. The New Year Festival celebration related royal justice and the return of the autumn rains within the complexity of the order that it handled. Once such connections seemed arbitrary, fanciful and a touch primitive. The modern world is relearning that the 'one world' and the 'global village' has its total functioning closely interconnected. Justice and the integrity of creation cannot be separated.

The Tutor traditions, by which we have characterized the presence of Wisdom within Israel's mainstream religious practice, were a particular witness to God as creator and its implications. Wisdom was a close ally to developing Hebrew monotheism in reflecting on 'the only God that mattered'. The integrity of Wisdom which insisted that there was no centre to the universe and that all human beings are equidistant from God brought a high moral dimension to reflection on monotheism. It enabled reflection upon God within a moral context which matched the awesomeness of the task. Wisdom insisted that even to speak of God totally relativized everything and everyone – God has no favourites. Everything partakes of the sacredness of being his handiwork. The generosity of God knows of no artificial boundaries. Human behaviour must take this into account or fail.

The contemporary application of Wisdom's principles and their relevance for a world where ethnic cleansing has become a way of life is evident. There is unfortunately much truth in Cupitt's statement:

> So far as the history of religions is concerned it is undeniable that religion is very close to culture, and God to ethnicity.[13]

In the name of religion, culture and ethnicity can become elevated to idols with horrendous implications. The doctrine of God as creator, prior and unassailable, alone stands between true religion which judges prejudices, and religious tribalism which confirms prejudices and legitimizes the worst excesses of human behaviour. Without a proper doctrine of God as creator, faith is not simply handicapped, it is ultimately manipulated and perverted. Religion is reduced to a badge of tribalism. The perspective of each faith-community needs to be continually cleansed by contact with the irreducible confession that God is without reservation the universal creator. He can be nobody's exclusive private possession. Wisdom achieves this for biblical theology.

It has been pointed out by J. Sacks that:

> It is no accident that the most intractable conflicts of recent years – Northern Ireland, the wars and massacres of the Middle East, even the emerging rivalries of Eastern Europe – have had a religious dimension.[14]

The full recognition of the presence of Wisdom in biblical theology and in particular the moral authority it brings to the whole Bible through 'the Old Testament to the Hebrew Scriptures' in Genesis 1–11 is vital. That alone can judge and not foster the human instinct to put oneself, and not God, at the centre of the world. The recognition of Wisdom and its true significance in biblical theology can achieve the vision which Sacks seeks:

> To have faith in God as creator and ruler of the universe is to do more than to believe that God has spoken to us. It is to believe that God has spoken to others, in a language which we may not understand.[15]

In many ways the whole contemporary human rights debate and the attempt to establish the reality of 'war crimes' that recognize a moral boundary which, even in war, should not be breached, is an expression in our own day of Wisdom's principles. It has been said that 'human rights' is the only internationally uniting vision of the twenty-first century and potentially more powerful than any global forces including commercial, political or cultural interests. Is the emergence of human beings from cosmic evolution with their sense of the moral, of altruism and of mystery sufficient to generate a consensus that can unite a multicultural world? If so, then Wisdom's embers have not been quenched. The closeness of this to a religious vision of the world is evident.

The final word must be to identify the radical openness of biblical monotheism. It is a consequence of the fact that the Hebrew Scriptures did indeed trigger the potential assembled by the Ancient Near East that was never otherwise released. Ancient Near Eastern religious reflection never truly broke loose from the pantheistic roots whence it emerged. Divinity was about maintenance, about the eternal return and the stable status quo. The only true 'act of God' was creation itself, and therefore anything novel was to be shunned. Ecclesiastes articulates the frustration of this dominant perspective:

> What has been is what will be,
> and what has been done is what will be done;
> there is nothing new under the sun. (Ecclesiastes 1:9)

Hebrew monotheism, uniquely in the Ancient Near East, articulated the implications of real transcendence; that is, the consequence of a distinction between creator and creature: God and the world he had made. It was a new perspective to be handled carefully. It gave humanity a terrible freedom in that it desacralized the created order, opening the way for a detached scientific approach to creation's processes, but also unleashing the potential for unrestrained abuse of the created order. The veil of mystery that had been taken away needed replacing in a new form.

However, the new theological achievement in Hebrew monotheism opened the way for what has become known as 'eschatology'. If God is other than his creation then he can act in a radically new way to transform it as a whole. Openness to the possibility of a new act of God is the exciting prediction of fully developed Hebrew monotheism. It is something quite different from the merely miraculous. It is about the possibility of God's initiative beyond the absolute end. It is, therefore, less about tinkering with creation's processes and more about transformation. It is less about repairing and more about redemption. There is something 'eschatological', that is something final and ultimate, about such an act. In terms of the Jerusalem theology it means that alongside creation, as the only event that truly made a difference, can be set the potential for a new creation. There can be a new divine act that truly makes a difference.

There is ambiguity in this theological development; indeed, it is analogous to the ambiguity of the developments recorded in the Yahwistic Primaeval History. The possibility of a new act of God liberated creation from bondage to the status quo. There could be change, the poor could be raised up, the inequalities of life might be overthrown, the human heart could ache for something different. Indeed, the 'people of God' might seek to anticipate God's new order by going to creation's darkest corners to proclaim the coming new equilibrium which would transform the relationships of the world's order.

Conversely, misplaced trust in God's 'new thing' might be coupled to a particular political aspiration. All too easily, frustrated nationalism could claim a vehicle for its promotion. The hope for a Messiah might raise up a political agitator claiming, with false optimism, divine sanction to be the gateway of God's intended future. The expectation of God's new initiative would also dash the hopes of those who felt they had reached the pitch of human endurance and therefore God must intervene. The new theory would be tested by the silence of God. The conflagration of Jerusalem in 70 CE was such a terrible moment. The prediction of God's new initiative that is an inalienable aspect of Hebrew monotheism had – and has – to be handled with care. Those who think they can read God's purpose without seeing through a glass darkly must beware.

If God can act eschatologically, if he can act to bring about a new creation, then it is difficult to know how human beings could perceive or comprehend it. Nevertheless, the prophets set themselves up as heralds and watchmen of the new dawn. A modern scientist who develops a theory which predicts certain outcomes has to search carefully for evidence in the 'real world' that confirms the theory. So the prophets looked for confirmation of Hebrew monotheism in evidence of God's new initiative at work in Israel's history. Indeed, from the moment the Yahwist had placed the call of Abraham in the setting of God's response to the instability of primaeval time, Israel's history was firmly placed in the arena of God's 'new thing'. Initially, it was anticipated that success and the universal 'trickle down' of the consequent blessings would be evidence of the divine activity in Israel's story. It was the tradition of Deutero-Isaiah, classically in Isaiah 53, which astoundingly and bravely put the moment of Israel's perceived failure and the humiliation of exile within that frame. The one who is made to serve in carrying creation honours the servant who suffers.

Hebrew monotheism leaves us with an open future. It predicts that if God is God, then human beings must be open to his radically new initiative. There is always a new horizon beyond which the prophetic word is true. Expectancy and excitement are abroad:

> For I am about to create new heavens and a new earth;
> the former things shall not be remembered or come to mind.
> (Isaiah 65:17)

There is a future in God whose curtain is not yet lifted.

Points for Discussion

1. 'It is a characteristic of Hebrew monotheism that it articulates complexity in the Godhead.' What do you think is meant by this? Are there inadequacies to strict unitarianism?

2. How far can it be argued that Hebrew monotheism is responsible for the Western scientific approach to the natural order? What are the biblical limits to human dominion?

3. If righteousness, justice and peace as biblical concepts give expression to a divinely gifted world perceived to be a delicate equilibrium in which everything is inter-connected

and morally tuned, how do we begin to give that insight a priority in the way we express our faith? To what key contemporary issues does this insight relate?

4. Is the notion of human rights close to a perception of a religious view of the world?

5. In what ways could it be argued that religious faith is essential to the survival of a healthy world?

6. 'Hebrew monotheism predicts that if God is God, then human beings must be open to his radically new initiative.' How do you understand the significance of that statement for your own faith?

Key Bible Passages

Genesis 12:1–3 (the call and blessing of Abraham – Yahwistic narrative); Exodus 24:1–2, 9–11 (communion with God at Sinai); Jeremiah 31:31–34 (a new covenant); Isaiah 65:1–25 (a new creation).

Further Reading

C. Westermann, *Genesis 1–11*, London and Minneapolis (1984), 'The Theological Meaning of the Primeval Story', pp. 600–606.

E. W. Nicholson, *God and His People*, Oxford (1986), chapter 10: 'The Covenant and the Distinctiveness of Israel's Faith', pp. 191–217.

J. Day, *Yahweh and the Gods and Goddesses of Canaan*, Sheffield (2000), chapter 8, 'Conclusion – The Canaanite Gods and Goddesses and the Rise of Monotheism', pp. 226–33.

Figure 8. The Menorah, or seven-branched candlestick that stood in the Jerusalem Temple. Reconstruction by N. Avigad from a plaster fragment recovered from beneath the floor of a Herodian building. (Israel Exploration Society.)

Endnotes

[1] E. W. Nicholson, *God and His People,* Oxford (1986) p. 202 makes the perhaps darker point that the potential monolatry of the Exodus was consolidated by the military conquest of the Promised Land: 'In the indisputably ancient traditions of Yahweh's deliverance of Israel's ancestors from bondage in Egypt and of his victories on behalf of the tribes of Israel against their enemies during the early generations of Israel's emergence in Canaan, Yahweh was acknowledged to be the God who alone stood at the foundation and beginning of Israel.'

[2] J. Day, *Yahweh and the Gods and Goddesses of Canaan,* Sheffield (2000), p. 233.

[3] Ps 7:17 cf. 9:2; 92:1.

[4] Genesis 1:2 corresponding to Genesis 7:11.

[5] Genesis 1:2b corresponding to Genesis 8:1b.

[6] Genesis 1:25 corresponding to Genesis 6:20.

[7] Genesis 1:22 and 1:28 corresponding to Genesis 8:17 and Genesis 9:1.

[8] John Day, *Yahweh and the Gods and Goddesses of Canaan,* p. 228.

[9] G. von Rad, *The Message of the Prophets,* London (1968), p. 154.

[10] 'Elias glich einem Vogel, der vor dem Morgen singt', J. Wellhausen, *Grundrisse zum Alten Testament,* ed. R. Smend, Munich, (1965), p. 90. First published as 'Israelitisch-jüdische Religion', *Die Kultur der Gegenwart* ed. P. Hinneberg, Berlin & Leipzig (1905).

[11] It may be that the Yahwist is deliberately allowing that although the human initiation of creation's disruption is central to his thesis, yet there is a 'corruption of heaven' beyond human control. Alternatively, Westermann maintains that even to the Yahwist's audience the activities of the sons of God would have been understood as a thinly veiled analogy of human behaviour (C. Westermann, *Genesis,* p. 143).

[12] C. Westermann, *Genesis,* p. 408.

[13] D. Cupitt, *Creation Out of Nothing,* London (1990), p. 122.

[14] J. Sacks, *The Persistence of Faith,* London (1991), p. 79.

[15] J. Sacks, *The Persistence of Faith,* p. 106.

The Primaeval History in its Separate Traditions

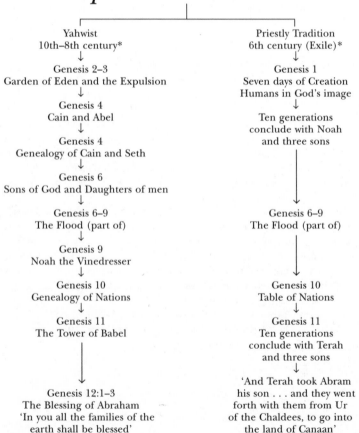

Yahwist 10th–8th century*	Priestly Tradition 6th century (Exile)*
↓	↓
Genesis 2–3 Garden of Eden and the Expulsion	Genesis 1 Seven days of Creation Humans in God's image
↓	↓
Genesis 4 Cain and Abel	Ten generations conclude with Noah and three sons
↓	
Genesis 4 Genealogy of Cain and Seth	
↓	
Genesis 6 Sons of God and Daughters of men	
↓	↓
Genesis 6–9 The Flood (part of)	Genesis 6–9 The Flood (part of)
↓	
Genesis 9 Noah the Vinedresser	
↓	
Genesis 10 Genealogy of Nations	Genesis 10 Table of Nations
↓	↓
Genesis 11 The Tower of Babel	Genesis 11 Ten generations conclude with Terah and three sons
	↓
↓	'And Terah took Abram
Genesis 12:1–3	his son . . . and they went
The Blessing of Abraham	forth with them from Ur
'In you all the families of the	of the Chaldees, to go into
earth shall be blessed'	the land of Canaan'

* Both traditions use very ancient material; the date refers to the assembling of the traditions.

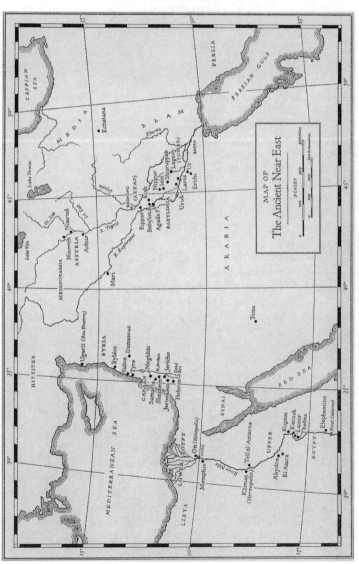

Figure 9. Map of the Ancient Near East.

Bibliography

Albright, W. F. *The Archaeology of Palestine and the Bible*, New York (1932) [second edition 1933].

──────, *Yahweh and the Gods of Canaan*, London (1968).

Allen, J. P. *Genesis in Egypt*, New Haven (1988).

Alonso-Schökel, L. 'Sapiential and Covenant Themes in Genesis 2–3', in ed. J. Crenshaw, *Studies in Ancient Israelite Wisdom*, New York (1976), pp. 468–80.

Alt, A. *Der Gott der Väter*, BWANT III:12, Stuttgart (1929) [English translation 'The God of the Fathers', *Essays in Old Testament History and Religion*, Oxford (1966), pp. 1–77].

Anderson, B. W., *Creation versus Chaos: The Reinterpretation of Mythical Symbolism in the Bible*, New York (1967).

──────, ed. *Creation in the Old Testament*, London (1984).

────── and W. Harrelson. *Israel's Prophetic Heritage*, London (1962).

Atwell, J. E. 'An Egyptian Source for Genesis 1', *Journal of Theological Studies*, New Series, 51 (2000), pp. 441–77.

Bahat, D. *The Illustrated Atlas of Jerusalem*, New York (1990).

Barton, J. *Isaiah 1–39*, Old Testament Guides, Sheffield (1995).

Begrich, J. 'Das priesterliche Heilsorakel', *ZAW* 52 (1934), pp. 81–92.

──────, *Studien zu Deuterojesaja*, BWANT 77, Stuttgart (1938) [reprint in Theologische Bücherei 20, München (1963)].

Bentzen, A. *King and Messiah*, London (1955) [first published as *Messias-Moses redivivus-Menschensohn*, Zurich (1948)].

Beyerlin, W. ed. *Near Eastern Religious texts Relating to the Old Testament*, London (1978) [first published Göttingen (1975)].

Blacker, C. and M. Loewe eds *Ancient Cosmologies*, London (1975).

Blenkinsopp, J. 'Second Isaiah – Prophet of Universalism', *JSOT* 41 (1988), pp. 83–103.

──────, *A History of Prophecy in Israel*, Philadelphia (1983).

──────, *Wisdom and Law in the Old Testament*, Oxford (1995).

Bonnard, P. *Le Second Isaïe, son disciple et leurs éditeurs*, Etudes Bibliques, Paris (1972).

Brandon, S. G. F. *Creation Legends of the Ancient Near East*, London (1963).
————, *Religion in Ancient History*, London (1973).
Bright, J. *A History of Israel*, London (1960).
Brown, W. P. *The Ethos of the Cosmos: The Genesis of Moral Imagination in the Bible*, Grand Rapids (1999).
Brueggemann, W. 'David and his Theologian', *CBQ* 30 (1968), pp. 156–181.
————, *In Man we Trust*, Richmond VA. (1972).
————, 'Unity and Dynamic in the Isaiah tradition', *JSOT* 29 (1984), pp. 89–107.
————, The Loss and Recovery of Creation in Old Testament Theology', *Theology Today*, 53:2 (July 1996), pp. 177–190.
————, *Hopeful Imagination: Prophetic Voices in Exile*, London (1992).
———— and Wolff, H. W. ed. *The Vitality of Old Testament Traditions*, Atlanta (1975) [second edition Atlanta (1982)].
Budde, K. *Jesajas Erleben: Eine gemeinverständliche Auslegung der Denkschrift des Propheten*, Gotha (1928).
Budge, E. A. Wallis, *The Book of the Dead*, London (1913) [reprinted New York (1960)].
————, *Hieratic Papyri in the British Museum*, Second Series (1923).
Caquot, A. 'La Naissance du Monde selon Canaan', *Sources Orientales* 1, Paris (1959).
Cassuto, U. *A Commentary on the Book of Genesis, Part I: From Adam to Noah*, English transl. Jerusalem (1961); Hebrew (1944). *Part II. From Noah to Abraham*, English transl. Jerusalem (1964); Hebrew (1949).
Castellino, G. R. 'Les Origines de la Civilisation selon les Textes Bibliques et les Textes Cunéiformes', *VTS* 4 (1957), pp. 116–37.
Childs, B. S. 'The Enemy from the North and the Chaos Tradition', *JBL* 78 (1959), pp. 187–98.
————, *Myth and Reality in the Old Testament*, SBT 27, London, second edition (1962) [first edition London (1960)].
————, *Introduction to the Old Testament as Scripture*, London (1979).
————, *Old Testament Theology in a Canonical Context*, London (1985).
————, *Isaiah*, Louisville (2001).
Clark, R. T. Rundle, *Myth and Symbol in Ancient Egypt*, London (1978) [first published London (1959)].
Clements, R. E. *Abraham and David*, SBT 5, London (1967).
————, Review Article of Rolf Rendtorff, *Das überlieferungsgeschichtliche Problem des Pentateuch*, Berlin (1977), *JSOT* 3 (1977), pp. 46–56.
————, *Isaiah 1–39*, New Century Bible, Grand Rapids and London (1980).
————, *Isaiah and the deliverance of Jerusalem*, JSOT Supplement Series 13, Sheffield (1980).

———, 'The Unity of the Book of Isaiah', *Interpretation* 36 (1982), pp. 117–29.

———, 'Beyond Tradition-History. Deutero-Isaianic Development of First Isaiah's Themes', *JSOT* 31 (1985), pp. 95–113.

Clifford, R. J. 'The Hebrew Scriptures and the Theology of Creation', *Theological Studies* 46 (1985), pp. 507–23.

Clines, D. J. A. *I, He, We and They: A Literary Approach to Isaiah 53*, JSOT Supplement Series I, Sheffield (1976).

Coats, G. W. 'The Yahwist as Theologian? A Critical Reflection', *JSOT* 3 (1977), pp. 28–32.

Collins, J. J. 'The Root of Immortality: Death in the Context of Jewish Wisdom', *HTR* 71 (1978), pp. 177–92.

Craigie, P. C. 'The Comparison of Hebrew Poetry: Psalm 104 in the light of Egyptian and Ugaritic Poetry', *Semitics* 4 (1974), pp. 10–21.

Crenshaw, J. L. ed. *Studies in Ancient Israelite Wisdom*, New York (1976).

———, 'Prolegomenon' in ed. J. L. Crenshaw, *Studies in Ancient Israelite Wisdom*, New York (1976), pp. 1–45.

———, *Old Testament Wisdom*, London (1982) [first published Atlanta (1981)].

Cross, F. M. 'The Council of Yahweh in Second Isaiah', *JNES* 12 (1953), pp. 274–8.

———, and Freedman, D. N. *Studies in Ancient Yahwistic Poetry*, Missoula (1975) [submitted as a Ph.D. thesis at John Hopkins University (1950)].

———, 'The Divine Warrior in Israel's Early Cult', in ed. A. Altmann, *Biblical Motifs*, Cambridge, Mass. (1966), pp. 11–30.

———, *Canaanite Myth and Hebrew Epic*, Cambridge, Mass. (1973).

Cupitt, D. *Creation out of Nothing*, London (1990).

Dalley, S. *Myths from Mesopotamia*, World Classics, Oxford (1991) [first published Oxford (1989)].

Daniel, G. *The First Civilizations*, London (1968).

Davidson, R. 'Universalism in Second Isaiah', *SJT* 16 (1963), pp. 166–85.

———, *Genesis 1–11*, Cambridge Bible Commentary, Cambridge (1973).

Davies, G. I. 'The Destiny of the Nations in the Book of Isaiah', in ed. J. Vermeylen, *The Book of Isaiah*, Leuven (1989), pp. 93–120.

———, 'Were there schools in Israel?' in ed. John Day *et al.*, *Wisdom in Ancient Israel*, Cambridge (1995), pp. 199–211.

Day, J. *God's Conflict with the Dragon and the Sea*, Cambridge (1985).

———, *Psalms*, Old Testament Guides, Sheffield (1990).

eds. *et al. Wisdom in Ancient Israel*, Cambridge (1995).

———, 'Foreign Semitic Influence on the Wisdom of Israel' in eds. *et al. Wisdom in Ancient Israel*, Cambridge (1995).

———, *Yahweh and the Gods and Goddesses of Canaan*, Sheffield (2000).

Dijk, J. van. 'Le Motif Cosmique dans la Pensée Sumérienne', *AO* 28 (1964/5), pp. 1–60.

Dillmann, A. *Genesis Critically and Exegetically Expounded*, I and II, Edinburgh (1897) [translation from German sixth edition (1892)].

Dion, P. E. 'Le genre littéraire sumérien de l' "hymne à soi-même" et quelques passages de Deutéro-Isaïe', *RB* 74 (1967), pp. 215–34.

———, 'L'universalisme religieux dans les différentes couches rédactionelles d'Isaïe 40–55', *Biblica* 51 (1970), pp. 161–82.

Driver, G. R. and J. C. Miles, *The Babylonian Laws*, Oxford (1952).

———, *Canaanite Myths and Legends*, Oxford (1956).

Duhm, B. *Das Buch Jesaia*, Handkommentar zum Alten Testament III, 1 Göttingen (1892).

Eakin, F. E. 'Yahwism and Baalism before the Exile', *JBL* 84 (1965), pp. 407–14.

———, 'The Reed Sea and Baalism', *JBL* 86 (1967), pp 378–84.

Eaton, J. H. 'The Origin of the Book of Isaiah', *VT* 9 (1959), pp. 138–57.

———, *Kingship and the Psalms*, London (1976).

———, *Festal Drama in Deutero-Isaiah*, London (1979).

Ebeling, E. *Tod und Leben nach den Vorstellungen der Babylonier*, Berlin and Leipzig (1931).

Edwards, I. E. S. *et al.*, edd. *The Cambridge Ancient History*, vols I and II, Cambridge (1970, 1971, 1973, 1975).

Eichrodt, W. 'In the Beginning: A Contribution to the Interpretation of the First Word of the Bible', in eds B. W. Anderson and W. Harrelson, *Israel's Prophetic Heritage: Essays in honour of James Muilenburg*, New York (1962).

Eissfeldt, O. 'El and Yahweh', *JSS* 1 (1956), pp. 25–37.

———, *The Old Testament: An Introduction*, Oxford (1965) [first published Tübingen (1934); translated from third edition Tübingen (1964)].

Emerton, J.A. 'The Teaching of Amenemope and Proverbs 22:17–24:22. Further Reflections on a Long-Standing Problem', *VT* 51 (2001), pp. 431–65.

Engnell, I. *Studies in Divine Kingship in the Ancient Near East*, second edition Oxford (1967) [first published Uppsala (1943)].

Erman, A. *Handbook of Egyptian Religion*, London (1907) [first published Berlin (1904)].

———, 'Eine ägyptische Quelle der "Sprüche Salomos", *Sitzungsberichte der Preussischen Akademie der Wissenschaften*, 15 (1924), pp. 86–92.

Faulkner, R. O. *The Ancient Egyptian Pyramid Texts*, Oxford (1969).

———, *The Ancient Egyptian Coffin Texts*, Warminster (1973).

———, *The Book of the Dead*, London 1972 (Revised 1985).

Fichtner, J. 'Isaiah among the Wise', in ed. J. L. Crenshaw, *Studies in Ancient Israelite Wisdom*, New York (1976), pp. 429–38 [originally published as "Jesaja unter den Weisen" *TLZ* 74 (1949), pp. 75–80].

Fisher, L. R. 'The Temple Quarter', *JSS* 8 (1963), pp. 34–41.

———, 'Creation at Ugarit and in the Old Testament', *VT* 15 (1965), pp. 313–24.

Fohrer, G. *An Introduction to the Old Testament*, London (1970) [first published Heidelberg (1965)].

———, *History of Israelite Religion*, London and Nashville (1973) [first published Berlin (1968)].

Forman, C. C. 'Koheleth's Use of Genesis', *Journal of Semitic Studies*, 5 (1960), pp. 256–63.

Frankfort, H. *et al. Before Philosophy. The Intellectual Adventure of Ancient Man*, Chicago (1946). [Published in Pelican Books from 1949.]

———, *Ancient Egyptian Religion*, New York (1948).

———, *Kingship and the Gods*, Chicago (1948).

Gammie, J. G. *et al.* eds *Israelite Wisdom: Theological and Literary Essays in Honour of Samuel Terrien*, Missoula (1978).

Gaster, T. H. *Myth, Legend and Custom in the Old Testament*, London (1969).

Gelston, A. 'Universalism in Second Isaiah', *JTS* 43 (1992), pp. 377–97.

Gerth, H. H. and C. W. Mills, *From Max Weber: Essays in Sociology*, London (1948).

Gibson, J. C. L. *Canaanite Myths and Legends*, Edinburgh (1978) [first edition by G. R. Driver, Edinburgh (1956)].

Ginsberg, H. L. 'The Arm of Yahweh', *JBL* 77 (1968), pp. 152–56.

Goldingay, J. 'The Arrangement of Isaiah 41–45', *VT* 29 (1979), pp. 289–99.

Golka, F. W. 'Die Königs-und Hofsprüche und der Ursprung der israelitischen Weisheit', *VT* 36 (1986), pp. 13–36.

———, *The Leopard's Spots: Biblical and African Wisdom in Proverbs*, Edinburgh (1993).

Gordon, C. H. *Ugaritic Textbook*, Rome (1965).

Gray, J. *The Canaanites*, London (1964).

———, *The Biblical Doctrine of the Reign of God*, Edinburgh (1979).

Griffiths, J. G. 'The Egyptian Derivation of the Name Moses', *Journal for Near Eastern Studies* 12 (1953), p. 225–231.

Gunkel, H. *Schöpfung und Chaos in Urzeit und Endzeit*, Göttingen (1895).

Habel, N. 'Yahweh, Maker of Heaven and Earth', *JBL* 91 (1972), pp. 321–27.

Hackett, J. *The Balaam Text from Deir 'Alla*, Harvard Semitic Monographs 31 (1980).

Hanson, P. D. *Isaiah 40–66*, Interpretation, Louisville (1995).

Harner P. B. 'The Salvation Oracle in Second Isaiah', *JBL* 88 (1969), pp. 418–34.

Hayes, J. H. 'The Tradition of Zion's Inviolability', *JBL* 82 (1963), pp. 419–26.

Heaton, E. W. *Solomon's New Men*, London (1974).

———, *The Old Testament Prophets*, London, second edition (1977), first published 1958.

———, *The School Tradition of the Old Testament*, Oxford (1994).

Heidel, A. *The Babylonian Genesis*, Chicago (1951) [first published Chicago (1942)].

Herbert, A. S. *Isaiah 40–66*, Cambridge Bible Commentary, Cambridge (1975).

Hermisson, H-J. 'Observations on the Creation Theology in Wisdom', in ed. B. W. Anderson, *Creation in the Old Testament*, pp. 118–34 [first published in eds J. G. Gammie *et al. Israelite Wisdom: Theological and Literary Essays in Honour of Samuel Terrien*, Missoula, Mont. (1978)].

Hiebert, T. *The Yahwist's Landscape: Nature and Religion in Early Israel*, New York (1996).

Hooke, S. H. ed. *Myth and Ritual*, London (1933).

———, *Babylonian and Assyrian Religion*, London (1953).

———, ed. *Myth, Ritual and Kingship*, London (1958).

Humbert, P. 'La relation de Genèse I et du Psaume 104 avec la liturgie du Nouvel-An israëlite', *RHPR* 15 (1935), pp. 1–27.

———, 'Mythe de création et mythe paradisiaque dans le second chapitre de la Genèse', *RHPR* 16 (1936), pp. 445–61.

———, 'Emploi et portée du verbe bārā' (créer) dans l'Ancien Testament', *TZ* 3 (1947), pp. 401–22.

Hvidberg, F. 'The Canaanite Background of Genesis 1–3', *VT* 10 (1960), pp. 285–94.

Hyatt, J. P. 'Was Yahweh Originally a Creator Deity?', *JBL* 86 (1967), pp. 369–77.

Jacobs, V. and I. Rosensohn Jacobs, 'The Myth of Môt and 'Al' eyan Ba'al', *HTR* 38 (1945), pp. 70–109.

Jacobsen, T. 'The Battle between Marduk and Tiamat', *JAOS* 88 (1968), pp. 104–8.

———, *Treasures of Darkness*, New Haven (1976).

James, T. G. H. *An Introduction to Ancient Egypt*, London (1979) [first published London (1964)].

Jamieson-Drake, D. W. *Scribes and Schools in Monarchic Judah*, Sheffield (1991).

Johnson, A. R. *Sacral Kingship in Ancient Israel*, Cardiff (1967).

Jones, D. 'The Traditio of the Oracles of Isaiah of Jerusalem', *ZAW* 67 (1955), pp. 226–46.

Kapelrud, A. S. *The Ras Shamra Discoveries and the Old Testament*, Oxford (1965) [translated from *Ras Sjamra-funnene og det Gamle Testament*, Oslo (1953)].

Kayatz, C. *Studien zu Proverbien 1–9*, Neukirchen (1966).

Kramer, S. N. 'Sumerian Literature and the Bible', *AB* XII (1959), pp. 185–204.

———, *Sumerian Mythology*, Torchbooks (1961) [first published Philadelphia (1944)].

———, ed. *Mythologies of the Ancient World*, Chicago (1961).

———, 'Sumerian Literature, A General Survey', in ed. G. E. Wright. *The Bible and the Ancient Near East, Essays in Honour of W. F. Albright*, London (1961), pp. 249–66.

———, *The Sumerians, their History, Culture and Character*, Chicago and London (1963).

———, *History begins at Sumer. Thirty-Nine Firsts in Man's recorded history* [third revised edition Philadelphia (1964)].

Lambert, W. G. *Babylonian Wisdom Literature*, Oxford (1960).

———, 'The Great Battle of the Mesopotamian Religious Year', *Iraq* 25 (1963), pp. 189 f.

———, 'A New Look at the Babylonian Background of Genesis', *JTS* XVI (1965), pp. 287–300.

———, and A. R. Millard, *Atra-ḥasīs, The Babylonian Story of the Flood*, Oxford (1969).

Lang, B. *Monotheism and the Prophetic Minority*, Sheffield (1983).

Leick, G. *Who's Who in the Ancient Near East*, London & New York (1999).

Lindars, B. 'Good Tidings to Zion: Interpreting Deutero-Isaiah Today', *BJRL* 68 (1985/6), pp. 473–97.

Lindblom, J. *The Servant Songs in Deutero-Isaiah*, Lund (1951).

Lipinski, E. 'Yāhweh Mâlāk', *Biblica* 44 (1963), pp. 405–60.

Ludwig, T. M. 'The Traditions of the Establishing of the Earth in Deutero-Isaiah', *JBL* 92 (1973), pp. 345–57.

McKane, W. *Prophets and Wise Men*, SBT 44, London (1965).

———, *Proverbs*, The Old Testament Library, Philadelphia (1970).

———, 'Prophet and Institution', *ZAW* 94 (1982), pp. 251–66.

Melugin, R. F. 'Deutero-Isaiah and Form Criticism', *VT* 21 (1971), pp. 326–37.

———, *The Formation of Isaiah 40–55*, BZAW, Berlin and New York (1976).

Mendenhall, G. E. 'Covenant Forms in Israelite Tradition', *BA* 17 (1954), pp. 50–76.

———, 'The Shady Side of Wisdom: The Date and Purpose of Genesis 3', eds. H. N. Bream *et al.* *A Light Unto My Path: Old Testament Studies in honour of Jacob M. Myers*, Philadelphia (1974), pp. 319–34.

Mettinger, T. N. D. *A Farewell to the Servant Songs*, Scripta Minora, Lund (1983).

Miller, P. D. 'El, The Creator of Earth', *BASOR* 239 (1980), pp. 43–6.

Moor, J. C. de *The Seasonal Pattern in the Ugaritic Myth of Ba'lu*, Neukirchen-Vluyn (1971).

Moran, W. L. 'New Evidence from Mari on the History of Prophecy', *Biblica* 50 (1969), pp. 15–56.

Morenz, S. *Egyptian Religion*, London (1973) [first published Stuttgart (1960)].

Morgan, Donn F. *Wisdom in the Old Testament Traditions*, Oxford (1981).

Mowinckel, S. *Jesaja-disiplene. Profeten fra Jesaja til Jeremia*, Oslo (1925).

———, *He that Cometh*, Oxford (1956) [first published as *Han som kommer*, Copenhagen (1951)].

———, *The Psalms in Israel's Worship I and II*, Oxford (1962 & 1982) [first published Oslo (1951)].

Muilenburg, J. 'Introduction to Isaiah 40 - 66', *The Interpreter's Bible* V, New York (1956), pp. 381–419.

Murphy, R. E. 'Assumptions and Problems in Old Testament Wisdom Research', *CBQ* XXIX (1967), pp. 407–10.

———, 'A Consideration of the Classification "Wisdom Psalms"', in ed. J. L. Crenshaw, *Studies in Ancient Israelite Wisdom*, New York (1976), pp. 456–67.

Murray, M. A. *The Splendour that was Egypt*, London (1964) [first published London (1949)].

Murray, R. *The Cosmic Covenant*, London (1992).

Nicholson, E. W. *Exodus and Sinai in History and Tradition*, Oxford (1973).

———, *God and His People*, Oxford (1986).

———, *The Pentateuch in the Twentieth Century*, Oxford (1998).

North, C. R. *The Suffering Servant in Deutero-Isaiah*, London (1948).

———, *The Second Isaiah*, Oxford (1964).

Noth, M. *A History of Pentateuchal Traditions*, Englewood Cliffs (1972) [first published *Überlieferungsgeschichte des Pentateuch*, Stuttgart (1948)].

———, *History of Israel*, second edition, London (1960) [first published *Geschichte Israels*, Göttingen (1950)].

———, and D. Winton Thomas eds *Wisdom in Israel and in the Ancient Near East*, Leiden (1955).

O'Connor, D. *A Short History of Ancient Egypt*, Pittsburgh (1990).

Oppenheim, A. Leo *Ancient Mesopotamia, Portrait of a Dead Civilization*, Chicago (1977) [first published Chicago (1964)].

Orlinsky, H. M. 'The So-Called "Servant of the Lord" and "Suffering Servant" in Second Isaiah', in H. M. Orlinsky and N. H. Snaith, *Studies on the Second Part of the Book of Isaiah*, *VTS* XIV, Leiden (1967).

Orlinsky, H. M. and N. H. Snaith *Studies on the Second Part of the Book of Isaiah*, VTS XIV, Leiden (1967).

Otzen, B. *et al. Myths in the Old Testament*, London (1980) [from *Myter i Det gamle Testamente*, second edition Copenhagen (1976)].

Parpola S. *Assyrian Prophecies*, State Archives of Assyria 9, Helsinki (1997).

Parrot, A. *The Tower of Babel*, London (1955) [translated from the second edition, *La Tour de Babel*, Neuchâtel (1954)].

Paul, S. M. 'Second Isaiah and Cuneiform Royal Inscriptions', *JAOS* 88 (1968), pp. 180–6.

Petersen, D. L. *The Prophetic Literature*, Louisville and London (2002).

Pettinato, G. 'The Royal Archives of Tell Mardikh-Ebla', *Biblical Archaeologist* 39/2, May (1976).

Pfeiffer, R. H. 'The Dual Origin of Hebrew Monotheism', *JBL* XLVI (1927), pp. 193–203.

———, *State Letters of Assyria*, American Oriental Series 6, New Haven (1935).

Plumley, J. M. 'The Cosmology of Ancient Egypt', in eds C. Blacker and M. Loewe, *Ancient Cosmologies*, London (1975), pp. 17–41.

———, 'The Religion of Ancient Egypt', in ed. A. Cotterell, *Encyclopedia of Ancient Civilizations*, London (1980).

Porteous, N. W. 'Jerusalem-Zion: The Growth of a Symbol', *Verbannung und Heimkehr*, Festschrift für Wilhelm Rudolph, Tübingen (1961), pp. 235–52.

Porter, S. E. *et* al. ed. *Crossing the Boundaries: Essays in Biblical Interpretation in Honour of Michael D. Goulder*, Leiden, New York & Koln (1994).

Pritchard, J. B. 'Man's Predicament in Eden', *RR* 13 (1948/9), pp. 5–23.

———, ed. *Ancient Near Eastern Texts Relating to the Old Testament*, Princeton (3rd Edition 1969).

Rad, G. von *Genesis*, London (1961) [translation of *Das erste Buch Muse, Genesis*, fifth edition, Göttingen (1958)].

———, *Old Testament Theology I*, London (1975) [first English edition London (1962); first published as *Theologie des Alten Testaments I, Die Theologie der historischen Überlieferungen Israels*, Munich (1957)].

———, *Old Testament Theology II*, London (1975) [first edition London (1965); first published as *Theologie des Alten Testaments II, Die Theologie der prophetischen Überlieferungen Israels*, Munich (1960)].

———, *The Problem of the Hexateuch and other Essays*, Edinburgh and London (1966) [first published Munich (1958)].

———, 'The Theological Problem of the Old Testament Doctrine of Creation', *The Problem of the Hexateuch and Other Essays*, pp. 131–43.

———, 'Job XXXVIII and Ancient Egyptian Wisdom', *The Problem of the Hexateuch and Other Essays*, pp. 281–91.

———, *Wisdom in Israel*, London (1972) [first published as *Weisheit in Israel*, Neukirchen-Vluyn (1970)].

———, 'The Joseph Narrative and Ancient Wisdom'. In ed. J. L. Crenshaw, *Studies in Ancient Israelite Wisdom*, New York (1976), pp. 439–47.

———, *The Message of the Prophets*, London (1968) [German edition Munich & Hamburg (1967)].

Reade, J. *Mesopotamia*, British Museum London (1991).

Reeves, D. *Making Sense of Religion*, London (1989).

Rendtorff, R. 'The "Yahwist" as Theologian? The Dilemma of Pentateuchal Criticism', *JSOT* 3 (1977), pp. 2–10. Originally published as 'Der "Jahwist" als Theologe? Zum Dilemma der Pentateuchkritik', *VTS* 28 (1975), pp. 158–66.

———, *Das überlieferungsgeschichtliche Problem des Pentateuch*, Berlin and New York (1977).

———, *The Old Testament, An Introduction*, London (1985) [translated from: *Das Alte Testament: Eine Einführung*, Neukirchen-Vluyn (1983)].

Ringgren, H. *Israelite Wisdom*, London (1966) [first published as *Israelitische Religion*, Stuttgart (1963)].

———, *Religions of the Ancient Near East*, London (1973) [first published Stockholm (1967)].

Roberts, B. J. 'The Second Isaiah Scroll from Qumran', *BJRL* 42 (1959), pp. 132–44.

Roberts, J. J. M. 'The Davidic Origin of the Zion Traditions', *JBL* 92 (1973), pp. 329–44.

———, 'Myth versus History', *CBQ* 38 (1976), pp. 1–13.

———, 'Isaiah in Old Testament Theology', *Interpretation* 36 (1982), pp. 130–43.

Rowley, H. H. *The Servant of the Lord and other Essays on the Old Testament*, London (1952).

Sacks, J. *The Persistence of Faith*, Reith Lectures 1990, London (1991).

Saggs, H. W. F. *The Greatness that was Babylon*, second edition London (1988) [first published London (1962)].

———, *Babylonians*, London (1995).

Sandars, N. K. *The Epic of Gilgamesh*, London (1972) [first published London (1960)].

Schmid, H. H. *Wesen und Geschichte der Weisheit*, BZAW 101, Berlin (1966).

———, *Gerechtigkeit als Weltordnung*, Tübingen (1968).

———, *Altorientalische Welt in der Alttestamentlichen Theologie*, Zurich (1974), [the first chapter (abridged) appears in English translation as 'Creation, Righteousness, and Salvation: "Creation Theology" as the Broad Horizon of Biblical Theology', in ed. B. W. Anderson, *Creation in the Old Testament*, London (1984), pp. 102–17].

———, *Der sogenannte Jahwist*, Zurich (1976).

———, 'In Search of New Approaches in Pentateuchal Research', *JSOT* 3 (1977), pp. 33–42.

Schmidt, W. H. *Die Schöpfungsgeschichte der Priesterschrift*, WMANT 17, Neukirchen-Vluyn (1964) [second edition revised (1967)].

———, *The Faith of the Old Testament*, Oxford (1986) [first English edition Oxford (1983); first published as *Alttestamentlicher Glaube in seiner Geschichte*, Neukirchen-Vluyn (1968)].

———, *Introduction to the Old Testament*, London (1984) [German first edition (1979); translation from second edition *Einführung in das Alte Testament*, Berlin (1982)].

Schoors, A. 'Les choses antérieures et les choses nouvelles dans les oracles deutéro-isaïens', *ETL* 40 (1964), pp. 19–47.

———, 'L'Eschatologie danï les prophéties du Deutero-Isase, *Recherches Bibliques* VIII, Bruges (1967), pp. 107–28.

———, 'The Rîb-pattern in Isaiah 40–55', *Bijdragen* XXX (1969), pp. 25–38.

———, *I am God your Saviour*, VTS XXXIV, Leiden (1973).

Scott, B. B. Y. 'Folk Proverbs of the Ancient Near East', *Transactions of the Royal Society of Canada*, XV (1961), pp. 47–56.

———, 'Solomon and the Beginnings of Wisdom in Israel', in ed. J. L. Crenshaw, *Studies in Ancient Israelite Wisdom*, New York (1976), pp. 84–101.

Scullion, J. *Isaiah 40–66*, Old Testament Message 12, Wilmington (1982).

Seale, M. S. *The Desert Bible, Nomadic Tribal Culture and Old Testament Interpretation*, London (1974).

Seters, J. van *Abraham in History and Tradition*, New Haven and London (1975).

———, 'The Yahwist as Theologian? A Response', *JSOT* 3 (1977), pp. 15–19.

———, *In Search of History*, New Haven and London (1983).

Skinner, J. *The Book of the Prophet Isaiah Chapters 40–66*, Cambridge Bible for Schools and Colleges, Cambridge (1917).

———, *Genesis: A Critical and Exegetical Commentary*, International Critical Commentary, Edinburgh (1930), second edition [first edition (1910)].

Smith, P. A. *Rhetoric and Redaction in Trito-Isaiah: The Structure, Growth and Authorship of Isaiah 56–66*, SVT 62, Leiden (1995).

Soggin, J. A. *Introduction to the Old Testament*, third edition, London (1989) [English translation from *Introduzione all'Antico Testamento*, fourth edition, Breschia (1987)].

Speiser, E. A. 'Word Plays on the Creation Epic's Version of the Founding of Babylon', *Orientalia* 25 (1956), pp. 317–23.

————, *Genesis*, The Anchor Bible, New York (1964).

Terrien, S. 'Quelques Remarques sur les Affinités de Job avec le Deutéro-Isaïe', *VTS* XV (1965), pp 295–310.

Vermeylen, J. 'Le motif de la création dans le Deutéro-Isaïe', in ed. F. Blanquart, *La Création dans l'Orient Ancien*, Lectio Divina 127: Editions du Cerf, Paris (1987), pp. 183–240.

————, ed. *The Book of Isaiah, Le Livre D'Isaïe*, Leuven (1989).

Volz, P. *Das Neujahrsfest Jahwes*, Tübingen (1912).

Waldow, H. E. von *Der traditionsgeschichtliche Hintergrund der prophetischen Gerichtsreden*, BZAW 85, Berlin (1963).

————, 'The Message of Deutero-Isaiah', *Interpretation* 22 (1968), pp. 259–87.

————, *Anlass und Hintergrund der Verkündigung des Deuterojesaja*, Dissertation, Bonn (1953).

Walters, C, 'Ancient Egypt', in ed. A. Cotterell, *The Encyclopedia of Ancient Civilizations*, London (1980).

Watson, P. L. 'The Death of "Death" in the Ugaritic Texts', *JAOS* 92 (1972), pp. 60–4.

Watts, J. D. W. *Isaiah 1–33*, Word Biblical Commentary, Waco (1985).

Weeks, S. *Early Israelite Wisdom*, Oxford (1994).

Weinfeld, M. 'God the Creator in Genesis 1 and in the Prophecy of Second Isaiah', *Tarbiz* 37 (1967/8), pp. 105–32.

Wellhausen, J. *Prolegomena to the History of Israel*, Edinburgh (1985) [translated from *Prolegomena zur Geschichte Israels*, Berlin, second edition (1883). First edition (1878)].

————, *Die Composition des Hexateuchs und der historischen Bücher des Alten Testaments*, Berlin (second edition 1889; third 1899).

Wensinck, A. J. 'The Semitic New Year and the Origin of Eschatology', *AO* 1 (1923), pp. 158–99.

Westermann, C. *The Praise of God in the Psalms*, London (1965) [from *Das Loben Gottes in den Psalmen*, Göttingen (1961)].

————, *Isaiah 40–66*, London (1968) first published as *Das Buch Jesaia, 40–66*, Das Alte Testament Deutsch 19, Göttingen (1966)].

————, *Creation*, London (1974) [from *Schöpfung*, Stuttgart-Berlin (1971)].

————, *Genesis 1–11: A Commentary*, London and Minneapolis (1984) [first published in *Biblischer Kommentar*, Neukirchen-Vluyn (1974). English translation from second German edition (1976)].

————, *Genesis*, Edinburgh (1988) [translated from the Dutch edition *Genesis: Een Praktische bijbelverklaring* I and II (1986)].

Whedbee, J. W. *Isaiah and Wisdom*, New York (1971).

Whybray, R. N. 'Proverbs 8: 22–31 and Its Supposed Prototypes', VT XV (1965), pp. 504–14. [Reproduced in ed. J. L. Crenshaw, *Studies in Ancient Israelite Wisdom*, pp. 390–400.]

———, *The Succession Narrative*, SBT (9), London (1968).

———, *The Heavenly Counsellor in Isaiah XL:13–14*, Cambridge (1971).

———, *The Book of Proverbs*, Cambridge Bible Commentary, Cambridge (1972).

———, *The Intellectual Tradition in the Old Testament*, Berlin and New York (1974).

———, *Isaiah 40–66*, The New Century Bible, London (1981) [first published London (1975)].

———, 'Response to Professor Rendtorff', *JSOT* 3 (1977), pp. 11–14.

———, *The Second Isaiah*, Sheffield (1983).

———, 'Two Recent Studies on Second Isaiah', *JSOT* 34 (1986), pp. 109–117.

———, 'The Structure and Composition of Proverbs 22:17–24:22' in ed. S. E. Porter *et al. Crossing the Boundaries*, Leiden, New York & Köln (1994), pp. 83–96.

Widengren, G. *The King and the Tree of Life in Ancient Near Eastern Religion*, Uppsala (1951).

Wilcox, P. and D. Paton-Williams, 'The Servant Songs in Deutero-Isaiah', *JSOT* 42 (1988), pp. 79–102.

Williamson, H. G. M. *The Book Called Isaiah*, Oxford (1994).

———, *Variations on a Theme: King, Messiah and Servant in the Book of Isaiah*, Carlisle (1998).

Wright, G. E. *The Old Testament Against its Environment*, London (1950).

———, *The God who Acts*, London (1952).

———, ed. *The Bible and the Ancient Near East*, essays in honour of W. F. Albright, London (1961).

Zimmerli, W. *The Law and the Prophets*, London (1965).

———, *Old Testament Theology in Outline*, Edinburgh (1978) [first published as *Grundriss der alttestamentlichen Theologie*, Stuttgart (1972)].

———, 'Concerning the Structure of Old Testament Wisdom', in ed. J. L. Crenshaw, *Studies in Ancient Israelite Wisdom*, New York (1976), pp. 175–207.

Index of Authors

Ancient Near Eastern Texts

Index of References